STUDIES AND TEXTS

40

Henry E. Huntington Library MS HM 55, fol. 1r.

THE LIFE OF ST. NORBERT
BY JOHN CAPGRAVE,
O.E.S.A. (1393-1464)

EDITED BY

CYRIL LAWRENCE SMETANA, O.S.A.
York University, Downsview, Ont.

PONTIFICAL INSTITUTE OF MEDIAEVAL STUDIES
TORONTO, ONTARIO, CANADA
1977

ACKNOWLEDGMENT

This book has been published with the help of a grant
from the Humanities Research Council of Canada,
using funds provided by the Canada Council.

Canadian Cataloguing in Publication Data

Capgrave, John, 1393-1464.
    The life of St. Norbert

(Studies and texts — Pontifical Institute of Mediaeval Studies ; 40 ISSN 0082-5328)

In verse. Translation of the Latin Vita Sancti Norberti.
The text is that of the unique ms. HM 55 in the Henry E. Huntington Library, San
Marino, Calif.

Bibliography: p.
Includes index.
ISBN 0-88844-040-5

1. Norbert, Saint, Abp. of Magdeburg, d. 1134.   I. Smetana, Cyril Lawrence,
1920-   II. Title.   III. Series: Pontifical Institute of Mediaeval Studies. Studies
and texts — Pontifical Institute of Mediaeval Studies ; 40.

BX4700.N8C37   1977   282'.092'4   C77-001043-1

Copyright 1977 by
PONTIFICAL INSTITUTE OF MEDIAEVAL STUDIES
59 QUEEN'S PARK CRESCENT EAST
TORONTO, ONTARIO, CANADA M5S 2C4

PRINTED BY UNIVERSA PRESS, WETTEREN, BELGIUM

Edmundo Colledge, O.S.A.
Collegae, Confratri, Amico

CONTENTS

Preface VII

Abbreviations IX

Introduction 1

LIFE OF SAINT NORBERT
  MS HM 55, Henry E. Huntingdon Library 19

Glossary 157

Bibliography 171

Scriptural Citations 175

Index 177

PREFACE

This volume in the Pontifical Institute Studies and Texts Series is a first edition of John Capgrave's *Life of St. Norbert*. In 1892 F. J. Furnivall had asked the curator of the Thomas Phillipps' Collection at Cheltenham, England for permission to publish it for the Early English Text Society but this request was refused. In 1924, after the manuscript had been sold to the Henry E. Huntington Library in San Marino, California, Professor William Clawson of University College, Toronto obtained permission to edit it, and in the same year he was assured by Sir Israel Gollancz that the Early English Text Society would welcome *Norbert* into its series. Professor Clawson announced his forthcoming edition four years later at a meeting of the Modern Language Association in Toronto, 27 December 1928. This edition never appeared although the text transcribed in several ledger volumes together with an introduction and notes can be found in the Thomas Fisher Rare Book Library, University of Toronto. Although he was not able to publish *Norbert* Prof. Clawson did submit his transcription to Professor Hans Kurath at Ann Arbor Michigan and thus ensured its inclusion in the *Middle English Dictionary* along with the other vernacular works of Capgrave. I had initially entertained the possibility of publishing Professor Clawson's work but very early decided upon a completely independent edition.

The following litany of persons and institutions indicates deep indebtedness but it cannot in any way intimate the generosity with which they shared their own expertise and their institutional facilities with me. First of all it is a happy duty to thank the authorities of the Henry E. Huntington Library for permission to edit *Norbert* and to Miss Jean Preston and Miss Mabel Fry for their generous and knowledgeable help. I am particularly grateful to Mrs. Jane E. Fredeman, then of the University of British Columbia, who graciously relinquished her plans to publish the manuscript in my favour. To Dr. Richard Hunt, his staff at the Bodleian Library and to all those who gave me such courteous help at Balliol College Library, the British Library and the Pontifical Institute Library, Toronto I am most grateful.

This edition was made possible through research and publication grants from the Humanities and Social Sciences Division of the Canada Council and through the continuing interest of the editorial board of the Pontifical Institute of Mediaeval Studies. I am also indebted to my colleagues at York University for two minor research grants which enabled me to examine the manuscript at San Marino, and to the staff of York's secretarial services for cordial and painstaking work over the past six years.

I am especially grateful to Professors Beryl Rowland and James Mason at York for their ready and courteous help in the preparation of the manuscript; to Frs. Rudolph Arbesmann, O.S.A., and Edwin Quain, S.J., and William Grauwen, O. Praem., for helpful criticism of my Introduction. I am happy to record that like Capgrave at West Dereham, I found "a very Julianes ham" with the Premonstratensians at West DePere, Wisconsin, and at Averbode, Belgium, because of the good graces of Frs. B. Mackin and G. C. Claridge, O. Praem.

My greatest single debt is to Fr. Edmund Colledge, O.S.A., Professor Emeritus of the Pontifical Institute of Mediaeval Studies, Toronto to whom I am dedicating this volume. His constant and patient guidance in the early stages of the transcription of *Norbert*, his sage but searing criticism of my early draft of the Introduction and his collaboration in our article on Capgrave's language and spelling are substantial contributions. The present edition may not meet the exacting standards of his own scholarship, but has greatly benefited from them.

York University   Cyril Lawrence SMETANA, O.S.A.
Downsview, Ontario
1975

ABBREVIATIONS

A	*Vita A*, MGH, SS 12
Anal. Boll.	*Analecta Bollandiana*
Anal. Praem.	*Analecta Praemonstratensia*
ASS	*Acta Sanctorum*
B	*Vita B*, PL 170: 1235-1364
DHGE	*Dictionnaire d'histoire et de géographie ecclésiastiques*
EETS	Early English Text Society
Mansi	*Sacrorum conciliorum nova et amplissima collectio* (ed. G. D. Mansi)
MED	*Middle English Dictionary*
MGH	*Monumenta Germaniae Historica*
Monast. Praem.	Backmund, *Monasticon Praemonstratense*
PL	Migne, *Patrologia Latina*
Rev. Ben.	*Revue Bénédictine*
RHE	*Revue d'histoire ecclésiastique*
TCBS	*Transactions of the Cambridge Bibliographical Society*

INTRODUCTION

The *Life of St. Norbert* by John Capgrave, MS HM 55 in the Henry E. Huntington Library, San Marino, California, is a unique manuscript. According to the author's own statement in the envoy, it was "made to the Abbot of Derham" by "Ion Capgraue" who translated it and completed it "Assumpcion weke" in "A thousand foure hundred and fourty euene" (ll. 4097-4108). This manuscript is probably the actual copy presented to John Wygenhale (l. 4102).

The oak boards which made up the original binding are covered with doe skin and held together on the inside covers by untanned thongs, one horizontal and two V-shaped. There is evidence that the volume had two leather strap-clasps, secured to the front with nails and fastened to the verso side by two diamond shaped hasps, the nail-holes of which are still visible.

The over-all dimensions with the cover are 17.3×26.6 cm.; the vellum folios are 17×25.8 cm. with written space 9.7×15.9 cm. The ruled frames and lines are visible in a greater part of the manuscript. The horizontal rulings are generally 5 cm. apart.

The text is written in a fifteenth-century cursive hand, which is probably not professional but very regular, on fifty-nine folios of vellum quartos. There are eight quires with eight folios each, except that the last gathering has only four folios and of these folio sixty has been cut off. Through excessive cropping a number of catchwords and signatures have been lost. Four of the seven catchwords are still visible: 'This her' (fol. 16v), 'Euene' (fol. 24v), 'haue 3^e' (fol. 32v), 'Ne no man' (fol. 40v). The first quire, the sixth and the last (a half-quire) lack signatures; some of the remaining signatures are barely visible; in some cases only the crown of the letter can be seen. In binding, fol. 44 and 45 have been reversed. Thus ll. 3081-3150 precede ll. 3011-3080 in the manuscript.

Except for fol. 59v, which has only the final two stanzas of the envoy, the other 58 folios have 5 stanzas each, in rime royal. The seven-line stanzas are divided by a paragraph-marker at the beginning of each stanza; the rhymes are consistently indicated on the right-hand side by horizontal lines drawn into the margin and joined by a vertical line to the corresponding rhyme-word. The fifth line of each stanza is invariably followed by a large comma; it is not joined to the other 'a' lines. The *Life* proper, preceded by a prologue of 9 stanzas and followed by an envoy of 2 stanzas, has 37 divisions introduced by capitals at the left and numerated with small Roman numerals at the right.

The manuscript itself is in a remarkable state of preservation. The illuminations are still vivid; the red and blue hues have not faded appreciably and the script is still dark and legible. The "ravages of time," however, are noticeable principally on fols. 1 and 2, and fols. 56 to 59. A combination of moisture and dirt has discoloured them. Only fol. 2 presents a problem to the reader; there a swath of faded script extends through the middle of the first stanza and sweeps down to the left into the second and third stanzas. The last fifty years have bleached this section, for the passage is quite legible on photostats made in the mid-twenties.

It is obvious from the quality of the illuminations and initials that Capgrave, in preparing this volume for presentation to his patron, took special pains not only to make it fair copy but also to make it a precious document. Five hundred years have not appreciably altered the illuminations, as the frontispiece of this edition shows. The historiated initial 'J' (fol. 1r) shows Capgrave, in an Austin Friar's black habit, kneeling to present a red-covered book to Wygenhale in the Premonstratensian white and seated on a canopied abbatial throne, against a green and pink diapered background. The letter proliferates across the upper edge and down the left side of the folio and round the bottom margin in a series of stylized blue and pink leaves. Golden flowers are attached to the flowing stem by light black lines.

The beginning of the *Life* is distinguished by an illuminated 'I' (fol. 2r). The initial itself is gold on a blue background and is filled with red. Delicate white tracery covers the whole background, and white flowers with gold centres reach out from the upper and lower left corners into the margin. Each chapter of the poem begins with a capital letter two lines high. The letters are in blue projected against a red frame which spills out along the left margins in a series of curls and loops.

There is no evidence that Capgrave's *Norbert* was subject to the kind of criticism he anticipates in the prologue (ll. 8-14); the marginal annotations, however, prove that someone used it and approved of statements on religious life in it. In the sixteenth century its margins served as a scribbler for practice in writing an indenture and for reckonings in an untutored and illegible hand.

The flyleaf at the back, once pasted to the undercover, is an unfinished page from a fourteenth-century lectionary. The office for the feast of St. Andrew occupies the greater part of the folio with directives for first Vespers; these are followed by the little chapter, an indication of the

Vesper hymn, the versicle and antiphon for the Magnificat and the oration proper to the feast. Three brief *lectiones* beginning 'passionem sci. andree' follow. The folio begins with the last few lines from Homily 37 of Gregory the Great (PL 76: 1257 D). This reading, traditionally used for the feasts of martyrs, may indicate that the preceding feast was that of St. Saturninus celebrated in the Roman calendar on the day previous to the feast of St. Andrew.

Sotheby's *Catalogue of Savile and another Collection of Ancient Manuscripta and Printed Books* (6 Feb. 1861) 22, under item no. 80 describes the present manuscript: "Capgrave, John, *The Life, Miracles and Visions of Saint Norbert with the Rules of Saint Austin, written in English Verse.*"[1] There is little likelihood that the manuscript could have ever contained the Rule of St. Augustine, and the purchaser of the manuscript, Sir Thomas Phillipps does not mention the Rule in his description of the manuscript.[2] Mention of the "Rules," however, might simply be analogous to the other items in the title: "Life Miracles and the Visions ...," and merely refer to the section of the Life where Norbert chooses St. Augustine's Rule as more suitable for his foundation than the suggested eremitical, anchorite or Cistercian way of life. This section (ll. 1212-1330) and a parallel passage from the *Additamenta ad Vitam* (ll. 3917-55) extol Augustine's Rule but contain no specific detail from its chapters. In fact neither the preoccupation with the white habit (ll. 1331-86) nor the austere statutes (ll. 1387-1533) reflect the spirit or the letter of the Rule, though they are important in defining the severely ascetical character of the first Premonstratensians.

Little can be said about the manuscript from the time it left Capgrave's hand until it was sold to Sir Thomas Phillipps in 1861.[3] The five signatures,[4] perhaps of owners, which occur at various places in the

---

[1] The British Library has the auctioneer's copy with annotations concerning price and buyer. The first 65 items belonged to the Savile collection; the rest appear under the non-committal rubric, "Another Property."

[2] Sir Thomas Phillipps did not copy the description from a sales catalogue; it is distinctly his own. Through the kindness of Prof. A. N. L. Munby and Dr. R. Hunt, I have a xerox copy of page 2 of this rare catalogue.

[3] The auctioneer entered "150" and "Powis" in the margin to item 80, i.e. *Norbert*. According to A. N. L. Munby, *The Formation of the Phillipps Library from 1841 to 1872* (Phillipps Studies No. 4; Cambridge, 1956) 77, "Powis" was one of the pseudonyms used by Sir Thomas in bidding for books.

[4] Newington Ladbrooke (fol. 1r), Arthur Hubbard (fols. 3r, 27r, 45r), Richard Clarke (fols. 13r, 49r erased), Ferdinand Newington (fol. 49r), Frances Barnad (fol. 28v.). Seymour de Ricci and W. J. Wilson, *Census of Medieval and Renaissance MSS in the*

manuscript, tell us very little. Of the five, I have been able to identify only one: the "Revd. Arthur Hubbard," whose name appears three times. According to the clergy lists in the Records Office of Essex, he was a resident of Epping and "lecturer" in the parish of Watford, Hertfordshire from 1846 to 1856.[5] Of the two whose signatures appear with dates on fol. 49r (Richard Clarke, 1729[6] and Ferdinand Newington, 1670) nothing has been ascertained.

Sotheby's sales catalogue (6 February 1861) provides the first public mention of the manuscript. From 1861 until 1923, when it was sold privately to the Henry E. Huntington Library,[7] the manuscript remained in the Phillipps Library at Cheltenham under the press mark Phillipps MS 24,309 (fol. 1). Furnivall, Munro and Bannister refer to the Norbert manuscript, but no one personally examined it.[8]

The Scribe and his Language

Norbert is confidently described in Sotheby's catalogue as "the original autograph of an hitherto unmentioned English Poem."[9] Furnivall quoted

United States and Canada (New York, 1935) 1: 46, enumerate the signatures, assign dates to all except Ladbrooke and thus establish the following chronology. "Owned by Frances Barnard (c. 1600); by Richard Clark (c. 1650); by Fordman Newington (1670); Newington Ladbrooke; Rev. Ar. Hubbard (c. 1750)." Some details in the description are patently wrong: 1) The name is Barnad, not 'Barnard'; 2) The name is Clarke, not 'Clark', and his name discernible through an erasure on fol. 49r has the date 1729; 3) Newington's name is clearly Ferdinand not 'Fordman'; Rev. Arthur Hubbard lived in the mid-nineteenth century not the 18th, as Sir Thomas Phillipps points out in his *Catalogue* p. 2: "sometimes of this XIX Century."

[5] This information was sent to me by K. C. Newton, County Archivist, Essex Record Office, Chelmsford, Essex, England.

[6] The date under Richard Clarke on fol. 49r (1729) is the year that Samuel Clarke, controversial ecclesiastic, theologian and preacher, died. Born at Norwich, he studied at Cambridge and was later dean of Norwich under the noted bibliophile, Bishop Moore. He subsequently became chaplain to Queen Anne and rector of St. James, Westminster. I have not been able to ascertain whether he had a son named Richard. It is interesting to imagine a transfer of the *Norbert* manuscript from the bishop to the dean and on to the dean's son, but it is pure speculation.

[7] de Ricci, *Census*, p. 46.

[8] F. J. Furnivall in his "Forewords" to John Capgrave, *Life of St. Katharine*, ed. Carl Horstmann, EETS, O.S. 100 (1893), pp. xiv-xv relies on the description in Sotheby's sales catalogue; J. Munro in his edition of John Capgrave, *Lives of St. Augustine ...*, EETS, O.S. 140 (1910), xi-xiv quotes from Dr. H. N. MacCracken's description; H. M. Bannister in John Capgrave, *Ye Solace of Pilgrimes*, ed. C. A. Mills (1911), p. xviii cites Furnivall.

[9] *Catalogue*, p. 22.

the description but questioned it.[10] Such caution had not been exercised by editors and cataloguers, who were all too prone to label Capgrave manuscripts autographs. H. M. Bannister was one of the first to question this prodigality in attribution.[11] Of the 10 manuscript he examined, he decided that only 3 could properly be called autographs: 1) *De illustribus Henricis*, Cambridge, CCC MS 408, 2) *The Lives of St. Augustine and St. Gilbert*, B.L. Add. MS 36704, 3) *Ye Solace of Pilgrimes*, Oxford, Bodleian MS 423. All three are written in the same hand — text and corrections. In the first of these he found proof "decisive and unanswerable"; i.e. three (of possibly four) remarks and revisions in the margins which "no one but Capgrave could have inserted ... ." He, furthermore, considered the expression on the fly-leaf of the second, "*Magister Johannes Capgrave ... fecit istum librum ...,*" an indication that Capgrave actually wrote the manuscript. Finally, the use of words and phrases in the third work identical with those in the *St. Augustine* convinced him "that the identity is undisputable."[12]

The question of Capgrave's autographs has been reopened recently. Dr. Lucas in an article on Capgrave as "Scribe and 'Publisher'"[13] examined seventeen extant manuscripts and held that six were written in Capgrave's own hand; Fr. Edmund Colledge in a more recent article, "The Capgrave 'Autographs'"[14] claimed that Capgrave himself was not the scribe of any of them. Prof. Lucas contended that ten of the twelve Capgrave manuscripts dating from his lifetime show the hand of one scribe who wrote two distinct scripts, Y and Z. The text of four of these was written in another hand but corrected in the Y-Z script; six were written and revised in the Y-Z script. The unprofessional rubrication, texts and revisions in red are by the same scribe.[15] Dr. Lucas argues that if this scribe is not the author, one is faced with the "implausible conjecture" of a scribe who, when he wrote a manuscript, was supervised at "almost every stroke," but who assumed editorial prerogatives when dealing with manuscripts written by others. Capgrave was, therefore, author, scribe, reviser and annotator of six manuscripts. This is corroborated with evidence of cumulative value by the

[10] Horstmann, *Katharine*, p. xiv.

[11] Mills, *Solace*, p. xii-xviii.

[12] *Ibid.*, p. xvii.

[13] Peter J. Lucas, "John Capgrave, O.S.A. (1393-1464), Scribe and 'Publisher'," *Transactions of the Cambridge Bibliographical Society* 5 (1969-1971) 1-35.

[14] Edmund Colledge, "The Capgrave 'Autographs'," *Trans. Camb. Bibl. Soc.* 6 (1974) 137-148.

[15] Lucas, "Scribe and 'Publisher'," p. 11.

"signatures" (*Feliciter*, or `Per Capgraue`) and the trefoil mark found in most of the manuscripts.

Fr. Colledge insists, as had Bannister, that neither the motto, trefoil nor even the unquestioned identity of the script in the text and revisions are evidence of a Capgrave autograph or holograph (p. 146). He considers it "inherently improbable" that an author could copy his own first draft and still make the many errors evident in the Capgrave manuscripts. Secondly, an author as careless as the scribe could not possibly have exercised the meticulous care of the corrector of the ten Capgrave manuscripts (pp. 146-7). Though Capgrave did not write the "faulty texts," his autograph is "in their emendations," since he is manifestly the "corrector" (p. 146). The texts were written by a scribe, layman or friar, granted by statute to friars "of defined academic or official standing" (p. 147).

There is no incontrovertible proof in *Norbert*, taken by itself, that Capgrave was the scribe or reviser. It is one of the four manuscripts in the *Y* script, however, and a strong case can be made for Capgrave's workmanship for certain revisions and remarks could have been made by no one but the author. For instance, the remark, pointed out by Bannister in the margin of *De illustribus Henricis*, `iam no*n* recordor *quoni*am ad man*us* no*n* est,` or the marginal note in the *Tretis*, `in my Concordia,` or the `va ... cat` used by the reviser to delete misplaced or erroneous passages are in the same *Y* script as the text.[16]

Furthermore, *Norbert* was neither written by the excessively careless scribe described by Fr. Colledge, nor emended by his punctilious corrector. In the 4109 lines (and some 30,000 words) of the text not a single passage is deleted. There are twenty erasures, seven expunctions and eight minor corrections. Yet, despite the obvious care expended by the reviser, he overlooked twice as many mistakes as he corrected.[17] The errors in *Norbert*

[16] Bannister in *Ye Solace*, p. xvi and Lucas, "Scribe and 'Publisher'," p. 8 marshall additional editorial remarks. The cumulative evidence of these together with the rubrications, the trefoil marks and signatures establish a strong presumption in favour of Capgrave as both author and scribe.

[17] I count 16 such failures, 9 of which occur between fols. 46r and 55v. Most of them are errors that an author proofreading his own work could easily overlook: 1) the omission of a letter: *dek* for *derk* (3590), *empour* for *emperour* (3684) where he failed to cross the *p*, *religio* for *religioun* (3346), *fudacion* for *fundacion*; 2) the failure to correct one letter: *te* for *to* (1295), *is* for *it* (2466), *him* for *hem* (1527), *he* for *þe* (3498), *him* for *his* (3766), *and* for *as* (193), *whei* for *whech* (3182); 3) failure to delete: *fi* (897), *noblel* for *noble* or *nobel* (796); 4) failure to complete *ph ... k* to *phisik* (1225). Finally, *The* for *Thei* (3170) and *þe* for *þei* (3495), though possible spellings, are singular in *Norbert* and most probably an oversight. These are, however, very minor failures.

are relatively few and minor and can certainly be ascribed to the inattention and disturbances which play havoc with the works of most mortal men; his corrections were an honest if not a completely successful attempt to make his presentation volume a fair copy. Though one cannot be apodictic, evidence points to Capgrave as scribe as well as author of *Norbert*.

Capgrave's language in the *Life of St. Norbert* has been treated in an article published by Fr. Colledge and myself in 1972.[18] There we show that despite minor variations, Capgrave's language conforms to what scholars have felt was the usage of King's Lynn during the fifteenth century.[19] The *Norbert* manuscript consistently avoids 'gh' spellings, using 'th' or 'tȝ' ('right'>'rith' or ritȝ'), a practice which Furnivall considered characteristic of texts written by Capgrave.[20]

The Author and his Works

John Capgrave was born in Lynn,[21] Norfolk, 21 April 1393. He entered the Order of the Hermits of St. Augustine about 1410, studied at the *concursorium* or *studium generale* in London and advanced to the *magisterium* at Cambridge, probably about 1425. He is not to be confused with another Austin friar of the same name who had been a student at Oxford in the last decade of the fourteenth century.[22] The twelve years following his studies

[18] E. Colledge and C. Smetana, "Capgrave's *Life of St. Norbert*: Diction, Dialect and Spelling," *Mediaeval Studies* 34 (1972) 422-434.

[19] See MED, pp. 8-11 and S. Moore, S. Meech, H. Whitehall, *Middle English Dialect Characteristics and Dialect Boundaries* (Ann Arbor, 1935).

[20] Furnivall took Horstmann to task for editing the *Life of St. Katharine* from B. L. Arundel MS 392 rather than from Oxford, Bodleian, Rawlinson MS 118, which he considered the obviously better text since it "had spellings and forms like those of the autograph *Chronicle*." Furnivall would be happy to know that *Norbert* has, as he had hoped, "no *gh*, and that its other forms match those of the Gg. *Chronicle* (once Moore 40) at Cambridge [CCC MS 167]." (*St. Katharine*, pp. xxv, xlv).

[21] Fr. Alberic de Meijer's "John Capgrave, O.E.S.A.," *Augustiniana* 5 (1955) 400-440, is the most recent biography. Fr. de Meijer has sifted through the materials of earlier biographical notices, and has thrown considerable light on some of the obscurities and resolved a few contradictions. E. J. Fredeman, *The Life and English Writings of John Capgrave* (Ph. D. dissertation, University of British Columbia, 1970) 1-69, has fleshed out the skeleton biography of de Meijer with data concerning Augustinian life and education in the fifteenth century.

[22] The fact that two friars bore the same name has given rise to no little confusion. Bale and subsequent biographers made our Capgrave a native of Kent and a graduate of Oxford; but Capgrave gives Lynn, Norfolk as his 'cuntre' (*St. Katharine*, l. 16) and Cambridge as his university (*St. Augustine*, p. 61). Fr. de Meijer, *Augustiniana* 5, pp. 405-406, drawing on the Registers of the Augustinian General Archives in Rome, proves that

offer no record of the monastery to which he was assigned nor of the kind of work in which he was involved. Extant manuscripts, however, and a long list of works no longer extant but attributed to him by his early biographers,[23] suggest that this period was devoted to scholarly activity. The earliest dated works were written between October 1437 and August 1440.[24]

It is presumed that he was prior of the monastery in his native Lynn, since he informs us that he was host to Henry VI, who visited the monastery there in 1446.[25] Capgrave's own visit to Rome, sometime between 1447 and 1452, is documented in his *Ye Solace of Pilgrimes.*[26] General Registers of the Order twice confirm his election as Prior Provincial of the English Province.[27] It is unlikely that he was elected for a third term of office, since in the dedicatory letter to Bishop Gray in his *Super Actus Apostolorum*, written about 1457, he mentions that he is now free from the cares of his office.[28] Before he died on 12 August 1464, he had completed two more works, *De fidei symbolis* and the first vernacular history of England, *The Chronicle of England.*[29]

a John Capgrave was given permission to attend Oxford in 1390, three years before our author was born. Nothing else is known of the elder John Capgrave, though it is inferred from the Registers that he was a native of Kent which was part of the Oxford *limes* of the English Province.

[23] For a complete list of the works attributed to Capgrave see A. de Meijer, *Augustiniana* 7 (1957) 531-575.

[24] The colophons of both the *Genesis* and *Exodus* (de Meijer, *Augustiniana* 7 (1957) 532n, 534n) note the date of the beginning and the ending of the respective works; the envoy of *Norbert*, (ll. 4105 and 4108) specifies the week of 15 August 1440 as time of completion.

[25] *Liber de illustribus Henricis*, ed. F. C. Hingeston (Rolls Series 1, London, 1858), p. 137. The whole tenor of the passage suggests that he was not merely a guide but was acting in an official capacity. See Lucas, "Scribe and 'Publisher'," pp. 12-16.

[26] Regarding the date of Capgrave's Roman trip see de Meijer, *Augustiniana* 5 (1955) 422. There is no reason to quarrel with his contention that Capgrave was in Rome during the Holy Year, 1450.

[27] The Register on 8 May 1454 in the Archives of the Augustinian General in Rome confirms Capgrave's election at Winchester in the preceding year; on 4 February 1456 his reelection in Lynn in 1455. The documents are quoted in de Meijer, *Augustiniana* 5 (1955) 400-401. Furnivall is wrong in supposing that he was provincial in 1461 (*Katharine*, p. xiii); John Bury was elected provincial in 1459.

[28] Dedicatory Epistle, *Actus* fol. 2r: 'et nunc a sollicitudine officii mei penitus absolutus.'

[29] Though it bears no date, *De fidei*, may well be his last work, as he alludes to approaching death; the *Chronicle*, dedicated to Edward IV shortly after his accession to the throne (4 March 1461), speaks only of his declining powers: "Now is age come, and I

We owe our first knowledge of Capgrave as an author to Leland and Bale,[30] who give lists of his works (defective and misleading in many ways). According to these, Capgrave's commentaries covered almost all the protocanonical books of the Old Testament and all the books of the New Testament. His four lives of the saints, not mentioned by his early biographers, are all translations from Latin into the vernacular; two in prose and two in verse. His venture into history produced *De illustribus Henricis* and *The Chronicle of England*. These two works, though largely derivative, contain a number of personal views, facts, and experiences important for an appreciation of his life and character. *Ye Solace of Pilgrimes*, a guide book to the topography and monuments of Rome, is valuable for its highly accurate transcriptions of inscriptions still visible and invaluable as a record of those no longer legible.

The extant works generally give the impression that they were intended for a specific patron rather than for the public at large. Only three of the twelve works envisage a wider audience; *Katharine* and *Ye Solace* address the general reader,[31] and Capgrave's dedication to Bishop Gray of the *Super Actus Apostolorum* seems to solicit approval for wider publication.[32]

If proliferation of manuscripts and contemporary notices were the sole criteria of scholarly reputation, one would be forced to conclude that Capgrave was little known. His name is not found in the catalogues of illustrious men of the Augustinian Order, yet a marginal note in General Archives of the Order in Rome dated 13 October 1390, erroneously attached to a reference to the elder John Capgrave, describes him as *doctissimus omnium anglorum ordinis nostri*.[33] Apparently, then, his reputation was not merely a local one. Bale's encomium both particularizes his field of endeavour and universalizes his fame: *Philosophus enim ac Theologus illa aetate praecipuus*.[34]

---

want ny al that schulde long to a studier." (See de Meijer, *Augustiniana* 7 (1957) 543n and 561n.)

[30] John Leland, *Commentarii de scriptoribus Britannicis*, ed. A. Hall (Oxford, 1709) vol. 2; John Bale, *Illustrium Maioris Britanniae scriptorum* (Wesel, 1549).

[31] *Katharine* (ll. 244-248): "Ye that reed it pray for hem alle/That to this werk either travayled or payde." *Ye Solace of Pilgrimes* (p. 1, ll. 25-26) "Onto all men of my nacioun þat schal rede þis present book."

[32] *Super Actus Apostolorum* fol. 2r: '... bona que ibi sunt pia auctoritate roborata, mala autem si sunt euellere studeatis, ut sic liber, a dominatione vestra procedens, asterisco vel obelo consignatus, securius ad alios descendit, tanta auctoritate vallatus.'

[33] See de Meijer, *Augustiniana* 5 (1955) 405.

[34] Bale, *Illustrium*, fol. 201v.

Of the forty-three works attributed to Capgrave,[35] twelve are extant and with the present edition all the vernacular works have been published. His four Latin theological-biblical works have not as yet found an editor. In the following list I give all the extant works in the order in which they were most probably written together with all extant manuscripts and the editions of each.[36]

a. *Commentarius in Genesim* (1437-38)
    Oxford, Bodleian Library, MS Oriel 32, 181 fols.
b. *Commentarius in Exodum* (1439-40)
    Oxford, Bodleian Library, MS Duke Humphrey b. 1, 187 fols.
c. *Life of St. Norbert* (1440)
    San Marino, California, The Henry E. Huntington
        Library, MS HM 55, fols. 1-59.
d. *Life of St. Katharine* (c. 1445)
    Oxford, Bodleian Library, MS Rawlinson Poet. 118, x + 130 fols.
    London, British Library, MS Arundel 168 no. 9, fols. 15-65v.
                                    396 no. 1, fols. 1-118.
                                    20 no. 1, fols. 1-43.
    ed. Carl Horstmann, EETS, OS 100 (London, 1893).
e. *De illustribus Henricis* (c. 1447)[37]
    Cambridge, Corpus Christi College, MS 408, 72 fols.
    London, British Library, MS Tiberius A VIII, 101 fols.
    ed. Francis C. Hingeston, Rolls Series 1 (London, 1858).
f. *Life of St. Augustine* (c. 1451)
    London, British Library, MS Add. 36704 no. 1, fols. 5-45.
    ed. J. J. Munro, EETS, OS 140 (London, 1910).
g. *Life of St. Gilbert of Sempringham* (1451)[38]

---

[35] The *Nova legenda Anglie* has falsely been attributed to Capgrave and this from a very early date. Fr. de Meijer notes that the author was John of Tynemouth and states that Capgrave was at most the editor, yet numbers it among Capgrave's "most famous works." Peter J. Lucas, "John Capgrave and the *Nova legenda Anglie*: A Survey," *The Library*, Ser. 5, 25 (1970) 10, concludes that it was probably attributed to Capgrave through the errors of the early biographers, Bale and Leland, and that it were "far better if his name were dissociated from *NLA*."

[36] This section relies on the Bibliography of Capgrave's works compiled by de Meijer, *Augustiniana* 7 (1957) 531-75; the manuscript references have been checked against my own notes on them.

[37] This treats of 6 emperors, 6 kings and 12 other nobles, bishops and writers who bore the name Henry.

[38] The date of *Gilbert* is 1451; yet in the *Tretys* which he promised to append to it, Capgrave mentions *Norbert* and the fact that he had composed it for "the abbot of

London, British Library, MS Add. 36704 no. 2, fols. 46-116.
ed. J. J. Munro, EETS, OS 140 (London, 1910).

h. *Tretis of the Orderes that be undyr the Reule of oure Fader Seynt Augustin* (1451, from a sermon of 1422)[39]
London, British Library, MS Add, 36704 no. 3, fols. 116v-119
ed. J. J. Munro, EETS, OS 140 (London, 1910)

i *Ye Solace of Pilgrimes* (c. 1451)[40]
Oxford, Bodleian Library MS 423, no. 5, fols. 355-414
Oxford, Balliol College MS 190 (fragment)
Oxford, All Souls MS 17 (fragment)
ed. C. A. Mills, British and American Archaeological
  Society of Rome (London, 1911).

j. *Super Actus Apostolorum* (c. 1457)
Oxford, Balliol College MS 189, 178 fols.

k. *The Chronicle of England* (c. 1462)[41]
Cambridge, University Library, MS Gg. 4. 12, 204 fols.
Cambridge, Corpus Christi College, MS 167, 196 fols.
ed. Francis C. Hingeston, Rolls Series 1 (London, 1858).

l. *De fidei symbolis* (c. 1462)[42]
Oxford, Balliol College MS 190, 116 fols.
Oxford, All Souls College MS 17, 113 fols.

Capgrave's Source

By a strange irony the *Vita Sancti Norberti*,[43] long believed to be the

---

Derham þat deyid last" (see pp. 64 ll. 10-14 and 147, l. 34 in Munro's edition). This anticipates Wygenhale's death by fully 10 years. Wygenhale's will, extant in the Norwich Archives Centre, is dated 14 January 1461.

[39] This brief treatise is based on a sermon which Capgrave delivered in 1422. Augustine is portrayed as Jacob and 12 religious orders who followed the Augustinian Rule as his sons. The Hebrew meaning of the name of each son is found to be relevant to the particular order. The work is more ingenious than convincing.

[40] It is divided into three parts: I. Monuments of pagan Rome; II. The great basilicas and 'station' churches; III. (unfinished) 13 other churches of Rome.

[41] This work, dedicated to Edward IV, was not given a title by Capgrave. The editorial title, "Chronicle of England," is a misnomer. It begins in the manner of a universal history; only at the year 1216 does it focus on "the regne of the Kyngis of Englond." It ends with a reference to the Council of Basle (convened 22 July 1431). Peter J. Lucas is reediting it for EETS.

[42] This is more an anthology of creeds than an essay on doctrine; the commentaries are excerpted from the Church Fathers.

[43] PL 170: 1253-1343. In subsequent references the citation will consist of PL and the

primary source for Norbert's life, since it was composed under the direction of an early disciple,[44] incorporated as such into the Bollandists' *Acta Sanctorum*[45] and used in part as a reading for his feast day in the Roman Breviary, is now generally known as the *Vita B*. In the middle of the last century Roger Wilmans discovered a briefer version of the *Vita* and called it *A*,[46] because he thought it could be proved that it was earlier and more authentic than the popular and often copied *B*.[47] In his opinion *B* was an expansion and to some extent a falsification of the more authoritative and factual *A*. Though not all scholars accepted Wilmans' conclusions, they have accepted his nomenclature.[48]

Wilmans' edition, which prints the text of *A* together with the expansions from *B*, leaves no doubt that the texts are closely related, in fact identical in the disposition of material, chronology, and even in wording. There is, however, a marked difference in outlook, attitude and style, explained in part by the fact that *B* is French in origin, while *A* is German. *A*, furthermore, tends to stress the fundamentally apostolic and evangelistic orientation of the saint, *B* his contemplative and ascetical character. Whether *B* is an expanded and rhetorically rounded-off version of *A*, or *A* an abbreviated form of *B*, or both *B* and *A* derive from an unknown common source,[49] has not been answered to anyone's satisfaction in the past

pertinent column numbers of the *Vita S. Norberti* in Migne. I use this text since it is generally more accessible and certainly more convenient than the oversize volumes of the *Acta Sanctorum*. I have chosen to cite the column numbers rather than the chapter divisions as found in the manuscript versions and indicated in Migne.

[44] See, for instance, D. Papebroch's remarks in his "Commentarius Praevius" PL 1242 C-D.

[45] ASS 21 (Junii I) 797-800.

[46] Berlin, MS Theol. lat. f.m. 79, published in MGH, SS 12: 663-706.

[47] There are 24 extant manuscripts of the *Vita B*; of these six are fragmentary. See R. V. Waefelghem, *Répertoire des sources imprimées et manuscrites relative à l'histoire et à liturgie des monastères de l'ordre de Prémontré* (Brussels, 1930). N. Backmund, *Die mittelalterlichen Geschichtsschreiber des Prämonstratenserordens* (Bibliotheca Analectorum Praemonstratensium, Fasc. 10; Averbode, 1972) 103, lists the extant manuscripts.

[48] For a summary of the earlier reactions to Wilmans' opinions regarding the primacy of *Vita A* see O. Mannl, O. Praem., "Zur Literatur über den heiligen Norbert," *Anal. Praem.* 35 (1959) 5-14. This is a reprint of an article which first appeared in 1890. See also V. Fumagalli, "Note sulle 'Vitae' di Norberto di Xanten," *Aevum* 39 (1965) 348-356, and a critique of it by W. M. Grauwen, "De 'Vitae' van Norbertus," *Anal. Praem.* 42 (1966) 322-326.

[49] Wilmans believed that there may have been a third *Vita* composed in the reign of Innocent III (p. 668). This *Vita* could account, he felt, for details in later printed biographies which are neither in *A* or *B*. R. Rosenmund, *Die ältesten Biographien des*

hundred years of scholarship.[50] It is, however, not a crucial question here, since it can be demonstrated that Capgrave used *B* as his source.

Wherever Capgrave's *Norbert* and *Vita A* agree, the same materials are found in *B*, but *B* contains many more facts, incidents, moralizations, and generalizations found in *Norbert* but not in *A*.[51] At the same time in no instance does Capgrave include material peculiar to *A* alone.[52] Finally, he uses the *Additamenta fratrum cappenbergensium* which regularly accompanies versions of *B*. Capgrave's *Norbert* is in spirit, content and style, definitely that of *Vita B*.

The changes Capgrave made in translating his text are hardly original or innovative. Capgrave belongs to the same school of hagiography as the author of the *Vita B*; for him, as for his 'auctour', edification was the end and wonderment the means. *Mirabilia* — miracles, visions, diabolical encounters, and exorcisms — were grist for his mill; and *B* abounds in the strange and the marvellous. Apparently neither Capgrave nor his source was interested in delineating a profile of Norbert; God's favour was evident in the extraordinary power of the saint's preaching, in his clairvoyance and particularly in his victories over Satan. He is, therefore, content to convey both the *sensus* and even the *verbum* so far as the exigencies of his verse permit.

---

heiligen Norbert (Berlin, 1874), rejected Wilmans' contention that *A* was the original *Vita*. He contended that both *A* and *B* were dependent upon a common source, a *Vita* 'a', no longer extant.

[50] The most recent work on Norbert's life is by Fr. Wm. M. Grauwen, O. Praem., "Norbert van Maagdenburg (Gennep, Xanten)," *Nationaal Biografisch Woordenboek* (Brussels, 1968) 3: 610-625. His doctoral dissertation, *Norbertus, aartsbisschop van Maagdenburg 1126-1134* (Brussels, 1971) 4 vols., will be printed in the Flemish series by L'Academie royale des Sciences, Lettres et Beaux-Arts de Belgie. Gerlinde Niemeyer, Oberstaatsarchivrätin, Münster, West Germany, is working on a new edition of the *Vita Norberti* for MGH.

[51] Several larger issues stand out: Norbert's regulations regarding fasting and the mode of travelling (PL 1294B: *Norbert* ll. 1443-1450); the criticisms levelled at Norbert for the choice of the rugged site of Prémontré (PL 1284: *Norbert* ll. 1633-45); an encounter with the devil at a well (PL 1310A-11C: *Norbert* ll. 2381-2415); the tame-wolf stories (PL 1316A-19C: *Norbert* ll. 2514-2653); variant details in the election of Norbert as archbishop of Magdeburg (PL 1322B-23C: *Norbert* ll. 2865-2933); the Premonstratensians in Magdeburg (PL 1325D-26B: *Norbert* ll. 3102-43); Norbert's selection of a successor at Prémontré (PL 1328C-29C: *Norbert* ll. 3326-92); the antipope's attempt to 'buy' Rome (PL 1331C-32A: *Norbert* ll. 3540-56).

[52] The barren mother who conceived a child through Norbert's prayers (MGH, SS. 12, p. 681, ll. 17-48); Norbert's power against Satan (MGH, SS 12: p. 690, ll. 18-33); Norbert's stand against papal weakness and imperial arrogance (MGH, SS 12: p. 701, l. 13, p. 703, l. 2).

Capgrave's contribution to the life of St. Norbert is minimal. Except for the prologue (ll. 1-70) and the envoy (ll. 4099-4109) he makes no major changes in disposition of material, nor does he add any new incidents or facts. He frequently refers to the source before him and to his complete dependence on it, but he is by no means a slave to the text. He questions the meaning of some passages, explains others, criticizes the author for his rambling narrative and for his failure to provide precise information. Yet he makes no effort to correct these faults once he has made it clear that they are not his own.

He exercises editorial prerogative more by excision than by addition. He glosses over, for instance, an early appearance of Satan (PL 1271B) perhaps since there is a much more sensational confrontation later in the story (PL 1320C-21B). Again he disregards a scene of peacemaking, which of its nature demanded mere human diplomacy (PL 1278B-79A), in favour of a later passage which shows Norbert as an inspired and charismatic peacemaker (PL 1280C-81C). Naturally he does not include the invidious remark about the thieving novice: *Anglicus enim erat* (PL 1295C). It is more difficult to understand why he chooses to omit passages and incidents that might have added lustre to Norbert's image, or passages important for the sequence of the narrative. He passes over in silence such remarkable events as Norbert's discovery of the relics of St. Gereon in Cologne (PL 1290C-91A), and his victory over Tanchelin, the heretic of Antwerp (PL 1311A-13A). He also misses an opportunity to add an interesting dimension to Norbert as a searcher of souls by omitting incidents where he accepts Godfrey of Cappenberg, though already married, for the religious life and rejects the yet unmarried Theobald (PL 1304D-08B). In the latter case the omission renders Norbert's involvement in the marriage arrangements (ll. 2787-2821) gratuitous. A more serious lapse is his failure to report Norbert's journey to St. Gilles (PL 1272B) after his denunciation by the Council of Fritzlar, an omission which renders his appearance at Orleans and Valenciennes inexplicable. Since all eighteen manuscripts of *Vita B* preserve the entire life of Norbert with only slight variations, it seems unlikely that this crucial journey to obtain Pope Gelasius's permission to preach was lacking in the text Capgrave used. In fact, B.L. Harleian MS 3935, probably from a northern abbey of the Premonstratensians, omits only one chapter (PL 1265C-1268B). Since Capgrave usually follows his source closely, it seems that omissions may be the result of inadvertence.[53]

---

[53] Variations in text and the omission of a few chapters of the *Vita B* in some manuscripts would hardly warrant calling them versions. Capgrave's omissions, however,

Capgrave reproduces most of the speeches and dialogue of his original, yet they become uniquely his own. A touch of local colour, a proverbial tag or colloquial turn and the past becomes present, the characters of the twelfth century speak with a fifteenth century Norfolk accent.[54] Yet the sum of his additions to the speeches of *B* is a meagre 100 lines. Some of these are expansions of a speech, others, narrative recast into speech or dialogue;[55] most of his additions, however, are in the form of apostrophes, aspirations, and blessings.[56]

Capgrave's *Norbert* reproduces the portrait in *B*, except that in tracing the outlines he has attempted to heighten those features which present the more ideal and exemplary picture. He suppresses anything that might conceivably detract from the ideal aspects of the Saint: Norbert as a worldly courtier,[57] the ugly scene where Norbert's newfound zeal for reform provokes a fellow canon to spit in his face; the terrifying scene where the drunken mob at Magdeburg threatens to kill him.[58] One certainly does not expect a "warts and all" school of medieval hagiography, but Capgrave does retouch *B*'s picture of Norbert. And this is to the detriment of the saint, for with the suppression of details some of the warmth and humanity has evaporated.[59]

are more numerous and may suggest either editorial intention or authorial inattention, but hardly a truncated source. The pattern of omissions corresponds in no way to that of the fifteen manuscripts used by Chrysostomus van der Sterre in the seventeenth century and reprinted by Migne in PL 170, or to that of the eight manuscripts I have personally examined.

[54] *Norbert,* ll. 1581-1582; 2015-2016; 2033-2035; 2477-2478.

[55] Expanded speeches: *Norbert,* ll. 954-972; 1849-1855; 1926-1929; 2744-2772; 2880-2887; 2957-2980; 3030-3037; 3386-3436. Speeches from narrative: *Norbert* ll. 544-550; 1276-1281; 1364-1379; 1690-1697; 2079-2081; 2279-2281; 2288-2294; 2297-2302; 2479-2513; 3288-3311.

[56] *Norbert,* ll. 195-196; 1211; 2181-2184; 2355-2359; 2981-2984; 2987-2989; 3460; 3668-3672; 3834-3835; 3901.

[57] Compare the positive picture in *Nobert* (ll. 120-126) with the less flattering description in *B* (PL 1259B): "nihil sibi denegare, neque intentatum relinquens, quod propriae voluntatis suggeret appetitus; non attendens quid liceat, et quid non deceat non cavens, dum tantum quod libet suppetat, et quod displicet non obsistat; ... civis saeculi hujus egregius, et inclytus Babyloniae colonus; religionis et quietis impatiens, inquietudini et impatientiae servus."

[58] PL 1265A: '... sputis etiam, incredibili arreptus dementia, foedavit faciem ejus,' and PL 1335-36.

[59] Compare, for instance, the staid scene in *Norbert* (ll. 483-489) and the emotionally charged meeting in *B* (Norbert is finally recognized by his old friend Bishop Burchard): 'Episcopus autem intuens hominem, et intra se vehementissime admirans ac stupens, collacrymatus est; non enim se poterat continere; mota quippe sunt viscera ejus super

On the whole, however, Capgrave has successfully rendered his Latin source into English. If not a masterly work, *Norbert* is a competent one. His use of decasyllabic verse in rhyme royale stanza is not completely regular. Many of the lines are iambic pentameter and many more can be so scanned, if one considers the extra syllables as anacrusis. Verses vary, however, between eight and twelve syllables and a strong four-stress rhythm, reminiscent of the old alliterative metre, pulses in many of the lines. His 'numbers,' if not entirely smooth and fluid, do not hobble along. An occasional finely chiseled phrase, his penchant for lively dialogue and dramatic scenes, though not sufficient to raise *Norbert* to the level of fine poetry, rescue it from the flatness of the fifteenth-century rhymers.

Editorial Practice

Punctuation, capitalization and word division follow modern conventions. The scribe of *Norbert* uses punctuation sparingly; in the 4109 lines of the poem there are only twenty-nine periods. Some of these are used after Roman numerals, others to separate identical words as *to.to* (l. 1129) or *it.it* (l. 2587), where ordinarily a comma would be used; only half function as periods. The large red comma at the fifth verse of every seven-line stanza, the paragraph marker at its beginning and the oblique stroke have no rhetorical or grammatical significance.[60] The former two, in fact, are often countersigns, since they signal neither a pause nor the beginning of a new unit.

This edition preserves the spelling of the manuscript except that the '*þ*' has been substituted for the '*y*', the "degenerate wynn form"[61] of the thorn. The scribe substitutes *Th* when it occurs initially in the verse; he alternates between *th* and *ʒ* (*With* or *witʒ*) when it occurs within the verse. His *ʒ* represents consonantal *y* as in *ʒere*, and also *z* as in *neʒyng*. The scribe does not distinguish between vocalic and consonantal *I*. My transcription follows this practice, though where long *I* represents a past participial prefix, I have joined it to the base word and have treated it as a lowercase letter.

---

eum. Et irruens collo ejus, ac pio ejulatu exclamans, cum suspirio dixit: "O Norberte, quid umquam de te talia crederet aut cogitaret?"' (PL 1274 B-C).

[60] For Capgrave's later use of these symbols and their functions see Peter J. Lucas, "Sense Units and the Use of Punctuation-Markers in John Capgrave's *Chronicle*," *Archivum Linguisticum*, N.S. 2 (1971) 1-24.

[61] C. E. Wright, *English Vernacular Hands From the Twelfth to the Fifteenth Centuries* (Oxford, 1960), p. 21. Here he analyzes the hand in the *Life of St. Gilbert* which is identical with that in *Norbert*.

Abbreviations and contractions have been expanded without the use of italics.[62] There are several abbreviations, however, that merit mention. The curl on final *r* has been regularly expanded to *re*.[63] An examination of words with and without the curl on final *r* shows that the scribe is not given to idle flourishes.[64] Words with the curl are in many cases spelled *re* elsewhere in the text, while words without the flourish, e.g. *ir, yr, or*, are consistently free of fanciful or otiose strokes.[65] The case is not quite so clear with regard to words that end in double *l*, for the *l*'s are invariably crossed with a light horizontal line. In some cases words are spelled *lle*, but these are usually in rhymes, where Capgrave is at pains to achieve a visual rhyme sequence even at the expense of consistency. I have therefore considered the horizontal bar on the *ll* as otiose except where there are numerous examples of *lle* spellings, as in the case of *alle, dwelle, telle, felle, fille*.[66] The suspension over *u* in *ou* is transcribed as a nasal suspension, and the loop after the *g* in *among* as *-is*.[67] I have let the ampersand symbol stand but have spelled out the Roman numerals in the text. Finally, round brackets are used to indicate words or letters omitted in the manuscript, square brackets for conjectural readings and angle brackets for corrections.

The scribe generally indicates superscript words and letters by a vertical stroke, less frequently by a double stroke or a caret. Most of these signs are in the same or similar ink. When they are in red ink, they are duly noted in the apparatus.

---

[62] The abbreviations and contractions in *Norbert* are for the most part the conventional symbols used in Latin texts: *con, -er, m/n, per-, pro-, re/ri/ra* and *us*. The *-er* abbreviation also signifies *ir/-yr*, but is never used as in Latin for *-ur* or *-tur*. Again, the scribe's sign for *-es/-is/-ys* is differentiated from the Latin *-us/-os/-is* in that it is formed with a left rather than a right loop-stroke.

[63] Wright, *Vernacular Hands*, p. 21, "It is a question whether the ' after 'r' is for 're' or whether it has become a meaningless scribal flourish."

[64] Dr. Lucas has sufficiently demonstrated Capgrave's thorough attention to minute details and his extraordinary consistency in spelling and punctuation in the *Chronicle*. See Peter J. Lucas, "John Capgrave," *TCBS* 5 (1969-1971) 19-27; "Sense-Units," 1-24 and "Consistency and Correctness in the Orthographic Usage of John Capgrave's *Chronicle*," *Studia Neophilologica* 45 (1973) 323-355.

[65] His consistency is not necessarily impugned by occasional spellings such as *wherefore*, or by the fact that *emperoure, daungere, fadere* and *seculere* are not spelled out.

[66] *Alle* occurs as often as *all* with horizontal stroke; in 23 of 28 occurrences *dwelle* is spelled out, in 38 of 42 cases the scribe spells *telle*.

[67] Wright, *Vernacular Hands*, p. 21: "Nor is it certain whether the 'es' symbol after 'g' in *among* (l. 9) is to be extended or not."

THE LIFE OF ST. NORBERT

Oye, grace & pees, loue, feith & charite
Euyr rest upon ȝour goodly religious breest,
To whom þat I with moost humylite
Euyr recomende me lowly as ȝoure preest.
And þouȝ I be of rymeris now þe leest,   5
Ȝet wil I now, obeying ȝoure comaundment,
Put me in daungere in þis werk present.

Who schal þese dayis make now ony þing
But it schal be tosed & pulled as wolle?
Summe schul sey alle þis is flateryng;   10
Summe of charite schul preise it at þe fulle.
Now lete hem rende, lete hem hale & pulle,
Swech maner puple, for I have myn entent,
So I plese him þat ȝaue me comaundment

To make þis werk of þat noble with,   15
Norbert called, wich with ful hye grace,
Made a ordre þat schewith now very lith
Of good ensaumple to men in euery place.
Ȝe noble men, if þat ȝe list to race,
Or rende my leuys þat I to ȝou write,   20
Ȝe may weel doo it; I schal ȝou neuyr wite.

In ȝoure correccioun put I þis matere
For I wil sewe & translate þis story,
And wele I wote ȝoure hertis be so clere,
So ful of charite withouten trechery,   25
Ȝe wil not put on me no vyleny
But I deserue it, and þat schal I nowt,
As I hope, neythir in speche ne þowt.

4   me *added to the right and above* recommende

1 The prologue of 10 stanzas and an epilogue of 3 stanzas are addressed to John
Wygenhale, Abbot of the Premonstratensian house at West Dereham, Norfolk. See note
on ll. 4102 ff.

In þis story rith þus I wil procede
Of þis same seynt to telle þe lyf real,   30
Both of his diete and eke of his wede.
Of his lettirrure alsoo tellen I schal.
Lete neuyr his lif fro ȝoure hertis fal,
Ȝe men of ordre þat be to him named.
Alle þat forȝete him iwis þei schal be blamed.   35

fol. 1v   I myselue, thou þat I mech ferther be
Fro his patronage, ȝet haue I deuocioun
Ful special, leueth weel, in his benygnyte,
Rith for þis cause and þis conclusion:
That he schuld kepe me fro alle illusioun   40
Of myn enmye bodely and goostly eke.
Seyntis be ny to hem þat hem seke.

The secunde cause eke whi I him loue,
For sothe, is for breþerin me þinkith we be,
His ordre and oure if ȝe wil it proue,   45
Beholdeth here lyfe, beholde here vnyte
Of here professioun, & therby proue may ȝe
That of o reule þei and we be alle.
Wherefore o kynrod men may us now calle

Vndir o fadir & doctoure of oure feith,   50
Floure of doctoris, Austyn is his name;
And we his childyr, what euyr ony man seith.
The cherch, þe world euyr beretȝ out þis fame.
It is no vylony to men of worthi name
Whech be endewid witȝ possession temporal,   55
Thouȝ othir pore men to here alyauns fal.

40   me *added above the final* e *of* kepe
48   d *inserted suprascript after* an
71-128   PL 1257-59*

* The juxtaposition of numbers above indicates Capgrave's indebtedness to his source.
Thus *Norbert,* ll. 71 ff., the beginning of chapter i, is a poetic version of *Vita B* in PL
170: 1257-59. As in my introduction, PL with the column numbers always indicates
volume 170 of Migne.

Thus endith þis prologe, my goodly fadir dere,
Whech I write to ʒou witʒ ful pure entent,
Thankyng ʒou euyr of ʒoure hertly chere
Whech ʒe make us whan we are oute sent.   60
And if ʒe list þat þis book present
May be receyued in ʒoure fraternyte,
Onto ʒoure name dedicate þan schal it be.

O lord Ihesu, of alle religious men
Abbot and maystir, bryng us to vnyte,   65
And ʒeue us grace witʒ þi comaundmentis ten
To fulfill þe councell whech were ʒoue be þe,
That we may dwelle in parfith charite
Whil we be here. & aftir oure endyng day
To se þat ioye whech þat lesteth ay.   70

fol. 2r   There was a man sumtyme dwelling here,   i
    As oure book seith, in þat ilk same tyde
That Pascase þe pope, to God lef and dere,
The cherch of Rome gouerned fere and wyde.
Herry the ʒonger was lord & alsoo gyde   75
Ouyr alle þe empyr þat tyme as seith oure book:
The ʒere of Crist veryly, if ʒe wil look,

---

34 The Norbertines, or Premonstratensians, were founded by St. Norbert at Prémontré in 1121. In England they were known as the White Canons from their garb of white or unbleached material. See ll. 1331 ff. and note; 1463 ff.; 1481 and note.

48 Norbert's choice of the rule of St. Augustine perhaps suggests his preference for a canonical rather than a more contemplative and monastic form of religious life. See the note on ll. 1252 ff.

65 Capgrave's prayer for unity is symptomatic of his own interest in stemming the rivalry between orders and particularly the bitter dispute between the Hermits and the Canons of St. Augustine. His *Concordia* or *De Augustino et suis sequacibus* (now lost), the *Tretis of tho orderes þat be vndyr þe reule of oure fader Seynt Augustin*, and the lives of St. Norbert and St. Gilbert, both founders of other Orders, show his continual preoccupation with the questions of unity and charity among religious groups.

73 Pope Paschal II (1099-1118), a Benedictine monk, succeeded Urban II. His reign was marked by a threefold struggle: 1) with the antipopes; 2) with Henry V, the emperor, over the question of Investiture; 3) with those who opposed his strong determination to reform the church in head and members.

75 Henry V (1106-1125) helped depose his father, Henry IV, for the latter's intransigence in the Investiture struggle. He, however, continued the fight for supremacy in this matter more passionately than his father and was, like his father, excommunicated.

A thousand a hundred & fiftene thertoo.
This mannys name Norbert thoo þei called
Of Teutonye nacioun, the story seith rith soo.   80
Whech word made me of stody al apalled;
For whethir it is a cyte weel iwalled,
Or ellis a cuntre, auctouris touch him nowt.
But aftirward whann I was bettir beþowt

I supposed þan þis cuntre stant in Germayne,   85
Because þis man of whech we haue now told
Was sumtyme dwellinge in þe cite of Colayne
With Frederik þe bisschop þat was man ful bold.
He was eke longing onto þe grete houshold
Of Herry þe emperoure; wherfore suppose now we   90
That þere abouten stant in þat same cuntre.

The townes name is touched here alsoo,
The place of Seyntis sumtyme called Troye.
Thus seith oure story and eke ferthermoo
Of his kynrod, with ful mykyl ioye,   95
Telleth he forth a man þat was ful koye,
And eke ful trewe. This seyntis fadere is
Herdbert, be name; his modir hith Hadwidis.

Herman of Laon, *Liber de restauratione Monasterii Sancti Martini Tornacensis*, MGH, SS 14, p. 315 tells us that Norbert was chaplain to the emperor on his journey to Rome, and that the humiliation of the Pope at the emperor's hands led to Norbert's conversion: 'Penitentia ductus, pedibus domini pape se prostravit et absolutione ab eo suscepta, secularem vitam relinquens in Franciam venit.' This 'instant conversion' is doubtful. Neither *A* nor *B* mention the incident, and *B* definitely places the conversion in 1115. See W. H. Grauwen, "Norbert," *Nationaal Biografisch Woordenboek* (Belgium, 1968) 3: 612.

78 Norbert was born sometime between 1080 and 1085; 1115 represents, therefore, his new birth or conversion.

80 It is not clear why Capgrave should be mystified by the phrase, 'vir quidam, nomine Norbertus, natione Teutonicus' (PL 1257A). This was traditionally the collective name for the German people; it stems from one of the tribes defeated by the Romans. A reader has suggested that *apalled* might mean 'tired' or 'anxious' because he did not find Norbert mentioned in books relating to *Teutonye*.

88 Frederick, archbishop of Cologne (1100-1131), was the son of Berthold, duke of Schwartzenburg. *Vita B* does not characterize the archbishop; Capgrave's *þat was man ful bold* may be due to the exigencies of rhyme, but there is more truth than poetry in it. He made outright war on Henry V and actually defeated the emperor's troops. Though he officiated at the crowning of Lothair III, he subsequently suffered suspension as the result

Both of Frensch and of Germayn kynde
Was þis man born be swech dyuersite   100
Of matrimony; and ferþermore, as I fynde,
Whan in his modir newly conceyued was he,
A heuenely vision with a voys had sche
Rith in hir sleep, and þus he to hire sayde:
"Be mery & glad, woman, & not afrayde;   105

fol. 2v For he þat is now in þi wombe conceyuyd
A herchbisschop schal be." Thus seid þe voys certayn;
And as he seyd sche was nowt deceyuyd,
But bare a childe and þerof was sche fayn.
He grew to age, to myth and eke to mayn.   110
Fayre of stature, lene he was and long,
Lith of lymys, loth to do ony wrong.

---

of an altercation with him. It is not clear whether his struggle against the emperors was always prompted by zeal for the house of the Lord or for the political advantage of his own family.

93 Xanten in Rhenish Prussia, formerly the capital of the Duchy of Cleves. The name is probably from 'ad sanctos' (martyres): St. Victor and companion martyrs. The original burial ground of the martyrs was discovered by Walter Bader on 1 Nov. 1933 (see *Die Stiftskirche des Hl. Viktor zu Xanten* 1, 1, *Grabfeld, Märtyrgrab und Bauten unter dem Kanonikerchor vom 4 Jhr. bis um oder nach 752-68*, ed. Walter Bader (Kevelaer, 1960)). Though neither *A* nor *B* — nor any other source, for that matter — offer corroboration for Xanten as Norbert's birthplace, it was generally accepted that he was born there. As late as 1946 Dr. H. Engelskirchen could write: "Die gesunde Tradition hat denn auch nicht bloss nie an dem Geburtsort Xanten gezweifelt, sondern sogar genau die Stelle in der Stadt festgehalten, die als 'locus natalis' anzusprechen sei." ("Nova Nobertina. Neue Forschungsergebnisse über Norbert von Xanten," *Anal. Praem.* 22-23 (1946-47) 135.) E. Valvekens, *Norbert van Gennep* (Brugge, 1944) dissents from this view. See W. Grauwen, O. Praem., "S. Norbertus" *Anal. Praem.* 41 (1965) 310-311 for an evaluation of the problem. *Troye*, the other name given by Capgrave, is from his source: 'quod antiquitus Troja dicebatur' (PL 1257A). This is most probably a corruption of 'Colonia Trajana,' the name of the Roman settlement near Xanten.

98 PL 1257: 'genere de illustri Francorum et Germanorum Salicorum prosapia ortus.' Until recently it has been accepted that Norbert was of noble rank. N. Backmund, *Geschichtsschreiber des Praemonstratenserordens*, pp. 99-100, states that Norbert's biographers, beginning with *B*, have greatly exaggerated his lineage. In saying, however, that *A* knows nothing of his nobility, he misses the nuance of *A*: '... in aula imperiali, necnon in ecclesia Coloniensi non minimus haberetur' (MGH SS 12:671), as well as the witness of Herman of Laon (see note to l. 75 above). His lifelong association with the royal court, his familiarity with emperors and prince-bishops and his own election as archbishop suggest that he was well-born.

107 PL 1258A is less specific: magnus apud Deum futurus est et apud homines. There

Amongis grete men he was ful wel itawt,
Amongis þe mene meke of spirith & goost.
For as I seide ere, if ȝe forȝete it nawt,   115
With þe emperoure dwellyng in his hoost
Was he sumwhile, but in certayn moost
With the erchbisschop, of whech we spak ere;
Welkome here and welkom was he þere.

What for his cunnyng, what for his gentilnesse,   120
Of alle maner men ful grete loue had he.
His condiciones proporcioned were, I gesse,
Vnto his persone, for ful fayre was he,
Mery in word, of hert and hand ful fre,
Large for to ȝeue and to take aschamed,   125
Neuyr in no cumpanye for his condicioun blamed.

Thus it befell aftir þat up on day   ii
     With o seruaunt he schul a iornay make
With fresch hors and with ful fresch aray
In grete hast his viage for to take.   130
But sone he gan oute of his pride awake
Whann he was fesed witȝ leuene & þundirblast,
Whech made hym and his child agast.

Fer fro towne, fer fro busch was he,
Ther was no couert. At þat tyme happed soo   135
To cure him fro fere in his aduersite
Thus is he falle. His child cryed euyr: "Hoo,
Maystir, leue now, lete us no ferther goo;
Turne hom agayn." Lich onto Balaam asse,
Swech a warnyng me þinkith þat þis wasse.   140

113, 114   *abbreviation for* is *added to* among
127-175   PL 1260A-61B
130   make *expunged*; take *added*
165   him *added above and to the right of* for

---

are, however, some manuscripts, according to the editor's note (PL 1258 n. 22) which
have: 'quoniam archiepiscopus futurus est, quem gestas in ventre.'
   120 This stanza is a rather close translation of PL 1259A; but Capgrave omits the less
flattering details of Norbert's character: non attendens quid liceat, et quid non deceat non

fol. 3r   He went swech weyis as were displesaunce
Onto oure lord, rith þus men may suppose;
For he was chosen, of Goddis puruyaunce,
Onto heyer lyf. God wold him not lose
To saue his soule; þus he fesed his kose.   145
As þouȝ he had be very new Seynt Poule,
Thus cryed oure lord pryuyly to his soule:

"Norbert, Norbert, tende now onto me.
Why pursuest me? Whi art þou inobedient
Onto my counceles, witȝ whech I enspired þe?   150
Turne aȝen lest þat þou be schent,
And to my seruyse sette more þin entent.
Forsake þis vanyte, if þou wilt me plese,
Thy ioly lif wil turne the to no ese.

Thi body is made for to seruen me.   155
Why wringist þiselue thus fro my seruyse?
I wyl þou wite it, ful hard it is to the
To wynse or grucch aȝens me in ony wyse.
My scharp prik is sette in swech a sise,
There may no man scapen my daungere.   160
Turne aȝen, þerfor, fro þi lif seculere!"

Whil he lay þus in sownyng on þe ground
Ther cam a clap of þundir fro aboue.
Grete was þe fyre, hidous was þe sound;
Gresse and herbes before him gan he schoue,   165
And in the ground, men myth it aftir proue,
Smet it a pitte with ful grete strength,
As mech as a man both in brede & length.

---

cavens, ... civis saeculi hujus egregius, et inclytus Babyloniae colonus; ... religionis et
quietis impatiens, inquietudinis et impatientiae servus (PL 1259B).
    128 PL 1260A: festinaret ad locum quemdam Freden nomine; probably Marien-
Freden, a few miles from Xanten. See H. Engelskirchen, "Nova Nobertina," *Anal. Praem.*
22-23 (1946-47) 132-136.
    139 Num. 22: 28.
    146 Pl. Lefèvre, O. Praem. ("L'Episode de la conversion de S. Norbert et la tradition

The sory sauoure of brimston & of fere
Fulfillid here hedes and here clothes eke.   170
He lay ful stille, þere was with him no chere,
His wittis were ded, his strength for to seke.
Thus onto God in hert he gan to speke:
"What wil I do, lord?" He answered, witʒouten lees:
"Fle euele, do good and seke pees."   175

fol. 3v   Now riseth he up, astoyned and adrad;   iii
           He fleth þe pres, þe besinesse he had ere,
There he was wone to singe & be ful glad.
Now are his corage, his wordes & his chere
Turned onto sadnesse. A redy, a good skolere,   180
To holy ordres he hastith now; in al wise
His stody is now to lerne dyuyne seruyse.

And for þat cause onto an abbey beside
Called Sigebergense he takith his viage.
There he castith him for a tyme abide,   185
Rith as a bird to hold him in a cage;
For now his wil, his stody & his corage
Is set to leue þe world withouten more
And lerne religion, on whech he stodieth sore.

175   *period after* pees *in light ink*
176-245   PL 1261B-64D
193   <as> *MS* and
194   eke *added above and to the right of* mad
210   *period after* curtesye

---

hagiographique du 'Vita Norberti,'" *RHE* 56 (1961) 813-826), after a careful com-
parison of the manuscripts suggests that the episode is a fabrication. The topos, however,
which sees parallel incidents between the biblical characters and the saint's life is, in
England, certainly as old as Bede's hagiographical essays. The biblical reference here is to
the conversion of St. Paul recorded in Acts 9: 1-9. See also H. Engelskirchen, "Zur
Bekehrung des hl. Norberts," *Anal. Praem.* 31 (1955) 344-45.
    175 Ps. 34: 15.
    184 A Benedictine abbey at Siegburg in Rhenisch-Prussia, about 15 miles from
Cologne. It is significant for Norbert's later reform spirit that this monastery under Abbot
Cuno (1105-1126) was prominent in the monastic reforms of the 12th century. See J.
Semmler, *Die Klosterreform von Siegburg* (Bonn, 1959).

There took he ordre of presthod, as it is seyd,   190
Amongis þoo munkis, & fourty dayes euene
Was he with hem, in here obseruauns teyid,
In swech weyis ⟨as⟩ leden to heuene.
This made þe þundir, þis mad eke þe leuene;
Euyr God be þanked of his sondes alle.   195
Thouȝ we turne fro him, aȝen he wil us calle.

Onto his cuntre where þat he was bore
Turneth he aȝen hastily, a ful grete pase,
Where he was norched long tyme before.
A noble cherch stant in that same plase   200
Ful of seculere chanonis, men ful of grase.
There lyueth he now in deuoute prayere,
In habite and seruyse as chanoun seculere.

There was a vse in þat cherch þat tyme,
If ony straungere cam of worthi degre,   205
The deen went to him sone aftir pryme
With his conchanones eythir too or thre.
Swech manere profir to him þann mad he:
To synge þe masse conuentual solemply.
Of ful grete norture & ful grete curtesy   210

fol. 4r   Thus ded þay to Norbert whan he was come
The first day euene, witȝouten ony more;
And he obeyid mekely here custome,
Sang þe masse as þouȝ he of houshold wore.
Thei song here servyse, as þei had do ȝore,   215
Til þei to þe gospell cam, & whan þat was doo,
With ful grete spiritȝ he turned hem ontoo.

190 *B* informs us that Norbert went to the archbishop of Cologne with the request:
'Diaconus et presbyter simul volo fieri' (PL 1262B). The archbishop complied with this
canonical irregularity. Later Norbert received absolution from this irregularity from Pope
Gelasius II (PL 1272C). Capgrave mentions neither incident.
197 PL 1263C makes it clear that Norbert went back to the church where he had been
a secular canon previous to his conversion; Capgrave does not. In Capgrave Norbert
emerges as a visitor; in *Vita B* his attempt to reform the canons is more credible.

He seyde a sermoun, ful sad and ful deuoute.
Vnware to alle men þat he schuld preche,
The holy goost, whech he bare aboute, 220
Stered him to þis holy, þis deuoute speche.
What schuld I lenger ony prolonging seche
To vttyr my matere? Þe most þing he þere spak
Was who we schuld throwe boldly at oure bak

Alle wordly welth and þe intricacioun 225
Of worldly felicite. This was his sentens:
Alle þing þat is here schal fall adown
Or we be ware, schal fayle of permanens.
Wherfore, concluded he þere in here presens,
These wordly plesaunses ar fals & onstable, 230
Schort of tyme, wrecchid in prys, euyr able

To turne to corrupcioun, onworthi to loue,
Not able to possessioun but fayling ioye.
Blynd pryde is þis world, as I seid aboue,
Welth is in moment, witnesse of Troye; 235
Sekirnesse is onsikyr, rest is but noye.
Swech þingis seyde he þann and many moo
That made here hertis ful of care and woo.

For al þe ende of his tale turned he to hem
Whech he preched onto & for þis entent 240
Seyde he þis sermoun to þo same men:
He was fro God as a messagere isent
Rith on hem as þei þat tyme ment.
He seide, eke, no þing vnpunchid schal be,
That is doo onclenly aȝens honeste. 245

246-315 PL 1268C-70A

238 PL 1264 continues the story of Norbert's attempt to reform the canons. After a time he became intolerable to the community and one ignoble cleric, ʻsputis etiam, incredibili arreptus dementia, foedavit faciem ejus' (1265A).

246 The spider story was popular in the 12th century. The identical story is related of Conrad of Constance (MGH, SS 4: 433); it is told with some changes in the life of Vitalis of Savigny ("*Vitae BB. Vitalis et Gaufridi*," *Anal. Boll.* 1 (1882) 376-377). The spider appears again in the life of a later Premonstratensian, Hermann Joseph (see K. Koch and E. Hegel, *Die Vita des Prämonstratensers Hermann Joseph von Steinfeld* (Köln, 1958) 70). For a study of the legend cf. P. Browe, *Die eucharistischen Wunder des Mit-*

fol. 4v   Aftir þis not longe tyme as I wene,   iiii
      He sayde a masse in a ful lowe voute,
Where felle a caas of stoynyng & of tene
Vnto him, eke ful desesy in thoute,
But fynaly it harmed hym rith noute.   250
This was þe caas whil he was at masse
And sayde his orisones, þe more and þe lasse.

Aftir sacry him befel this caas:
A ereyn dropped oute euene fro aboue —
The chalis onkewred at þat tyme waas —   255
In he felle and þere he gan to houe.
This man is astoyned with fere & with loue,
Feer for venym, love for þe sacrament.
But in his feith, swech an hardinesse he hent,

That al he soupith þe ereyn and þe blood.   260
He saide oute his masse & made a fayre ende,
But sore astoyned and fesed in his mood
Is þis man. Now ȝe wote weel, þe ereynis kende,
Withouten tryacle take it, wil sone bende
To cruell deth, thus supposed this man.   265
Wherfore, with face ful pale and ful wan,

He abidith his chaunce what schal befalle.
He cryeth onto God to send him counfort,
And in his prayere, as he gan to calle,
Oure lord with mercy mad to him resort,   270
And as oure book ful notabily can report,
Before þe autere where he gan knele,
Aboute his nose ȝekyng gan he fele.

Wherfore with handis bisily rith anoon
Onto þat place to scrat it mad he hast   275
With his fyngeris scharply on þe boon.
And in a neȝyng sodeynly þoo he brast.
With þat neȝyng alsoo eke he cast
The grete ereyn rith oute at his nose;
Whech was a miracule ful grete, I suppose.   280

---

telalters (Breslauer Studien zur historischen Theologie, N.S. 4; Breslau, 1938) 63-67.

fol. 5r   Now wil I ask þis, if euery man be bounde,
            Whann þat he stant in swech manere chaunce,
            To receyue onclennesse whech is ifounde
            On þe autere in only habundaunce?
            Doctouris of Ytaile and eke þei of Fraunce   285
            And Englisch men eke sey 'nay' thertoo.
            Eke þei telle us who that we schal doo.

            Thei sey alle þis: it schal be taken oute,
            Leyd on þe patene or on sum othir þing,
            And aftirward withouten ony doute   290
            Put forth in þe lauatory forth in wasching.
            This seynt at þat tyme of age was ful ȝing
            And had not lerned alle þing be stodye;
            Or ellis God ded þis his name to magnifie.

            Thus lyued he longe in þat ilk same stede,   295
            As summe men sey he was þere thre ȝere,
            Vsing here seruyse as weel as here wede.
            Eke sumtyme among to þat place wold he stere
            Whech we spak of now not long ere,
            Sigebergense Abbey. It stant fro Coleyn   300
            Miles thre, alle þese bokes so seyn.

            There was a monasterye eke þei called Rode,
            And thedir went Norbert ofter in þe ȝere,
            For þe persones of lyuyng there were ful gode;
            Of habite were thei chanonys seculere.   305
            Sumtyme eke visited he a ful holy sere,
            A hermyth, Lydulf was þoo his name,
            A man of ful grete and ful holy fame.

316-392   PL 1270A-71A
326   man *added above and to the right of* lewid

   285 Capgrave's opinion can be documented from one of the *Doctouris ... of Fraunce*,
Jacques de Vitry: 'Si autem musca uel aranea in calicem ceciderit, non est tutum propter
uomitem muscam uel araneam cum sanguine sumere. Debet igitur sacerdos diligenter et
pluries muscam uel araneam abluere et aquam ablutionis sumere. Id uero quod ablutum
est comburatur et cinis in piscina reponatur uel in liquida substantia recipiatur. Quidam
tamen sacerdotes ex tanta fide quandoque muscam et araneam cum sanguine receperunt,

Swech man soutʒ he in þoo dayes
To lerne lettirure, to lerne eke prudens.   310
To dyuers men made he dyuers asayes;
To vse vertu and to voyde necligens
Was ʒoue al his bysi studious eloquens.
This was his lyf alle these thre ʒere.
Saue sumtyme in preching þe puple wold he lere.   315

fol. 5v   In this same tyme, at a town called Frixlare,   v
          Was gadered a gret councell to reformacioun
Of holy cherch, & many prelates were þare.
But principal of alle and most dominacioun
Had a worthi man of þat same nacion,   320
Conone called, special legate fro þe pope;
Of certeyn defautes gan he visite & grope.

---

quod eis nil nocuerunt.' *The Historia Occidentalis of Jacques de Vitry*, ed. J. F. Hin-
nebusch (Fribourg, 1972), pp. 245-46. I am grateful to Fr. Colledge for having brought
this passage to my attention.

298 St. Victor, Xanten. See ll. 202-203 above.

300 Capgrave confuses this priory, 'Sigebergense quoddam monachorum coenobium'
(PL 1269C), with the abbey (mentioned in l. 184) 'Sigebergense quoddam magnae ac
praeclarae famae caenobium' (PL 1263B). Siegburg Abbey was near Cologne; the priory
was at Fürstenberg near Xanten. It was founded in 1119 as a daughter monastery of the
Abbey. Norbert and his brother Heribert figure prominently as patrons of the priory.

302 *Rode*: Klosterrath in Rolduc, Province of Limburg, Holland. At one time this was
an abbey of the Augustinian Canons. See Chas. Dereine, *Les Chanoines réguliers au
diocèse du Liège avant Saint Norbert* (Louvain, 1952).

307 *Lydulf*: C. Dereine ("Le premier Ordo de Prémontré," *Revue Bénédictine* 58
(1948) 91 n. 4) reviews various opinions concerning the identity of this man and
suggests that the hermit in question was most probably a certain Liutolf of Lonnecken in
the diocese of Trier.

316 Fritzlar, in Hesse, was the scene of the council in 1118 at which Henry V was excommunicated — cum propter praedictam culpam, tum propter tyrranidem quam exer-
cebat in ecclesia — according to the anonymous chronicler of St. Trudo (Mansi, 21:
179). As a member of the royal household it is understandable why Norbert should come
under attack.

321 Cuno (or Kuno) (d. 1122), legate to numerous councils and synods in the early
12th century, was both in character and teaching an eminent representative of reform in
this period. There is an international flavour about his life and work. A German by birth,
he studied in England and after the Norman Conquest first served William and Mathilda
as chaplain; later he became Cardinal bishop of Preneste. See "Conon" DHGE.

The bisschoppis þat were þere mad deposicioun
Of a grete defaute, as þei þoutȝ alle:
Thei seide it was a ful grete presumpcioun   325
That swech a lewid man in despite of hem alle
Schuld preche in here diosise, Norbert þei him calle.
Thus sayde þe prelates onto þe legate,
And he consideryng here auctorite and astate

Ded somown þis man in alle hasty wise.   330
He is come to councell to ȝeue his answere.
These bisschoppis accused him before here iustise
As þouȝ he of feith an heretik were.
The first poynt þei put aȝens him there
Was þat he preched witȝoute auctorite.   335
They put eke on him þat in his sermones had he

Many inuectif wordes aȝens here astaat,
Whech was to hem grete slaundir þei sayde.
Thei saide eke how he had take a new habitȝ laat
Of holy religion and not down ilayde   340
The propirtee of wordly good. Al þis þei upbrayde,
And whi he þrew awey al precious wede,
Whech was not þe custom in þat ilk stede.

Aȝens þese obieccionis þis man witȝ meke voys
Stood vp to answere, and asked silens.   345
First with his hand he blessed him witȝ þe croys
And aftir þat he spak in open audiens
Swech maner wordes, and in swech sentens:
"If I be accused as of religioun here,
What is my religioun now may ȝe here: 350

fol. 6r   Very religion, as þe holi apostill seith,
Clene and ondefiled before þe fadir of heuene,
Is to visite fadirles & wydowis of oure feith
In al here tribulacioun, & with þe werkis seuene
Hem to amende, & eke his lif ful euene   355
Must be so dressed þat he be euyr clene
Fro alle foule werkis whech in þis world are sene.

If I for my preching be now for to blame,
Wherfore seruyth þat scripture þat seith in þis wyse:
Whoso turne his broþir from euele fame,   360
And fro euele lif he getith him a prise,
For he is cause þat his broþir schal rise,
And saue his soule; he hiditȝ eke þe multitude
Of all grete synnes, as scripture can conclude.

And for ȝe speke of powere vsurped of me,   365
Whan I took my presthod þe bisschop to me saide:
Take þe holy goost witȝ þis new degre,
Loke þou be as clene as only mayde,
Be not aferd, aschamed, ne afrayde
To preche Goddis word, but bere it about   370
Boldly and sadly onto euery rout.

ȝet for my clothing ȝe put in me blame.
Hereth now Seynt Petir what he of cloþis seith:
Precious cloþing, before þe hye name
Of oure lord God, is not acceptable in feith.   375
Othir mo exsaumples þe gospell forth leith:
Who Ion þe baptist was clad al in here
Both body and leggis, swech as chameles bere.

And eke Seynt Cycile, þat glorious mayde,
Wered next hir skyn a hayir ful boystous.   380
Oure God eke, as þe scripture sayde,
Mad to Adam & Eue cloþis meruelous
Of bestis skynnes; þei were not corious.
Wherfor blame ȝe þing þat is onblamed?
Swech wordis of slaundir were bettir onnamed."   385

333 Capgrave heightens the tone of the accusations by a suggestion of heresy; there is
nothing in the B text to suggest this.
351 James 1: 27.
354 *þe werkes seuene*: the corporal works of mercy (Matt. 25: 35-37).
360-364 James 5: 20 and 1 Pet. 4: 8.
367 PL 1270D-1217A: Accipite potestatem, et estote relatores verborum Dei.
378 Matt. 3: 4.
379 St. Cecilia, the early Roman virgin and martyr.
382 Gen. 3: 21.

fol. 6v   Thus scaped he þis daungere be þe proteccioun
Of oure lord God; and Conone, þe legate,
Accepted ful goodly his excusacyoun.
He made at on þat ere were at debate,
And þouȝ þat þis man were no graduate,   390
Ȝet ȝaue he him leue to schryue and to preche,
As a post of þe cherch & a goostly leche.

Whan he had take þus þis general licens   vi
    To preche to þe puple ouyral where he cam,
With too deuote felawis ful of innocens,   395
Swech as he was, his iornay sone he nam
Ouyr þe feldys, þe marys and þe dam.
Went þai rith forth, þei spared no hardnesse;
Here hertis were ȝoue only to hardynesse.

Barefote þei went both in frost and hayl   400
That it was wondir who þei myth endure.
And whan his felawis for feyntness gun fayl
He fayled neuyr; so besy on his cure
Was þis Norbert; for a hauk to lure
Hasteth ful sone, so ded he to encrese   405
Vertue in soules, I sey ȝou doutlese.

Thei went in reyn, thei went in þe snow
Onto þe kne sumtyme, sumtyme to þe thy.
Were þe weye hy or elles were it low,
Thei spared rith nowt, a grete cause why: 410
Brennyng charyte made þese folk hardy
To doo these dedis to Goddis plesaunce,
And eke to here neybouris goostly gouernaunce.

393-539   PL 1272B, 1273A-75C
408   *MS period between* sumtyme *and* sumtyme

386 There is nothing in the *B* text to lend colour to Capgrave's contention that Norbert received permission to preach from Cuno, the legate. On the contrary it states that
Norbert, realizing that all were against hi:n, renounced his benefices, sold his property
and gave all but ten marks to the poor. He then set out for St. Gilles in the diocese of
Nimes where Pope Gelasius was living in exile. The Pope absolved him from the

His mete was comounly neythir flesch ne fisch,
But bred, herbis, frute & swech oþir þing;   415
Saue on þe Sunday had he in his disch
Fisch-mete & not often, & in þe euenyng
Was his refeccioun and his counfortyng,
For he wold faste alle þe day before,
As þei bere witnesse þat his felawis wore.   420

fol. 7r   His body rested not alle þe long day;
His goost was bysy both be day and nyth.
What for prayere and prechyng be þe way
And stody at eue how þat he schuld fyth
Aȝens his goostly enmye as a knyth   425
Swech was his lyf whil he lyued here;
Of othir þingis here aftir schul ȝe here.

With þese too felawys, as we seyd wel late,
Went he forth preching be town and be cyte
To Orgliaunce first, & þan forth in his gate,   430
As in his lyf ful pleynly rede may ȝe.
Thei coupled to hem a man of anoþir cuntre
Or þei to Valens cam, as ȝe schal here.
A sodekyn he was & a ful noble skolere.

Thei came to Valens rith on Palme Suneue,   435
And on þe Sunday Norbert, þis noble man,
Made a sermone of trew and rith byleue.
As he þat ful weel and eke ful treuly can,
Expleite þe message of Crist þat al þing wan
To his subieccioun be his owne blood sched.   440
The puple compelled him to rest & goo to bed

---

irregularity of his ordination and gave him permission to preach, ubique terrarum vellet et posset (PL 1273A). Capgrave short-circuits the story here by failing to include the episode, though later he refers to this permission from Pope Gelasius. See ll. 666 ff. below.

417 PL 1273B: piscibus namque seu vino rarissime utebatur.

430 Capgrave's omission of the visit to Pope Gelasius confuses Norbert's itinerary and renders his appearance at Orleans (*Orgliaunce*) less credible. In the *B* text, of course, it is a stop on his northward trek from the south of France.

433 Valenciennes is some 300 miles northeast of Orleans and over 500 miles north of St. Gilles.

And to refresch his wery membris alle.
But he nold consent in no manere wise;
Therfore oure lord, on whom alle men calle,
Whech is protectour to us and eke iustise,   445
Turned his entent alle in othir wise:
That he abidith now, wheydir he wil or nawt.
Thus hath þe puple al here desire icawt.

His felawis, alle thre of whech we spak ere,
Are now falle seek; wherfor he mote abyde.   450
Eke happed so, þat whilis he taried þere,
A grete bisschop be þat cyte gan ryde.
On Wednysday, aftir þat holy Palme tyde,
Cam he to towne, & Norbert knew him weel.
Thei had ete togedyr many a good meel   455

fol. 7v   In þe emperouris of Almayn, as I ere told.
But of þis aftir. Lete us now first speke
Of his felawis whech were of houshold,
And lyn alle thre ful febil and ful seke.
Thei deyid alle thre rith in Estern weke,   460
And went onto God for here good lyuyng.
Too of hem þat tyme chose here byrying

Rith in þe subarbes of þat cyte, Valens,
In a cherch to Seynt Petyr dedycate.
Rith be þe market is here residens;   465
There layde þai down here carnel astate,
And left þis worldly desese and debate.
The þird felaw was made a munk þere
And lith rith among hem, as ȝe may here.

Now wil I telle, as I began wel ere,   470
Off þis bisschop, Brocard was his name,
Cameracense his title, whan he was logged þere.
This ich Norbert, for werynesse ny lame,
Herd men sore speke of þis bisschoppis fame.
Streit he goth onto þe bisschoppis in,   475
But ere he myth into þe hostell wyn

466   Th of There *expunged by red dots but no correction made; I have let*
       it stand though it might be Where

He fond a clerk stondyng at þe ʒate
Longyng to houshold, & mekly he him prayde
That to his lord he schal make a gate,
And sey a man, ful pore and louly arayde,   480
Wold speke witʒ him fful mekly as a mayde.
This clerk his message doth, & in him browt.
The bisschop, as ʒet for soth, knew him nowt

Til he had told him certeyn toknes trewe,
Wherby he knew him, and sodeynly anoon   485
The bisschop on him ful sore gan to rewe.
He cryed lowde: "O God, þat art but oon!
Who wende sumtyme þat Norbert schuld þus goon
In swech aray, ful bare and euele iclad?"
This clerk stood by witʒ countenauns ful sad,   490

fol. 8r   And at here chere toke he ful grete heed.
But he no þing vndirstant of here langage
Because he was not born in þat same steed
Where þei were bore, but come on pilgrimage
Fro Ytaile, men wene. Now alle his corage,   495
And many day before it, set in þis wise:
To leue þe world & drawe to Goddis seruyse.

The bisschop turned onto þe clerk ful sone.
"Seest þou þis man," he seith, "þat stant here?
He and I were felawis ful long agone   500
In þe emperouris hous, ful leef & ful dere.
Now is his cloþing chaunged and his chere.
I sey the, ferþermore, he himself myth be
Rith as I am and of þe same degre."

471 Burchard, bishop of Cambrai (1115-1131). See *Gallia Christiana* 3: 27 and
Cyrille-Jean Destombes, *Histoire de l'église de Cambrai* (Lille, 1890-91) 2: 56-70.
  503 Both the *A* and *B* versions of the *Vita* quote Bishop Burchard as stating that Norbert refused the see of Cambrai. It is corroborated by Herman the Monk, *De miraculis S.
Mariae Laudunensis* (ed. R. Wilmans) MGH, SS. 12: 659 and in the short biography of
Burchard, *Gallia Christiana* 3: 27. Whether Norbert refused because of his worldliness, as
the bishop's words suggest — 'homo nobilis et deliciis affluens in tantum ut episcopatum
meum cum ei offerretur respueret' (PL 1274C) — or because of his opposition to lay investiture, as the editor of the *B* version suggests in a note (PL 1274, note 46), is not
known.

Alle þese ich wordes noted weel þis clerk,   505
And in his brest bare he hem ful stille.
The day was ny don, for it gan to derk.
Therfore Norbert be þis bisschoppis wille
Taketh now his leue; he hatȝ spoke his fille.
Hom he wil certayn, his felawis now ontoo;   510
He kepte hem not longe, but biried hem rith soo

As we have discried now a litil aboue.
He himselue is now ful seek ifalle.
This bisschoppis clerk euyr gan loke & houe,
If God fro þis world þis man schuld now calle.   515
Euery day went he fro his lordis halle
To loke at þis pore man, for sikir his entent
Onto holy lyf for euyrmore now is bent.

And schort tale to make, whan he was heil,
He mad ful connaunt witȝ him for to wende.   520
"O lord God," seid Norbert, "aftir thi fleil
Of tribulacioun ful weel can þou sende
Thi schynyng counfor goodly to þi frende.
Euyr be þou þanked, lord, of þi sonde,
And euyr be we bounde in þi loue bonde."   525

fol. 8v   This clerk, whech I spak of, gan take hys leue
To go to his cuntre to dispose certeyn þingis
Whech þat his kynrod onto him ded leue.
Norbert was aferd of swech taryingis:
"Brothir," he seith, "if þi message þat þou bringis 530
Be sent be God, it schal neuyr be distroyed
Ne with no temptacyoun of þe deuele anoyed."

Neuyrþelasse, þe man hatȝ now caut leue,
Went hom and cam aȝen ful constauntly;
For in his purpos so weel gan he preue,   535
That euyr he folowid his steppis by and by.
Thus are þai ioyned in sted fast cumpany;
Thus are þai ioyned in stedfast cumpany;
For too breþerin with loue ioyned in oon
Are lich a strong cyte, as seith Salamon.

540-623   PL 1280C-81C

Fro þe cite of Valens onto a town beside   vii   540
   Is he now goo, Gemlacum þei it calle.
Euery man is bysy for to goo and ryde
To here his sermoun, thus thei seide alle:
"We know not of oureself what schal befalle.
Lete us turne to God, be þis mannys counsaile;   545
His good doctrine may us mech avayle.

He is a bryngere of pees, a distroyer of werre;
He is ful of vertu, ful of sobirnesse;
Al manere þing that is oute of herre
He bryngith to pees and to stedfastnesse."   550
Thus seide þe puple of him, as I gesse.
But whann he had prechid, þei leued it weel more;
Thei seide he was in erde a heuenely tresore.

Now happed þoo dayes, in þat same cuntre,
That too princes at grete debate ware.   555
Wherfore of þe puple requyrid þo was he,
This same Norbert, þat he schuld not spare,
But pleynly and platly bid hem beware.
These too princes, þei leue no lengere soo,
Because þat mech care and eke mech woo   560

fol. 9r   Was wrouʒ in þat cuntre rith for here sake
In manslaut and robbery, enuye and debate.
This noble man streit gan his iornay take
Onto þese men þat were so obstinate.
The first of hem he gan thus to rate: 565
"Take heed, good man, what þat þou art.
Alle þat þou weldist it is Goddis part.

563   h *imperfectly erased after* t *of* streit

514 Capgrave's nameless clerk was Hugo: 'qui proximo post eum loco successit in regimine Praemonstratae Ecclesiae' (PL 1275D-76A). Norbert's popularity as a preacher, the attempts to trip him in his speech, his training of Hugo and his success as a peacemaker (PL 1275D-1280C), are not treated by Capgrave.
538-9 Prov. 18: 19 (Capgrave's addition).
541 Gembloux, Belgium, about 25 miles northeast of Valenciennes.

Thi ricchesse, þi powere comth fro God aboue,
And I am his seruaunt þat bringe þe þis message.
Thou schal not obeye me for myn owne loue,   570
But for Goddis loue I bidde þe þat þou swage
Alle þi malyce and thi bittyr corage,
And drawe onto vnyte, as þou art bounde.
Forȝeue þi neybouris here on þis grounde

Alle here trespaas whech þei do to þe,   575
If þou wilt þat God ouir þi defautes alle
Be propicious, lord of his hie mageste,
Whan þou to him for mercy haue nede to calle.
This þing þat I ask onto þi profitȝ wil falle,
It wil ese þe cuntre, releue þe pore men,   580
Whech debate destroyed, as we weel ken."

Whan þat þis lord had herd þis man speke,
He beheld his chere, for lich a aungell he schoon:
So britȝ he was for alle his penauns, þis freke,
This noble prince as stoyned as ony stoon;   585
Alle his entrayles were turbuled ritȝ anoon.
Witȝ spirit of pite fulfillid he gan answere:
"God þank þou, sere, for þat ȝe list to lere

Swech as I am both loue and charyte.
I wil obeye onto ȝou in alle maner wyse,   590
Rith as ȝe wil, ritȝ so schal it be.
I am aferd of þat hye iustyse,
That whann he sittith in his grete assyse,
He wil elles dampne me but I do sum good."
Thus was þis man chaunged of his mood.   595

fol. 9v   Whann he hatȝ conquerid þis man, he is now goon
To conuerte þe othir, but he sped nowt.
The sower of discord, as hard as ony stoon,
Had congeled his hert, his wil & his thowt.
He considered not who dere Crist had him bowt;   600
Ne entended non charyte no more þan a beste.
Wherfore Norbert of his message seste.

571   þ *written above the line after* bidde
591   it *written over an erasure*
601   no *written above and to the right of* charyte

He sey þe felle eye, þe contenaunce & þe chere,
The wordis of þe man & alle þe disposicioun.
Therfore him thoutʒ he schuld not as yere   605
The precious stonys of goostly exhortacyoun
Throwe onwysely before þe onclene nacyoun
Of slutty hoggis; bettir it was, him thoutʒ.
To go forth in his weye & throw him rith noutʒ.

Saue whan he went fro him þus he sayde   610
Onto his felaw: "Seest þou þis man?
I trowe he be frentyk, and in brayn afrayde,
For he no reson considre now ne can.
There schal com a day whann he schal sore ban
That he refused pees, for I telle þe in trewth   615
He schal fall to mischef & þat is grete rewth.

He schal be take with enmyes & sore ibounde,
Betyn and troden down as a renegate."
As þe holy man seid, so was it founde;
For anoþir man witʒ whom he kept debate   620
Took him prisonere and made him desolate.
This telle we now, þat ʒe may se herby
This holy man had spiritʒ of prophesy.

Fro þens goth he forth onto anoþir town,   viii
   Thei called it Colroys in here langage.   625
There seide he þann a noble sermoun,
In whech he gan trete who men schuld aswage
Here yrous desires and angry corage,
And drawe onto pees in al manere wyse,
For dred of þat hye and rithfull iustyse.   630

623   *period after* prophesy
624-658   PL 1281C-82A

606 Matt. 7: 6.
625 PL 1281C has *Colrois*; *A*, MGH 677 has *Koriletum*. Coriletum is in the Province
of Tournai near Gembloux, Belgium.

fol. 10r Aftyr þe sermoun he seide to hem alle
That he wolde reforme alle maner discord
Whech was amongis hem; & þei gunne sore calle
In name Iesu, whech is oure lord,
That he schuld brynge to loue & concord 635
To men þere present or he thens went.
He was ful glad to serue here entent.

And whil þat he laboured on þe o side,
The othir man fled, and out of cherch he goth.
He took his hors, awey for to ryde, 640
Smet sore with his spores, as he were wroth;
For to abyde þat loueday was he ful loth.
But oure blessed lord, þat al erde hatȝ fyrid,
Ded bettir with him þann he desired.

The hors stood stille, he wold no ferþer goo; 645
Thus was þis man constreyned to repentaunce.
Into þe cherche he cam with mech care and woo;
He told Goddis seruaunt al þis wondir chaunce,
Prayid him for charite to ȝeue him penaunce
For his defaute, and in obedience 650
Of alle his synnis with him to dispence.

This is þe holy messager of God and of pees,
The very palme of paradys, þe dowe of innocens,
The turtill of perseueraunce þat can neuyr sees
To morne for his make whann he wantith presens 655
Of swech þing as he loueth: I mene þe absens
Of oure lord God, whech wantitȝ euery nacyoun
Tyl þat þei deye & chaunge habitacioun.

Alle þese þingis, þat we haue teld in ȝour audiens, ix
Are but a fewe of many þat he dede, 660
Ere he gadered his breþerin, men of consciens,
To dwelle togidir in þat same stede
In whech he dwelt, þe world for to trede
Alle vndir fote. But now wil we telle
What þat to him in þat ȝere befelle. 665

643   *oblique dash used to separate* lord *and* þat
659-770 PL 1282B-84B

fol. 10v In þat same ȝere deyid the pope Gelas,
      Of whech pope had Norbert auctorite
      To preche and to teche as his vsage was.
      The cardinalis aftir his deth witȝ gret vnyte
      Chosen anothir man, Kalixt hith he,   670
      Bisschop of Vyenne, a holy man for þe nonys.
      Chosen was he rith witȝinne þe wonys

      Of þe abbey of Cloyne, as seith þe story.
      And aftir he was creat rith sone anoon,
      With will and hert ful meke & ful holy,   675
      He sette a grete counsell for reformacyoun
      Of holy cherch; rith in the Frensch nacioun
      At Reymys was it sette. Thedir is Norbert goo
      For this ich cause and for no moo:

      To haue new letterys of confirmacioun   680
      Of his holy legacye as he had ere,
      To drawe witȝ preching men to here sauacioun,
      And þe weyis of heuene hem for to lere.
      He sped sone his erand whan he cam there.
      Rith for his fame and his good leuyng,   685
      Euery man hatȝ ioye to here his comonyng.

      Abbotis and priouris were bysi in þat place
      To have relaxacioun of here obseruaunce;
      But oure Norbert refused swech maner grace.
      A man, he seid, mith not do to mech plesaunce   690
      To oure lord Crist, whech witȝ a launce
      Suffered for us þat ich brood wounde.
      Swech perseueraunce euyr in þis man is founde.

693   *period at the end of the e-stroke of* founde

649 PL 1282A: et prostratus veniam petens, quod prius ab eo petebatur, quantocius gratanter annuit: et absolutionem, quod sanctum Dei virum offenderat, petiit et accepit.
  666 Cf. note to l. 386.
  678 Convoked by Calixtus II, the council met at Rheims on 20 October 1119 with 427 prelates in attendance. The main issues were simony and the investiture struggle (Mansi 21: 233-256).

The pope in his letteris commended him to a man
Thei called Bartholome, bisschop of Laudune,   695
And prayed him be mouth þat he schuld tan
Good heed at þis man and him sustene.
The same Bartholome had kynrod, as I wene,
In þat same cyte & in þe cuntre aboute,
Good men of leuyng witȝouten ony doute.   700

fol. 11r   And þerfor desired he þat þis ich Norbert
Schuld dwelle amongis hem & hem gouerne.
The man refused it witȝ wordes ful couert,
With reuerens as he myth goodly him werne.
He seyde himselue had more nede to lerne   705
Thann be a techere or a ledere ellis
Of swech men as in þat cuntre dwellis.

Tho cam þe pope onto that same cytee
With whom þe bisschop gan comoun his conceyt.
He seide he was loth, if it myth othir bee,   710
That þis holy man whech was so weel iteyt
Schuld go fro his diosise; he had leuer spend his weyt
Of syluyr & gold onto his plesaunce,
So weel him plesed his noble gouernaunce.

Be þe popes counsell he offered him a place   715
To dwelle in a cherch of Seynt Martyne,
In whech dwelled chanonis ful fayre of face,
But not seruyng God in seruyse dyuyne
So as Norbert wold. He knew hem sumtyme,
And noted hem bettir þann þat þei wende.   720
Longe he refused it but ȝit at þe ende,

726   hem *inserted above and to the right of* bryng
735   *Though* quarter *can stand alone (see MED), the meter seems to*
          demand ȝere

695 Bartholomew de Joux, bishop of Laon (1113-1150?). In 1150 or 1151 he
resigned his see and became a monk at Fusciano, a monastery he himself had founded in
1128. His epitaph records his patronage of Norbert:

Dans Praemonstratum per devia euntibus aptum.
Monstrat iter, sequitur quod novus ordo patrum.

Because he schuld not be inobedient
Onto þe pope ne to þe bisschop onkende,
Only for here plesaunce he gann consent,
So þat þe chanonis here vsage wold amende.   725
He seyde pleynly he wold bryng hem to þat ende,
Þat þei schul lyue as þe aposteles ded sumtyme.
He was amongis hem at mateyns & at pryme

And alle othir owris, but þai myth not acord
With his hard preceptis. Þei seide þat he   730
Schul not regne ouyr hem ne be here lord
Because he was so ful of souereynte,
And wold compelle hem in harder lyf to be
Thann euyr þei were in ony tyme before.
There dwelt he þouȝ a quarter (ȝere) and more.   735

fol. 11v The bisschop norchid him witȝ ful fadirly chere.
He profered him mete, he profered drynk eke,
To refresch his membris whech at þat tyme were
Ful wery and dul & for laboure seke.
But swech counfortis myth him not leke.   740
The more he stered him onto sustenauns,
The more þis man ȝaue hym to penauns.

But for his good chere þat he ȝaue him bodely,
This same Norbert made retribucyoun
With noble chaunge in counfort gostely,   745
For many a holy word & swete consolacyoun
Had þis bisschop of his gest to his sauacyoun.
Thus were þei both ful gode and ful kende,
Ech of hem þat he had gan othir lende.

Legibus instituens Norberti Martinianos
Urbicolas, mores corrigit hisce malos.
                                        Gallia Christiana 9: 532.
716 Bishop Bartholomew gave St. Martin's to the Premonstratensians in 1124. It was
the second of the proto-abbeys. See N. Backmund, *Monasticon Praemonstratense*
(Straubing, 1952), 2: 509-512.

The bisschop ledde him al aboute þe cuntre   750
To loke where he wold dwelle and abyde.
He chase neythir town, ne village, ne cyte,
But a desolat place chase he þere beside.
Men called it Premonstrat þat ilk same tyde.
This place chase he for to dwelle in,   755
He and his felawis þat wold folow him.

Ful rithfully is þe name called Premonstrate,
For Premonstrate in oure language he soundiȝ þus:
A place schewid before whech was desolate,
And aftir schuld be inhabit witȝ folk vertuous.   760
It was schewid be name þan; now is it plenteuous
Of schewyng in dede as we se at yȝe.
Euyr be it soo thorw Goddis mercyȝe!

Rith as þe verytees whech are in owre feith
Were schewid be figuris in þe elde testament,   765
Rith so þis ordre whech Norbert forth leith
Ful of religioun, ful of holy entent,
Took in þis place a very fundament,
As in a figure schewyd mystily
Amongis busschis & breris hid ful pryuyly.   770

771-833   PL 1284B-85A
786   *period after* gon
790   ne *added above and to the right of* eue
796   *MS* noblel *with an expunction dot under the first* l

750 The fact that Callixtus II handed Norbert over to the care of the bishop of Laon has been interpreted as papal disapproval of Norbert's itinerant apostolate and a means to channel his energies and abilities into a "safe" project. This is the opinion of H. Grundmann, *Religiöse Bewegungen im Mittelalter* (Berlin, 1935), p. 44: "Allem Anschein nach war aber, weder der Papst noch der Bischof von Laon dazu bereit Norbert weiterhin wie bisher herumzugehen lassen." Chas. Dereine S. J., "Les Origines de Prémontré," *RHE* 42 (1947) 377 sees the Pope's attitude as one of "l'estime et la bienveillance, non la défiance ou l'hostilité, ..."
754 Prémontré in the forest of Coucy, Soissons. The charter of grant signed by Bishop Bartholomew and his chapter is printed in PL 1359-1364. See Fr. Petit, O. Praem, "Pourquoi saint Norbert a choisi Prémontré," *Anal. Praem.* 40 (1964) 5-16.
758 The etymology is Capgrave's. A. A. King, *Liturgies of the Religious Orders* (London, 1955), p. 157 notes a similarly pious etymology in the life of B. Godfrey (*ASS*, Januarii 2 (13 Januarii) 135): 'Venit ad locum vere juxta nomen suum, a Domino

fol. 12r   In this same place made he a solempne avow   x
        To dwelle þere witʒ þis condicion: if God wold him sende
Felawes good and sad to drawe in þe plow
Of holy religioun. For sekir now his mende
Was euyr sette only onto þat same ende: 775
That he wil make a college aftir his lyf;
Vpon þis conclusion is he inquysityf.

For þat cause eke he walketʒ al aboute,
He sowith þe seed whech Crist broutʒ fro heuene.
To euery puple, to euery parisch and route   780
Preched he the gospell, witʒ ful mylde steuene.
His wordes þoo happed for to falle ful euene
Into good ground. Whann he to Camerace cam,
There turned he to God a noble ʒong man.

Thei called him Euermode; he was enspired soo   785
That whan Norbert was gon in þat same place
Where as he preched, now is Euermode goo
To knele and pray þat God schuld send him grace
Owt of his hert þis worldly lust to race.
Euene as of Crist was seyde in prophecye: 790
"Thei schul worchep, lord, þi steppis holye."

So of þis man may be seyde in dede
That his steppes of grace ʒoue swech a prende
Onto his foloweris, þat þei ful sone ʒede
The same weyis to whech he gan wende.   795
This nobel Euermode now so sore gan bende
Onto þe skole of his maystir dere,
That he forsaketh al þing þat is here.

---

praemonstratum, electum et praedestinatum.' *B* states it more factually: 'Elegit locum valde desertum et solitarium, qui ab incolis antiquitus Praemonstratum vocabatur' (PL 1284B).

768 MED quotes this as 'fundament'; the text has *fundament*.

783 Cambrai, Nord, France, southeast of Douai. See H. Lancelin, *Histoire du diocèse de Cambrai* (Valenciennes, 1946).

785 Evermode was later bishop of Ratzeburg where he earned the title "Apostle of the Wends." He died in about 1178 and his cult was approved by Benedict XIII in 1728. See ASS Februarii 3: 47-51 and A. Zak, "Episcopatus ordinis Praemonstratensis," *Anal. Praem.* 4 (1928) 297.

791 Isa. 60: 14.

He was so special aftir to this man,
That þere is non but he, if I schuld sey soth,   800
Doth þat plesaunce; ne non eke do can
Swech maner dedis of religion as he doth.
He had charge of soule and body both;
He had in comaundment eke, as I gesse,
To bery his body alle the bysynesse.   805

fol. 12v This was þe secund felaw þat was chose.
Anothir þere was, whech at a town Niuigelle
Dwelled sum while, rith as men suppose;
But in sykirnesse this may we wel telle,
That þere he had him & led him to his celle.   810
Antony hith he, if ȝe will algate knowe,
Of witte studious, of hert he was ful lowe.

The thirde he had chosen longe before:
He was þe bisschoppis clerk Cameracense.
These thre and he were þe very tresore,   815
The very ground of þis ordre in existense,
Fulfillid witȝ pite, replete with innocense.
Who & whann he gadered his noumbir hertoo,
Of special callyng þis book touchitȝ no moo.

But thus mech he seith, þat in þat same lente   820
Whech folowid aftir he gat him felawis þirtene;
So þat in Passioun weke with hem alle he wente
Streit to Premonstrate, þere held þei, as I wene,
Here first Estern. Thus was þis couent isene
And eke igadered in that holy tyme   825
Ful conueniently, acordyng to oure ryme.

807   at *written above and to the right of* whech
824   T *of* Thus *capitalized*
828   Toward the holy lond *over an erasure*
834-980   PL 1285A-87A
841   *final* e *of* grete *blotted*
849   hem *written above and to the right of* Witȝ

805 *Vita B's* reference to this is clearer: 'Et post discessum suum, locum sepulturae suae ei commendaret' (PL 1284C).

For euene as Israel out of Egipt went
Toward the holy lond at þe fest of Pase,
Rith euene so þese men fro þe world are hent
As fro Egipt, & to religioun go a pase   830
As to Ierusalem, where þei gynne to brase
Alle Moyses tabernacule, witȝ his instrumentis,
Whech tokneth oure cherch, witȝ þe sacramentis.

Thus upon Cryst, whech is very ground   xi
    Of alle godnesse, biggid is this place   835
Of whik stones sware and no þing round,
Ful of veynys grauen all with grace.
The grete werkman aboue he ded race,
Alle þis werk goostly in here soule.
So techith us þe noble clerk Seynt Poule.   840

fol. 13r Thei made here place, þei made a grete hostel
In whech pore men, pilgrymis, and alle nedy
Were refreschid fro here hungir fel,
Fro here mischeuys; for al þing was þere redy,
Of bounteuousnesse þat hous was ful sedy.   845
But þe deuele, enmye to alle goode dedys,
Had grete envye with swech maner sedys.

He had enuye with hem þat were deuoute,
Witȝ hem þat lithly trespas wold forȝeue;
The grete fasteres stered he witȝouten doute   850
That þei schuld suppe whan it was late at eue.
To Goddis seruauntis he is a wikked reue,
For he wil lede hem from þe flok erraunt,
And make hem eke of here synne avaunt.

807 Nivelle, Belgium, 17 miles south of Brussels.
814 Burchard, see l. 471 *supra*.
818 PL 1285A: In hoc, ubi collegerit, vel quomodo socios alios Deus illi contulerit, non est immorandum.
827 Exod. 13: 14.
831 The MED, s.v. 'brasen', quotes this line: As to Ierbum [sic] wher þei gynne to brase/Att [sic] Moyses tabernacule (cf. Exod. 27: 2). I am not at all sure what this passage means. Certainly the tabernacle was not built at Jerusalem, nor is there work in brass in connection with Iyeabarim (Num. 21: 11 and 33: 44). A reader has suggested that the word is possibly from *bracen* in the sense of 'fasten or join one thing to another.'
840 2 Cor. 3: 1-6.

In especyal who þat he serued oon   855
Of þat same hous now schal ȝe here.
Goddis grace ful plenteuously þoo schoon
On þat same man & namely in prayere
Wold he stand astoyned in his chere
A long tyme sum while, so grete ioye had he   860
In contemplacyon of þe trynyte.

And in þis ilk same contemplacyoun
The deuele appered to him in þis wyse:
"Be glad," he seith, "þou man of þi sauacyoun,
For þou schal se veryly er þou ryse   865
For þi deuocyoun and þi good seruyse
The blissed trynyte, rith euene in his blis.
Lift up þin yȝe and se man where he is."

With þat word þe deuele apperd him too,
A fayre creature, rith as him thoutȝ,   870
O body stood before his presens þoo
With thre hedys ful sotilly iwroutȝ.
And þus he seid: "Man, drede þe rith noutȝ.
I am þe trynyte, whech þou often callest;
To þi desire alle sodeynly þou fallest!"   875

fol. 13v This man beþoutȝ him þoo in þis traunce
That inspiracioun whech comth fro aboue
Is sette in swech plith and swech gouernaunce,
It feseth no man ne maketȝ no grete schoue
Of no boystous stormys; but as a spirit of loue   880
It comth ful esily as a pipelyng wynde.
Helies avisioun stood in swech a kynde.

Thoo took he heed, þis man, & gan to þink,
For he herd a stormy, blasty clowde schoue.
Eke he felt in sauoure a wel foule stink,   885
Thorw whech ful sone he gan to trete & proue
That þis avision cam not fro aboue,
But rathere he dempt, in his estimacioun,
That it was a foul & fendly temptacioun.

897   *MS* fi *between* þi *and* selue *not expunged*

He caute a counfort herof in his herte,   890
And gan to speke with ful bold chere:
"O þou wrecch onworþi þat maist not asterte
The hand of God, þou þat were so dere,
For Goddis signacule for soth þou were
And witȝ pride þou lost þat faire figure.   895
O þou onkende, þou simulate creature!

Who art þou hardy þiselue for to feyne
That þou art þe trynyte, God moost of mith,
And art now dampned in so horible peyne
For þi grete trespaas as it is ful rith?   900
Awey fro me, awey þou enmye of lith,
Louere of derknes with þi fraudes alle!
In þi temptacyones I hope I schal neuyr falle.

He went away fro him as for a while,
For he cast him eft to come agayn   905
For to tempte him witȝ anothir wile.
And so he ded, to sey þe sothe certayn.
This man was vsed to grete fasting, þei sayn,
Haunted in prayere, redy to alle obediens.
There mytȝ no man fro his grete abstinens   910

fol. 14r Him drawe ne lette, so grete was his corage.
Scarse on þe Sunday wold he his fast breke;
Wherfore Sathanas witȝ his leonis rage
Cast him sikirly on him for to wreke.
Comen was lenton, euene þe first weke,   915
Whech þat we calle Puluir Wednisday;
Than cast he him his maistryis for to assay.

881 PL 1285C quotes the "sibilum aurae lenis" (1 Kings 19: 12) but not Elijah's vision.

894 *signacule*: signaculum similitudinis Dei (PL 1285C). In l. 2759, another confrontation with the devil, he uses *merke* (PL 1320B) for the same phrase. The OED, s.v. 'signacle', gives evidence that the word was used by the Aureate poets.

916 *Puluir Wednisday*: Ash Wednesday. MED cites Agnes Paston, *Paston Letters* 1: 270, "Wretyn at Norwyche on Pulver Wednesday."

Swech a hungir, swech a grete appetite
Fel on þis man whan it was late at eue,
That sikir, he seide, he must fille his delite;   920
Of God ne prelate wold he take no leue.
And lenten metis whech þei gun him ʒeue
Mith him not plese; but he mut nedis certayn
Ete buttir and chese to turne him into mayn.

Owre fader, Norbert, was not þann present,   925
But forth in preching as was þan his vsage.
The conuent seyde: "Brothir, take entent
What tyme it is, and of ʒoure appetite swage.
Childyr in þe world þat be but ʒong of age
Spare swech metes; þann is it to us schame,   930
We þat take upon us so hye a name

Of religioun, þat we schal be more large
In oure excesse þan þei þat be seculere."
Here ammoniciones he sette at no charge,
But þus he seide witʒ ful boistous chere: 935
"These metes & drinkis whech þat God mad here
Vpon erde, whi schuld we hem not vse?
I wil ʒe wite it that I wyl noon refuse."

But at þe last his breþerin gote þis of him:
That he schal ete euery day to meles.   940
Flesch and white, loke he neuyr so grym,
Schal he not ete. Lete him ete eles,
Tench or peke, his part now no deles
Of ony flesch whech þat he wold haue,
Thei wil not ʒeue it him, þouʒ he alday craue.   945

fol. 14v Thei dred þe speche, þe clatering eke of men
That so newe a religioun, whech þere was begunne,
Schuld so sone be broken, for if þei it ken,
They schul clatir it lowde openly in þe sunne.
Now are þe dayis of lentoun ny irunne.   950
Pase comth fast, and Norbert is com hom.
Alle þis temptacioun, he knew it ritʒ anon.

981-1211 PL 1287A-90A

Vnto his felawis he seide be the weye:
"It is not weel at hom at oure hous;
A grete waioure now treuly dare I leye.   955
There is a dede do there ful perilous."
His breþerin of his comyng were desirous;
Thei mette with him sothly ere he cam,
And teld þe caas whech was falle at ham.

"Allas," he seide, "whi wold ʒe do þis dede,   960
To lese þe soule of oure brothir so dere?
Where is he now?" and forth he to him ʒede.
He fond him fat, bolnyd and rody of chere.
With angry look, with yʒne brennyng clere,
Behelde he his maistir, astoyned as man wood.   965
He maketh no curtesie, ne avaleth no hood.

His blessed maistir vndirstood þis euerydeel,
That he was ouyrcome with temptacyoun.
He made hem drawe fro him al his meel.
"Glotenye," he seith, "hath þis condycioun,   970
Oonly fastyng is his sauacyoun
Lete him ete bred and watir al þis weke;
Hereaftirward bettir it wil him leke."

Whann he had fastid al þat lymyth tyme,
He turned deuoute, sad and obediente;   975
Sayde his mateyns, masse and his pryme
Witʒ more deuocyoun, with more sad entente.
His bodely fatnesse was impedimente
To his deuocyoun rith as seith oure book;
Thus was he voyded fro þe deueles crook.   980

fol. 15r Uoyded fro this man was þus þe fende   xii
          Be prayere, diligens and merite eke
Of oure fader Norbert and alle hatʒ an ende,
For pees and rest, whech were to seke
In this holy place are turned now to meke,   985
Both men and condicionis, & eke þis Norberd
Forth is to preche in Cristis vyneʒerd.

  968 PL 1286D: Videns ergo vir, cui Deus discretionem spirituum dederat, non esse
infirmitatis humanae, sed tentationis diabolicae.

The deuel hatȝ aspied ful sone his absens.
He bendith his bowe to loke if he may schete,
Or wayte for to hurt hem, whech in his presens   990
He durst neythir mech witȝ ne mete.
Euene as a theef lith in a strete
To wayte his avauntage whom he may wounde,
So waytith þis enmy, þis very hellehounde,

To slaundyr þis man, if that he may   995
Be ony weye lette him of his good viage.
This sawte vsed he many long day,
Til at þe last, as in a wood rage,
Certeyn persones of wit no þing sage
Gun sore to grucch of þe grete hardnesse   1000
Whech þat þei suffered vndir habit of holinesse.

There was eke so gret duresse in religioun
Thei myth not bere esily, as þei saide.
Wherfore witȝ venemous tunge, ful of detraccioun,
As men witȝ obstinacye alle afrayde,   1005
Seid þei had witȝ grete deuocioun assayde
This maner religioun: but no man mytȝ it bere,
So ful of noye was it and ful of dere.

And alle þis slaundir was put on þis man:
That he was vndiscrete in the makyng   1010
Of swech statutes of whech no man may ne can
Bere, ne sustene. For þe grete wakyng
Made he hedis all ful of akyng
And eke here fastyng wel more hem schent.
Thei saide þei had leuyr þe statutes were brent   1015

fol. 15v Than þei schuld kepe hem rith for her scharpnesse.
Alle þis ilk langage was be þe fend isowyn,
In defamyng of þis mannes holinesse,
That his good purpos schuld not forth growyn.
Oure enmye is wont euyrmore to throwyn   1020
His wikkid seed amongis þe good corn;
But on good lond it wil not longe be born.

1002   *erasure after* eke
1029   Wt *added in the left hand margin*

And for þe mannes name was þus defamed
God ordeyned a remedy to rere it ageyn,
With whech mene he was more inamed   1025
Than euyr he was before. For as clerkys seyn,
The deuele, whech is euyrmore in peyn,
Exalteth seyntes with his temptacioun,
With whech þat he supposed to brynge al adown.

At Nyuygelle dwelt he þat same tyde,   1030
For þere was he receyued most specialy.
His name was sprongen þoo fer and wyde
Thorwoute þe land, in euery cumpany.
Thedir cam a man, as seith oure story,
Witȝ his ȝong doutyr, of þe deuele obsessed,   1035
Vexid a long tyme, laboured and pressed.

With wepyng eyne þe fadir of þis childe
Prayed oure Norbert for Iesu sake
That he wold on þis creature so wilde
Haue pite and reuth & to his tuycioun take;   1040
Conioure þe deuele so he myth hire forsake.
And at þe leest, he prayed him, þat he
Wold onys se hire for seyn charyte.

Norbert answerd witȝ wordis ful mylde:
"Bring hire onto me, and we wil asay."   1045
The mayde was a fayre & a ȝong childe,
Twelue ȝere of age at that same day.
The puple presed fore to se þis aray;
And þis Cristis preest ded on his vestiment.
Both aube and stole, witȝ ful holy entent.   1050

989. Ps. 7: 13.
1030 Nivelle; see note on l. 807.
1035 *B* (PL 1288A) is more specific: 'Jam per annum a daemonio fuerat vexata.'
1050 *aube and stole*: liturgical attire consisting of a white tunic reaching to the feet
and a band of cloth worn around the neck.

fol. 16r   He coniured þe deuele be þe grete vertue
            Of Cristis passion, þat he schuld obeye
            And turne to swech place as to him was due.
            Many longe gospellis ouir hire gan he seye,
            This maydenes body to clense & to feye.   1055
            The deuele witȝinne scorned him among:
            "Swech harp haue I herd," he seid, "and swech song.

            But neythir for þe, ne for no man here,
            Schal I forsake now my dwellyng place.
            For whom schuld I go or for whos prayere?   1060
            The pileres of þe cherche, endewid witȝ grace,
            Owt of þis world haue take here pace;
            And þerfor I dwelle here in grete sikirnesse.
            No man may voyde me fro þis mayde, I gesse."

            Norbert þoo sore multiplied his orisones.   1065
            The deuele answerd: "Þou dost al in veyn,
            Thou chargest nowt me be þe holy bones
            Ne be þe brith blood whech fro þe veyn
            Of holy martires went, as ȝoure bokes seyn."
            And eke forth anoon, witȝouten ony more,   1070
            The deuel gan speke and no þing rore;

            But seide oute in Latyn al þat ilk book,
            Whech we Cantica Canticorum calle.
            Euery man gan sterten, waytyn and look,
            For þus þei seide at þat tyme alle,   1075
            Thei herd neuyr no wondir so sodeynly falle.
            For first þe maydin in Latyn al þis book spak,
            And aftir þat a exposicioun, witȝouten ony lak,

            Rehersed sche þerto; and ȝet aftir this
            In hir owne langage, in Teutony tunge,   1080
            Opened sche þese wordes witȝouten mys.
            This grete merveyle þorw þe town is runge,
            That swech a mayde of age so ȝonge
            Whech had not lerned but hire sauter only
            Schuld haue swech cunnyng of grete study.   1085

1057   he seid *written above and to the right of* herd
1069   went *added above and to the right of* martires

fol. 16v   For alle þis þing þis seynt was not aferd,
But euyr in on cryed on this fende
He schulde obeye þoo wordis þat he herd.
This goddis creature he schuld no lenger rende,
But take his viage & to othir place wende,   1090
Whereas he was wont for to dwelle.
The deuele answered, schort tale to telle:

"If þou wilt algatis," he seith, "þat I goo,
Lete me entyr þat munk þat stant þere."
For at þat tyme sikir it happed soo,   1095
A munk amongis þe puple to se and lere
Presed fast and ny, but mech care & fere
Had he in þe peticioun of þis newe logging.
Owre fadir Norbert, whech had ful clere knowyng

Of alle þe trantes whech þe deuele vseth,   1100
Cryed al lowde þat euery man myth here:
"Ʒe cristes puple, wondir no þing ne museth
On þis word þorw whech þe godman here
Is now dislaundred be þis fals lyere.
Euyr was his vsage to lye and slaundir men;   1105
Who trosteth to him þe treuth schal neuyr ken."

Ʒet hard and sore þis Norbert mad instaunce,
That þis spirit þis mayden schuld forsake.
To þis entent he ded many a obseruaunce.
The spirit witʒ boost gan to crye and crake.   1110
Grete thretis eke þoo he gan to make;
"If þou wilt," he seyde, "algatis þat I goo,
I schal clepe onto me of my felawis moo

And crye to hem: "O my blake felawis alle,
Help now, help now I be not ouyrthrowe;   1115
Doth Ʒoure laboure þat þis cherch may falle.
The grete arches þat stand al be rowe,
Lete us make hem for to ly ful lowe!
Alle þis wil we do, I sey þe withouten lees,
But if þou lat me frely dwelle in pees."   1120

1096 I have let *lere* stand, though 'here' would make better sense. The Latin text is of
no help: monachus quidam astabat (PL 1288C).

fol. 17r This herd þe puple and þei fled anoon.
Norbert abydeth and is no þing agast,
But he abydith stabyly as a stoon;
He seid his orisones & his blessingis fast.
The mayde roos up and both hire handis cast   1125
Onto þe stole þat hing aboute his nek.
Sche held him soo þat he gan to qwek.

Summe stert to, to pulle awey hire hand.
"Let be," seid Norbert, "I bid ʒou touch hire nowt.
If sche hath powere of Crist witʒ þis band   1130
To bynde my nek, lete þe dede be wrowt.
Crist is my lord, for he hath me bowt;
I trost on him sche schal me no þing dere."
With þat word, hir hold sche gan leue þere.

The day went ʒerne & was wel ny ended.   1135
Therfore owre Norbert bad þei schuld in hast
Take þis mayde, þat sche schuld be amended.
Hand and foot he bad bynde hir fast,
Into a vessel of haliwatir þei schuld hire cast.
Because eke þat sche had fayre ʒelow here,   1140
Alle hire lokkis he comaunded þei schuld schere

For þis entent: he supposed þat be occasion
Of this beute, þe deuele had more powere
Ouyr this creature. But whan þis decaluacion
Was performed, þe deuel gan crye and bere: 1145
"Thou pilgrime of Fraunce," he seit, "what dost þou here?
What haue I do, wherto reuest me my rest?
May I not dwelle for þe in myn nest?

Alle euel happe and alle wikkyd chaunce
Falle upon the for thi vexacyoun   1150
That þou dost to me witʒ þin obseruaunce.
Thou hast reft me mech domynacioun
Onþank haue þou for þin occupacyoun."
Thus seide þe deuele, & because þe day was don,
He bad hire fadir lede hire hom anon   1155

1128 *MS period between* to *and* to
1133 I *added to* scha; *virgule used to separate* schal *from* me
1157 him *added above and to the right of* onclothid

fol. 17v And bryng hire ageyn þe next day to messe.
He onclothid him of his vestimentis alle,
And whann þe deuele sey him oute of his clothis dresse,
With lowde voys he began to lalle:
"A fayre happe is now to me falle.   1160
Thou has do a þing þat pleseth me ful weel,
Thou hast not þi purpos now neuyr a deel.

Now dost þou þing onto my plesaunce,
For þu leuyst þis werk for very werynesse,
For very ioye now I gynne for to daunce.   1165
Oure fadere Norbert, witʒ ful grete heuynesse
Onto his hostell gan him sone dresse,
For in his mynde hatʒ he mad þis avow
That he wil no mete ne no drynk take now,

Ne neuyr cast him for soupe ne byte,   1170
Onto þe tyme þat þis wikkid goost
Be voyded, and þat þis mayde be qwyte.
Thus was he fastyng al nytʒ with his hoost.
The othir day cam, & þis preste of vertu moost
Goth forth to cherche his messe for to synge.   1175
There is now rennyng; þere is now waytynge;

Euery man loketh wheithir þe deuele or he
Schal haue þe maystri. He bad þei schuld take
This ich mayden & be þe auter ny as it myth be,
Hold hire fast because sche gan to qwake.   1180
This religious preest seide: "Þou fende, awake.
Voyde now þis body." Þoo seid he gospellis feele
Ouyr þis mayden, to hire goostly hele.

The deuele answerd, as he had do before,
That he had herd swech harpes sownd or now.   1185
He sang his masse, wit orisones lesse & more.
Til sacry cam, & þan þe deuele sore low,
Lowde he cryed: "God, I make a vow.
Se, men, þe litil God betwyx þe handis too
Of ʒoure Norbert, how he it liftith, loo."   1190

fol. 18r Thus deueles are aknowe þat heretikes denye!
This man prayed sore witȝ grete deuocyoun
That oure lord God, for his grete mercye,
Schuld of his grace make a dyuorcyoun.
Ful hertily to God made he his mocyoun,   1195
So ferforth þat þe deuele felt peyne,
And with grete waymenting þoo gan he seyne:

"I wil go, I wil, lete me now pase.
Turment me no more, I am obedient."
With þat word his weye sone he tase,   1200
With horibile stynk at hire fundement,
And stynkyng vryne whech lay on þe pament.
Thus seide thei þat in presens were,
In ful mechil þoutȝ and mechil fere.

Thus wery and seek for very febilnesse,   1205
Is þe mayde bore to hire fadere hous,
And aftir witȝ kepyng was sche, as I gesse,
Heil of body and of soule vertuous.
Thus is sche recured be werkys meruelous
Of God and Seynt Norbert, whech was hire leche.   1210
Euyr to his patronage mote men seche!

Now wil we speke what maner gouernaunce   xiii
He sette in his cherch, Premonstracense.
Witȝ special exhortacion he gan hem auaunce,
Whann he visitid hem newly witȝ his presense.   1215
He sette þere þe reulis of clene consciense;
Both morw and eue he vsed hem to fede
How þei in all clennesse here lyf schuld lede.

1212-1330 PL 1291B-92D
1225   MS only ph k legible, but in l. 2849 Capgrave spells phisik

1191 This is not a contemporary theologian's reflection on Wycliffe's Eucharistic
views; Capgrave is translating the text rather closely: 'Fatentur daemones quod haeretici
negant' (PL 1289C).
1211 Capgrave omits the following incidents related by B: 1) Norbert's visit to
Cologne where he points out the lost relics of St. Gereon, patron of the cathedral; 2) Ermensendis, Countess of Namur's, request that Norbert send canons to Floreffe — cf.
Backmund, Monast. Praem. 2: 373-378.

Here hye purpos, whech þei had take,
He stered hem to kepe it witȝ holy entent.   1220
The wordly goodis whech þei had forsake,
And eke here hertis were fro hem bent.
His steryng was euyr so to hem sent
Þat þei schuld not turne aȝen to swech delite
Of whech be his ph[isik] þei had a vomyte.   1225

fol. 18v   He ferd lych a egle schakyng his wyngis,
Prouokyng his birdis here coors for to flye;
For in his exhortacionis euyr more he myngis
These worldly plesaunses to passe forbye
And entenden to swech ioyes þat are upon hye.   1230
He himselue vsed lo swech manere flith;
He ascendid wit orison both day and nyth

And rested euene þere where as his mynde
Was bore up witȝ contemplatif bysynesse.
Summe of his bretheryn eke witȝ þat same wynde   1235
Were so irauyschid into holynesse,
That fro þat place where þei sat, I gesse,
Thei þoutȝ þei flyed euene up to heuene.
So had þe gost endewid hem witȝ þe ȝiftis seuene.

Specialy þei loued soo þis ilk same man   1240
That þere is no reule now, ne no obseruance,
Whech ony clerk can hem bryng or tan,
That may plese hem, but only þe gouernaunce
Of oure Norbert, whech may be to hem plesaunce.
But al here lokyng and here goostly desere   1245
Is sette his lernyng and doctryne to here.

And þat hatȝ þis man considered, by hy discrecioun.
He þoutȝ þat þis þing was perilous in charge;
Wherfore discretely onto his congregacioun
Of grete liberte he graunted þis targe: 1250
That þei schul in here eleccion stand at here large
To chese hem what reule þat hem likitȝ best;
So schall here consciens be most in rest.

1239 ȝiftis seuene: i.e. gifts of the Holy Spirit. Cf. Isa. 11: 2.
1252 For the form of the Rule attributed to St. Augustine see Charles Dereine, S. J.,

This was his dreed þat aftir his desees
On schuld go þis weye, anothir schuld go þis.   1255
Therfor þat þei schuld dwelle in stable pees,
And renne þe weye þat turne not amys
But ledeth streyte to eterne blys,
He wold sette hem in a lif moost conuenient
Onto þe apostelis lif, þis was his entent.   1260

fol. 19r For sum men counseled hem ankeris for to be,
Summe ʒoue hem counsel to dwelle in wildirnesse
As hermytes al alone, but þe moost comounte
Seyde there is a ordre ful of holynesse;
Men clepe it Cistercienses, rith as I gesse.   1265
This ordre wil þei haue, many of hem,
For þat ordre was ful ryf þoo in þat rem.

But neuyrþelasse here alderis desire
Hangeth on here fadere and his eleccion.
Thei are so bounden witʒ þe strong bond of wire — 1270
I mene loue — þat in his discrecioun
Put þei now here lyf & alle here disposicioun,
Loke what he wil, þei wil stande thertoo.
He must do alle that schall there be doo.

Whan he had avisid him, þis reson gan he make: 1275
"Taketh heed," he seid, "what we haue be or now
Indifferently in clothis, þe white & þe blake,
Haue we be clad and eke oure avow
Hing moost sewirly on þat ich vow
Whech is now called Seynt Austenis reule.   1280
Aftyr þat, be my reed, schul we us reule."

1254   This was ... desees *written over an erased line*
1294   *MS* te Seynt

"Le premier Ordo de Prémontré," *Rev. Bén.* 58 (1948) 84-92. A critical edition of the
Rule has been published by Luc Verheijen, O.S.A., *La Regle de Saint Augustin*, 2 vols.
Etudes Augustiniennes (Paris, 1967).
1265 Dereine, "Le premier Ordo," pp. 91-92, has shown that Norbert's community
was definitely 'canonical' in its beginnings. There were, from the very beginning, some
who favoured a more monastic life-style, and these, under the leadership of the first ab-

The book was brout forth onto his presens
Red lef be lef, witʒouten werynesse.
He seyde it was a reule of ful grete sentens,
Ful of clerkly lyuyng and ful of holynesse.   1285
Wherfor sith on him was set al þis bysynesse:
To chese hem a lyf, he seid in wordis plat,
He wold non othir reule chese hem but þat.

It was ful ny Cristmasse. Þerfor at þat fest,
Cast he him þat his bretheryn alle   1290
Whech wold abyde, þe more and þe lest,
With on asent þe holy goost schuld calle,
And mekely to a fraternyte schuld þei falle,
Makyng here profession to God & t⟨o⟩ Seynt Austyn,
As very childirn and eyres of his kyn.   1295

fol. 19v Thann felle there dowtis in this same matere,
For dyuers exposiciones þat on þis reule were.
Wherfor here conscienses were not alle clere,
And therefore seide þei þat þei wold lere
Why þat þei schuld certeyn charges bere   1300
Whech were not of custome in othir houses kept.
For very fere summe of þis cumpany wept.

Summe were aferd, summe felle in ful grete dowt,
Sum were slawhere þanne þei were wont to be.
This is aspied and openly claterid owt.   1305
But whann he herd it, this holy man, he
Seyde to hem: "Felawis, drede not þis dyuersite.
Alle Goddis weyis are grounded, witʒouten ly,
Vpon his treuth and upon his mercy.

bot, Hugo, won out. See note on l. 3326 below. H. Heijman, "Untersuchungen über die Praemonstratenser-Gewohnheiten," *Anal. Praem.* 2 (1926) 5-32; 3 (1927) 5-27; 4 (1928) 5-29, shows the marked influence of the Cistercian *Charta Caritatis* and *Instituta Generalia*.

1297 On the various interpretations of the Rule see Charles Dereine, S. J., "Vie commune, règle de Saint Augustin et chanoines réguliers au xiᵉ siècle," *RHE* 41 (1946) 365-406 and "Enquête sur la règle de Saint Augustin," *Scriptorium* 2 (1948) 28-36.

Alþouȝ þese reules be dyuers in manere,   1310
ȝet are þei not contrarie in no wyse;
Thouȝ þese customes whech are vsed here,
Be othir men be set in othir assyse
In othir place as hem lest deuyse,
ȝet are þei grounded alle on o charite,   1315
Whech is loue of god & neybour here by the.

What wil ȝe seke more of parfithnesse,
Thann ȝe schal fynde in þis book expressid?
Of loue, of laboure, of abstinens, I gesse,
Schul ȝe haue here dischis redy dressed: 1320
Glotony witȝ fastyng is here al oppressed;
Cloþing is mesured, silens is commended;
And alle presumpcioun witȝ obediens is amended.

Here is alsoo doctryne treuly tawt,
Who euery ȝongere schal, witȝ meke entent,   1325
Worchep hem whech elde age hatȝ cawt.
The very reules of reguleris here are sent
As fro heuene, a goostly sauory present,
Be Austyn, oure aungell & messager in þis caas.
Loke þat no man now refuse his graas.   1330

fol. 20r   Now of here clothing, what maner obseruance,   xiiii
Or constitucioun, calle it what ȝe wil,
He ordeyned at þat tyme witȝ his puruyaunce
Wil we speke, and eke ȝoure eres fil.
Oure fader Norbert, be very proued skil,   1335
Ordeyned his abite aftir þe holy gospell,
As ȝe schal here me aftirward now tell.

1331-86   PL 1293A-93B
1354   *period between* graue *and* white; white *written over an erasure*
1356   ony *above* outen; *right stroke of the caret is red*

1331 Capgrave's preoccupation with the habit of the Premonstratensians reflects the concern of the ecclesiastical and religious authorities in the 15th century. Pope Martin V in a special letter to the English houses in 1429 insisted that they return to the traditional cut and colour of the habit. See B. F. Grassl, "Der Prämonstratenserorden, seine Geschichte und seine Ausbreitung bis zur Gegenwart," *Anal. Praem.* 10 (1934) 56. The

He to his subiectis seyde, whann þat þei were
Gadered togider in consultacyoun,
That he in no scripture neuyr coude lere,   1340
Ne in no apostelis episteles or exhortacyoun,
What maner coloures þei wered or of what facioun
Were here garmentis mad, whech þei vsed.
Vpon þis matere he seid he had mused.

If ony othir man be þere, þat is here   1345
That haue red it, ȝet is it no preiudicioun;
But þat oure Norbert may witȝ consciens clere,
Make swech habite in his institucioun
Rith as him likith, lesse þan ony prohibicioun
Were founde aȝen it, & þere schal non be founde.   1350
As I trowe, þouȝ malice wolde abounde.

Be þis auctorite began he hem to clothe.
He seide þe aungellis, whech at þe resurreccioun
Appered at þe graue, white clothes bothe,
Seyth þe gospell, þat þei had vpon.   1355
Eke þe cherch vseth withouten ony woon
That in wollen men schul here penauns doo.
This conclusion drow he of þese too:

Be þe gospellis, he seide, grete auctorite
And he þe use whech þe cherch vseth ȝit,   1360
He wolde his puple schuld conformed be
Rith to þis custome & not refuse it.
Thus witȝ his malle þe nayle hed he hit:
"Mi breþerin for here synnes penauns here schul doo;
Therfor in wollen clothis I wil þat þei goo.   1365

---

general chapter of the order held at Mechlin in 1434 threatened superiors with suspension unless they corrected abuses with regard to the habit and monastic tonsure. See J. B. Valvekens, "Acta et Decreta Capitulorum Generalium Ordinis Praemonstratensis," *Anal. Praem.* 44 (1968) 104-108 (published as a supplement (1966-68) with separate pagination). See also F. Petit, "Les vêtement des Prémontré au xiie siècle," *Anal. Praem.* 15 (1939) 17-24, R. Van Waefelghem, *Les premiers Statuts de l'ordre de Prémontré* (Analectes de l'odre de Prémontré 9; Brussels, 1913), p. 43, and ll. 1463 ff. with the note on l. 1481.
1353 Matt. 28: 3.

fol. 20v Mi bretheryn eke schul kepe innocens,
And lich aungelis very witnesse bere
Of resurreccioun where al indulgens
Of alle trespases, withouten ony fere,
Schal be schewyd. Þerfor þat þei schuld lere   1370
How þei schuld be clene in soule and brytʒ,
Here vttyr garment I wil þat it be whitʒ.

Both white to laboure and white to holynesse
Schul here germentis be aftir myn ordynaunce.
Alle my chanones þe more and þe lesse   1375
With swech clothyng I wil hem avaunce.
Sith ʒe haue put al in my gouernaunce,
Thus schul ʒe go, but aftyr we wil declare
This ich aray in more open langage & bare."

This rithful man lerned not for þis cause   1380
These obseruaunces onto his meke couent
That he schuld dampne, schortly in a clause,
Ony ordynaunce or ony comawndment
Of othir seyntis, but oonly his entent
Was þat þei whech schuld folow his weye   1385
Onto þis doctryne nedis þei must hem teye.

This same man Norbert was in demyng   xv
Streyt and hard, specialy where as synne
Schuld be punched. Þe holy goostis techyng
Made him swech þat he coude not blynne,   1390
But euyr soules to heuene wold he wynne.
Ful many men cam to him for grace,
And ere þei fro his presens onys myth pace

Here proude spirit was turned to mekenesse.
Thus was þis man a very instrument   1395
Of goostly solaas, sothly as I gesse.
Thei þat were with synne al torent,
And eke þei þat were ful sore ibrent
In fleschly lustis, he took þe blak cole
Of synne fro hem & made hem alle hole.   1400

1370   *red period between* schewyd *and* þerfor
1387-1533 PL 1293C-95A
1408   so *added above and to the right of* tyme; *insert mark in red*

fol. 21r His occupacyoun was of no wordly þing,
But euyr goostly as to rede or wryte
Holy Scripture and his mysty expownyng.
Sumtyme among letteris wold he endyte
To dyuers states to turne hem onto ryte. 1405
Thei myth not fayle, þei þat folowid his lore,
But encresed in vertu euyr more and more.

The mynde of hem was at þat tyme so sette,
Thei loued bettyr wrecchid clothis bare
And clutte þan hole or ony othir new iette; 1410
For gay clothing þei had no grete care.
Summe of hem took peces of eldere ware
And sowed hem on here newe garmentis fast.
So were here hertis to pouertee al icast,

Thei were aschamed rith, as seith oure book, 1415
Of newe clothis, because þei had forsake
All maner vanyte; wherfore þei wold not look
Ne loue neythir þese fresch clothis blake,
Ne precious whites wold þei noon take.
There was no werk to wrecchid to hem þei þouȝ. 1420
Obediens was of hem so swetely souȝ.

What þing was bode hem þei were redy to doo,
That if a houene had be hoot brennyng
Thei schuld rathere arunne in thertoo,
Than aȝen obediens made ony grucchyng. 1425
Thei dred more here maystiris offendyng
Than ony deth or ony bodely harm,
Brennyng charyte had mad hem so warm.

1402 The question of the writings by Norbert is problematic. Certainly none of his
diplomatic correspondence is extant. G. Madelaine, *Histoire de Saint Norbert* (3rd ed.;
Tongerloo, 1928), 2: 125, attributes five documents to Norbert: three official letters (if
the "Constitution for the Poor" is such) and two sermons. The authenticity of the sermons has been questioned. Leon Goovaerts, *Ecrivains, artistes et savants de l'order de
Prémontré* (Brussels, 1899) 1: 626-627 classifies Norbert's works under nine headings:
1) Commentaries on Scripture, 2) Homilies, 3) Books of revelations and personal visions,
4) Sermons to the people, 5) Defense of Innocent II, 6) Office of the BVM 'purissimi
conceptionis,' 7) Sermo ad fratres, 8) Spiritual admonitions, 9) Official letters. In only

Silens was dew in euery tyme and place,
For þei þat folowid him in his weye preching,   1430
Were so endewyd with þis noble grace,
That notwithstandyng þei were euyr walkyng
Amonges þe puple and herd mech clateryng,
There schulde no man, in ernest ne in borde,
Of here mouthes ones here a worde.   1435

fol. 21v And if hem happed in ony defaute to falle,
Anon þei schuld go down on here kne,
With hande and mouth mekely for to calle
On here maystir þat, for his grete pite,
He schuld forȝeue hem in alle maner degre   1440
Here defautes, both in dede and thoutȝ,
And for þe puple ne schame spared þei noutȝ.

He ordeyned eke þat his breþerin schuld fast
Euery day, and ete but o mele.
The hard religioun, whech was kept ful fast   1445
And ful streit, is now larged sum dele,
Because þat men are not disposed so wele
As þei were sumtyme, treuly þus I leue.
He wold not ȝeue his bretherin eke no leue

To ryde on hors; but on asses to ryde alwey   1450
It myth not be kept for many causes grete.
On is this, ȝe wote and se at ey
Thouȝ ȝe þe asse spore or ellis bete,
His slaw paas can he not forȝete.
Eke in þis cuntre þere may no man hem haue.   1455
Who schuld þese men þese impossibles saue

1446   red period after streit; erasure before is
1462   red period between he and þat
1475   d erased from lynand and e written over the a
1486   erasure of h of clothis; scribe first wrote clothyng

---

two instances (7 and 9) does he give citations of where they may be found. PL 1357B-
58C prints two sermons 'ad populum,' and two charters (1357D-1360B). A third sermon, 'Hortamur vos, fratres dilectissimi, ad sedulam Dei ...," is mentioned by J. B.
Schneyer, *Repertorium der lateinischen Sermones des Mittelalters für die Zeit von 1150-
1350*, part 4 (Münster, 1972) 390.

Withouten dispensyng, whech I wote ful weel,
That þei haue purchased as wise men schuld doo?
He wold eke þat in euery tyme and seel
His goostly childir witȝ swech clothis schuld goo   1460
Whech hide oure schame, it nedeth to sey no moo.
Swech reules ȝaue he þat mannys myty mynde
Schuld not be effeminate in no kynde.

And of here clothis, as we seid before,
He sette swech reules as are grete plesaunce   1465
Onto oure God and ȝet, ferþermore,
Ful profitable to bodely gouernaunce.
The flesch schuld growe ful of myschaunce,
Ne were he chastised witȝ bridil of areest.
That knewe þis seynt treuly witȝ þe best.   1470

fol. 22r   For notwithstandyng þat he himself wered
Nexte his skyn a scharp hayre alwey,
ȝet was his hert witȝ swech pite stered,
Than on his bretherin lesse wite wold he ley.
Both lynen and wollen, schortly for to sey,   1475
Bad he his felawis þat þei schuld were,
Wollen next here skyn he wold þei schuld bere,

Wollen eke to laboure, owtward schul þei use,
Rith as þe pope, Innocent called be name,
Hath confermed — no man may it refuse —   1480
In his bulle þat is of ful grete fame,
In whech bulle reherseth he the same
That þis noble, holy, discreet religioun
Hath used white clothis fro here institucioun.

But for because þat þere is dyuersite   1485
In oppiniones of þese clothis partyng
Now lynen now wollen, to make a vnyte
Of this matere and who I the wrytyng
Vndirstand, I will witȝ ony lettyng
Telle ȝou now, vndir þis protestacioun,   1490
That I take upon me here no diuinacyoun

1481 Capgrave is referring, no doubt, to the Bull "In eminenti apostolicae sedis specula" (27 July 1198) by Innocent III. The pertinent section reads: 'Auctoritate

As for to determyn who þis men schul hem clothe.
Wollen clothis these men vsen schal
In penaunce doyng and in laboure bothe.
And if thei do not, þei haue a grete fal   1495
Fro here reules, for þis sentens al
Spryngith oute of Norbertis swete doctryne,
And goth onto heuene rith as ony lyne.

Wollen schul þei haue to laboure & eke to penaunce
Lynand, for clennesse, wold he þei schuld were   1500
At þe autere þere þei doo here obseruaunce.
And at alle places, schortly for to here,
Where as þei serue God þis abite schul þei bere,
Of lynand cloth oonly for clennesse,
In othir places þei are not bounde, I gesse.   1505

fol. 22v   If men wil algate of here deuocyoun
Were lynend alwey I wil it not dispraue.
Lete euery man aftyr his discrecioun
His obseruaunces in his monastery haue;
But þis wold I, þe vnyte for to saue,   1510
That alle schuld go lich to kepe honeste
Euene as alle cleyme of o religioun to be.

Thre þingis, seide this man to his breþerin there,
Were neccessarie and profitable to euery congregacioun.
Eke he wold þat þei schuld hem lere,   1515
For þere is no hous, he seid, in no nacioun,
That euyr schal falle in ony grete tribulacioun,
Whech haunteth þese þingis: þe first of hem here
Is clennesse in cherch, & ₐaboute þe autere.

1527   MS him
1534-1603 PL 1295B-96A

___

apostolica roboramus et presentis scripti privilegio communimus: videlicet, ut ordo
canonicus, quemadmodum in Premonstratensi ecclesia secundum A(u)gustini regulam et
dispositionem recolende memorie Norberti, quondam Premonstratensis ordinis in-
stitutoris, et successorum suorum *in candido habitu institutus* esse dinoscitur, per omnes
eiusdem ordinis ecclesias perpetuis temporibus inviolabiliter observetur et eedem penitus
observantie ... ab omnibus eiusdem ordinis uniformiter teneantur' (italics mine). This letter is addressed: 'Petro, abbati Premonstratensi et ceteris abbatibus et canonicis ... in per-

The secund is, in þe chapetir, very confessioun   1520
Of alle here defautes þat euery brothir hatȝ doo.
The thirde is of worldly goodis dispensacioun
To þe pore men, þat be þe cuntre goo.
These thre þingis, if thei kepe hem soo,
Ony hous of religioun, þei schul neuyr fayle,   1525
Ne neuyr schul for ony myschef wayle.

Thus be word and ded he h⟨e⟩m schewyd
No othir þing to know but oure lord Iesu
For us crucified, and to lerned and lewid
He prechid þis doctrine with laboure ful dew.   1530
It made many a man him for to sew,
Folowyng his lyf with steppes of perseueraunce,
His exaumple was to hem swech plesaunce.

It happed on a day þat he fro Reymys went   xvi
    With certeyn of his felawis & too nouyces eke,   1535
Whech he newly fro þe world had hent,
And taute hem here elde customes for to breke.
As þei went be þe weye cheke be cheke,
And kept here silens þinkyng on heuene,
A voys fro þe sky sowndyd ful euene.   1540

fol. 23r   He cryed in here eres on the o side:
"This is þe felawchep of Norbert owre frende."
Thei gunne for to list in that same tide,
Than herd þei anothir voys in þe othir side wende:
"It is not his felawchep." Þis was þe ende   1545
Of þis heuenely warnyng. He ment þat oon of þese too
Was not in hert as he pretended, loo.

---

petuum.' See *Die Register Innocenz' III*, ed. Othmar Hageneder and Anton Haidacher
(Groz-Köln, 1964) 1: 481-482.
    1520 *chapetir: capitulum culparum*, a community meeting where individuals accused
themselves of faults and failings against the community.
    1534 Rheims or Reims. See note above on l. 678.

Alle herd þis voys, and alle astoyned were,
But non wist what it signified or ment.
Wherfore oure Norbert, with devoute prayere,   1550
Day be day now his orysones hath isent
Vnto almyty God omnipotent,
That he schuld wisse him þe tokenyng of þis cry,
Whech þat he herd comyng fro þe sky.

Tho felle in his hert a gelous suspecioun   1555
Of þese too newe chosen & of here gouernaunce.
With ful sad and avised consideracyoun,
He took gret heed who in his obseruaunce
Oon of hem was ful nys in his cuntenaunce,
Slaw in comyng to seruyse, vnbuxum to obediens,   1560
Vnstable in maneris and large of consciens,

The good fadere took him oside & þus to him saide:
"Brothir, what is þat þow berest in thi hert?
Telle me now boldly and be not afraide.
For this is ful sikir, þere may no þing astert,   1565
Thouȝ þing be neuyr so pryuy hid vndir schert,
It may not be hid fro goddis brith yȝe.
Wherfore brothir make now no lyȝe.

If þou be stable in þing þat is begunne,
ȝeue thank to God and bettir it more & more: 1570
If þou be wery of goodnes new iwonne,
And be alle this ordre settist no store,
Open now þin hert that þis goostly tresore
May entre to þi soule, for I the ensure
Treuth and falshed may not togidir endure."   1575

fol. 23v The feyned man answerd as he ment:
"What heileth þe, fadere, wenyst þow I wold stele
Ony of thi tresore, eythir book or vestiment?
Be not aferd her of neuyr a dele.
I wil no þing fro þe of myn hert concele.   1580
Thou art so pore þere may no man þe robbe,
We lese not in this house a heryng cobbe!

1590   had *inserted above line after* He
1604-1715 PL 1296B-97C

He þat hat rith nowt, as þe gospel seith,
Thing þat he semeth haue men schul fro him rende
And to him þat is rich and of grete heith   1585
Men schul ʒeue ʒiftis and godis him lende."
As þis man seid, so felle it at the hende.
For þere was a new brothir com to hem late,
Whech had seld his patrimony, or ellis late

He had take therof a good qwantyte   1590
And leyd it in a bagge behynde þe autere
Where as þei sunge. Þis man with grete sotilte,
And grete awaytyng, þis feyned scolere,
Hath stole þis mony rith fro the qwere,
Whilys þat his bretherin rested in here sleep,   1595
And as a theef awey thus he leep.

He left hem not a peny, in al here hous,
To bye witʒ al þing whech þei had nede.
This dede to the theef was ful perilous,
And to þe good men it was ful grete mede.   1600
God wold hem þe weyis of perfeccioun lede,
And lerne hem be smale þingis who þei schuld do in grete.
Therfor with temperal duresse he wold hem bete.

Now of þis ich place, called Premonstracense,   xvii
Whech God had ordeynyd þese men in to dwelle,   1605
Wil I to ʒow rith in schort sentens
Alle þe descripcioun of this place telle.
Many men at þat tyme to þat felauchip felle,
Forsook al þe world, & come to þat place,
Oonly in pouerte good lyf to purchace.   1610

fol. 24r   And for because þere was grete gaderyng
Of mech puple to that religioun,
In here wittis was huge disputyng
Of here edyfies and of here mansioun.
For þe place was onable to ony habitacioun.   1615
Vntild and row, ful of brusch and brere,
Rith nowt in þe pleyn but marys and mere.

1559 The *B* text (PL 1295C) informs us that the ill-starred novice was an English-
man. Capgrave, understandably, omits this comment.
1567 Heb. 4: 13.
1583 Matt. 25: 29.

A sory place and vnable, many men þoutȝ,
Ony congregacioun to dwelle in ony while.
For whan alle here comoditees were isoutȝ   1620
Of studious men whech were ordeyned to bile,
There was no good watyr witȝ in a myle,
But a litil pitte whech fro þe hillis cam
And party was it fillid witȝ a wosy dam.

Of þe same marys. Þere stood eke a chapell,   1625
Ful old and ruynous, ny at downgate,
There was alsoo, as the stories telle,
A fayre appelȝerd; but neythir hegge ne gate
Had it to spere owt, or owt men to late.
In this same place restid this good man   1630
With swech meny & vitaile as thedyr cam,

Hopyng in God þat he schuld hem sende
Lyuelood inow of his merciful puruyaunce.
Othir religious men, þat þedir ded wende,
Whan þei had considered alle þe gouernaunce   1635
Of þis holy lyuyng, & eke þe longe distaunce
Of ony good soyle, þei seid it was impossibilite
That in þat place ony good dwelling schuld be.

Thei seide, ferþermore, þis religioun mytȝ not stande
For streyt obseruaunce, & for þe onliklynesse   1640
Of þe sory ground, þei seide, in tyme comande
Men schuld renne awey for werynesse.
Oure fadere Norbert had hardid, as I gesse,
His stabil face aȝens swech impediment.
There myth noon aduersite make him repent.   1645

fol. 24v   Ȝet þat he schuld þe hertis of hem alle
Comfortyn more kendly þat were of his flok,
And eke for þe slaundir whech was be falle,
Of þe euele tungis whech can neuyr but knok
And clater in euele tyme — wold God þei had a lok 1650
To schet with here tunge! — For þese causes tweyne
This good man, schortly for to seyne,

1625   eke *added above and after* stood; *MS period between* marys *and* þere
1657   more *inserted above and to right of* made
1676   to þe crosse *written over an erasure;* þe *has* e *suprascript*

Goth aboute þe place himselue al alone,
Waytyng & consideryng how he schal bild his hous.
The wisest of his bretherin eke he had gone   1655
And take good heed who þis place perilous
Mith be craft & cost be made more gracyous
Than men seyde it was. Thus þei ded in dede
And prayed onto God þat he schuld hem spede.

But specialy he comawnded to his breþerin alle   1660
That þei schuld, with good entent & meke prayere,
Onto oure lord God inwardly calle,
That he schuld ȝeue hem councell as in þis matere.
For here deuoute prayeris God cam hem nere,
And schewid be avysiones who þei schuld doo   1665
In bildyng of here kirk and place þertoo.

On of hem sone aftir had þis reuelacioun:
He þoute he say rith in the same place
Where as þe cherche schuld be in his avysioun
A blessed sith swete and ful of grace.   1670
He loked upward with his goostly face
And sey, as him þouȝ, in þe eyir aboue
Euene as he was crucified for oure loue,

Owre lord Iesu Crist, & seuene bemes brith
Sey he at þat tyme come fro þe sky   1675
Whech to þe crosse sent forth here lyth.
He sey alsoo pilgrimys in ful grete hy
Knelyng on þe ground crying mercy.
Summe, as him þouȝ, come from þe eest,
Summe fro north & south, summe fro þe west.   1680

fol. 25r   Euene as þe foure dorys of þe cherch now
Are made in dede, so þei come he thoutȝ
With stauys and hattis & berdis ful row,
Of here aray þei but litil routȝ,
Thei set hem on here kne & deuoutly soutȝ   1685
The mercy of oure lord. Al þis sey þis man,
And whann he wook his weye hatȝ he tan

1643 *had hardid* .../ *His stabil face:* ' PL 1296C-D — Sciens quia firmavit faciem
suam Jesus ut iret in Jerusalem (Luke 9, 51), firmavit et ipse faciem suam.'

Streyt to þis Norbert to telle him þe cas.
He þankid oure lord God and þus he sayde:
"Euyr be þou worcheped for þi hye graas,   1690
And neuyr be þin honoure fro mannis hert layde,
For whann alle frenschipis haue be asayde,
Thann is þin best. Þou ȝeuest, lord, counfort
Of þing þat is passed, & eke, if we resort

Onto þi proteccioun for ony comyng nede,   1695
Þan ȝeuest þou us knowlech of þin hye grace."
Whann he had seid þus he put awey drede,
And seide to his felawis witȝ ful myry face:
Be now alle glad ȝe dwelleris in þis place,
Arme ȝou and make ȝou redy to al temptacioun   1700
For þe sotil Sathanas witȝ al his nacioun

Schal make asaute to wynne us if he can.
For this avision, I sey ȝou treuly,
Whech þat appered now to this man,
As it semeth to me it is a prophecy,   1705
That to oure hous schul come be weye & be sty
Very pilgrymys for þei schul forsake
Alle worldly lust, and a new lyf take

Thus expowne I þis mannys dremyng."   1710
And euene as he sey in his avisioun,
So was it fulfillid at þe endyng.
Both cherch, crucifixe, dores and þe ryng
Alle was imade rith as he deuysed;
Euene as he bad, so was it desised.   1715

1716-1799 PL 1297D-98B
1730   þe *added in red above and to the left of* realtee

1722   See note to l. 695.
1728 *frankis and ducatis*: The franc here is anachronistic, minted under King John II
of France in 1360 with the legend, *Johannis Dei gratia Francorum rex*; the ducat,
however, was used in Norbert's time and stems from Apulia where Roger II of Sicily was
Duke. Hence the inscription from which it receives its name: *Sit tibi, Christe, datus quem
tu regis, iste ducatus.*

Erratum: Insert line 1709

Of clennesse and pouerte & make her professioun.

Erratum: Notes

1736 *Ingeramne:* 'Ingelramno' (PL 1297D) is Enguerrand II who succeeded his father. He died in the Second Crusade.

fol. 25v   Thus afitr he had ordeyned his edificacioun   xviii
      In spirituale houses, mennys soules I mene,
It was ful neccessarie his material mansioun
Schuld be now reysid and set on þe grene.
At þe groundes takyng were, as I wene,   1720
Ful many worthi men, of whech þe principal
Was þe noble bisschop, whech men ded cal

Bartholome of Laudune, for þere was his se.
He halowid þe stones þat went to þe ground.
He stood be þe werkmen with grete solempnite,   1725
And ȝaue hem to þe werk ful many a pound
Of frankis and ducatis þat were ful round.
There was in presens eke a noble lord,
Whos name was as þese bokes record

Thomas, þe lord of þe realtee of Coty.   1730
He dred þis Norbert & loued him alsoo.
He counseled þe werkmen hastyly to hye,
That þis cherch schuld sone be doo.
And at þat tyme it happed soo,
He brouȝt þidir witȝ him his son ful ȝong;   1735
Thei called him Ingeramne in here tong.

Many othir worthi men at þat tyme were þere
Of spiritualte and temporalte, & alle þei saide:
"What man is þis þat hatȝ now no fere,
Ne for alle þese perelis is not dismaide?   1740
Who schuld þis ground þat was neuyr asayde
Bere swech a werk of so huge a witȝ?
Thei haue put in of ston ten ton tyth

1730 Thomas de Marle, Earl of Coucy (Conci); a member of the feudal family which
took its name from the locality, Coucy le Château. Thomas's cruelty and rapaciousness
caused his own father, Enguerrand I of Bove, to make war on him. The Council of
Beauvais in 1115 excommunicated him "comme scelerat et ennemi du nom cretien, à
cause de sa cruauté" (Mansi, "Concilium Bellovacense" 21: 123). Eugène A. Lefèvre-
Pontalis, Le Château de Coucy (Paris, 1909 (?)), pp. 9-15 gives a short history of the
family.
father. He died in the Second Crusade.

Into the ground and it takith no tak."
Thus seyde þei þann, iangeleris in þe route.   1745
Thei put in þe werk a ful grete lak,
But for al þis oure Norbert hatʒ no doute,
But þoutʒ þat þe werk, whech þei were aboute,
Because it was plantyng of God aboue,
Owt of his stabilnes it schuld not lithly moue.   1750

fol. 26r   Than felle þere betwix werkmen a strif,
For sum of hem were of Teutony nacyoun,
Sum Frensch were & had be alle here lyf.
But when þei were come in congregacioun,
Eche of hem to othir had indignacioun.   1755
Therefore to swage envye & al male entent
To hem swech gouernaunce þis man hath lent,

That the o nacyoun on the o side,
The othir on þe othir side schal werk & rere.
Thus roos þe werk, ful longe & ful wyde;   1760
For non of þoo werkmen þat were þere
Feynted ony tyme to laboure or to bere,
For þat þei wold here felauchep ouyrlede,
Alle þei erned ful weel here mede.

Thus in nyne monthes þe werk had a ende,   1765
And halowid it was of þe same holy man,
Bischop Bartholomew, whech was ful kende,
And bysi to doo and pay þat he can.
For he was þe first þat þe werk began,
And he was þe last, God doo him mede!   1770
Alle þe werkmen went in his wede.

1785   be *added to the right and above* must
1799   *period after* nede
1800-1995   PL 1298D-1301B

1749 Matt. 15: 13.
1784 The original decree is attributed to Pope Hyginus: 'Si motum fuerit altare, denuo consecretur ecclesia; si parietes mutantur et non altare, salibus tantum exorcizetur' (Gratian, *De Cons.* D 1, c. 19).

But þe onstable fortune þat medeleth alwey
Hir bittir happes witȝ hire swete chaunce
Turned here ioye so sodeynly þat thei
Had no cause to trippe ne to daunce.   1775
Of puple was there so grete habundaunce
That ilk day, þat þe cherch was consecrate,
That þere was mech prees & mech debate.

And þorw boistous presing of þe puple there
The grete autere þat stood in the qweer   1780
Was meued fro his place, so sore gun þei bere.
Than is þere a statute, if ȝe wil heer,
That whech tyme witȝ violens ony auteer
Whech was halowid, as þe lawys seyn,
Be meued fro his place, it must be blessed ageyn. 1785

fol. 26v So was þis, for in Seyn Martines octaue
Was it new consecrate & anoynted eke.
And for he schuld þe elde custome saue,
He ordeyned, þerfor, þat same day and weke
Schuld euyr more of his breþerin meke   1790
Be kepte holy as a dedicacyoun,
In memory and witnes of þat innouacyoun.

Lete þis now suffise of þis material descripcyoun
Of þis real place, for now wil we turne
To telle ȝou treuly his occupacyoun;   1795
Noutȝ only his, but also we schul returne
Alle þe condicioun of hem þat þere soiorne,
So as here actes rith were do in dede,
Folowyng non ordre, for it is no nede.

This man went oute to sowe his noble sedis   xix 1800
   Of holy preching as he was wone to doo.
He left at hom, as ful grete nede is,
His place weel bylid, he left ferþermoo
Discrete gouernoures our hem euene too:
On ouyr þe prestis was made president,   1805
Anothir preferred was ouyr þe lewid couent.

1786 i.e. in the week of 11 Nov.

He seid onto hem, whan he fro hem went,
That þei schuld kepe pees ouyr al þing
Betwix hemselue; for he seid no couent
May stand at debat, þou þere be medelyng,　　　　　　1810
Where þat here prelates kepe of charite þe ring.
Wherfor to þese too he comaunded holy loue,
That þei schuld kepe it for reuerens of God aboue.

Thus fro þe folde parted with loue and pees
Is þis schepherde, and forth now is igoo,　　　　　　1815
Holy lyuyng with preching to encrees.
Oure enmy, þe deuele, is glad now & no moo
Of þis departing, for mechil care and woo
Wrout he to hem in þe absens of þis man.
His sotill sautys to rere þoo he began.　　　　　　1820

fol. 27r　Lich a wolf þat comth to a folde,
First he feseth þe scheep with his chere,
And aftir ful slyly wil he now beholde
Who he may þrote hem both there and here;
Aftir with teeth wil he neyh hem nere.　　　　　　1825
Thus farith þis enmye in his sautes alle;
Who may avoide him, a victoure men him calle.

To þese men þat in this perfeccioun
Were falle al newly þus appered Sathan:
To sum of hem made he open apparicioun.　　　　　　1830
For he cam sumtyme lich a armed man;
Sumtyme wold he þe likenesse of many tan,
With scheld and swerd, arayed as here enmyes were
Whech þei had in þe world or þei come there.

There were so fesed þann rith as hem þoutȝ　　　　　1835
Here enmyes come to hem rith to here celle.
So ny vpon hem with cruelnesse þe soutȝ,
That þei were fayn, schortly for to telle,
Defende hem with book, clothis or belle,
Or what cam next to hand witȝ good speed,　　　　　1840
So were here hertis þoo fulfillid witȝ dreed.

1810　þou: *usual form* þouȝ
1837　þe: *usual form* þei

Thei þat were not temptid with this þing,
Ne sey no swech visiones, as thei sey,
Runne onto hem with ful grete snybbyng.
Thei asked why and for what cause now þey 1845
Broke here silence & exalte here voys so hey,
Hurled so aboutʒ with stones & staues eke?
Thei answerd aʒen, witʒ wordes no þing meke:

"Se ʒe not here," þei sei, "what puple is come
With swerd and spere to gore us if þei may, 1850
And eke with many sundry dyuers lome
Vpon us haue þei made assay?
We haue now fowtyn here al þis long day,
And no man helpeth us of his charite
Of alle þat dwelle in this fraternyte." 1855

fol. 27v The sadder men, þat bettyr avised were,
Seide onto hem it was illusioun.
For non of hem, but þei þat fel in fere,
Sey no þing of this temptacyoun.
Wherfor ful hastily witʒ exorʒiʒacyoun 1860
Thei mad haliwatir & fast þrew aboute.
Thus voyded þei þese illusionis & put hem oute.

Thei crouched hem, and fast þe fantasy fled.
The oþir men þat temptid were before
Begunne to bold & were no more adred, 1865
But witʒ huge voys gunne to crye and rore:
"Awey, ʒe fendis, and assayleth no more
Goddis puple þat cast to leue in pees."
Thus was þis batayle ended doutlees.

Whann þei þat were deceyued witʒ þis chaunce 1870
Had þus aspied þe deueles sotiltee,
Thei were more redy in parfitʒ sustenaunce
To suffir temptacioun & aspye þis vanytee.
ʒet sum of hem had aftir no pouste
To perseuere in here innocent lyf, 1875
But to þe world aʒen þei went ful ryf.

And þouȝ þe fend expulsed were fro hem
As for a while, ȝet cam he sone ageyn.
For þouȝ he swalowid hatȝ alle þe strem
Of þe grete se, ȝet his appetitȝ, as þei seyn,   1880
Is not saciate but if þat he may dreyn
The flood of Iordan into his þrote only,
Be whech figure derk and al mysty

I vndirstand þat, þouȝ þe deuele hatȝ wunne
Alle worldly men onto his domynacion,   1885
It is to litil to his open munne
And not fulfillid is his temptacioun
But if he may wynne with his vexacioun
Religious men whech schuld be more clene.
This is þe vndirstanding herof, I wene.   1890

fol. 28r   Now were receyued into þis holi place
Alle maner puple and of al manere degre;
There was non refused þat called on þis grace.
Aftir þe gospell seith rith soo ded he,
Oure fader Norbert. "Alle þat come to me,"   1895
Seid Crist oure lord, "I schal wel receyue;
No man fro myn handis schal hem weyue."

But amongis alle þese þe deceyuable spiritȝ
Took grete heed þat ydiotes summe were.
He knew his vesselis, þerfor he gan hem ditȝ,   1900
And eke araye hem venym for to bere.
He made hem soo to stody and to lere,
That þei þat vnnethe coude on book rede
Within a while, witȝouten ony drede,

Now can þei rede, now can þei vndirstande   1905
Dyuers materis and derk bokes olde.
They dare now boldly take upon hande
To teche and preche; þei wex now so bolde,
That notwitȝstandyng þei be but of þe folde,
ȝet dare þei preche in here prelates presens,   1910
And he ȝaue to hem ful meke audiens.

1880   is *after* appetitȝ *expunged*

On of hem boldly took on hande
Danyeles profecies to expowne & teche.
Of þe ten hornes he gan vndirstande
Wondir doctrine and ful wondir speche.   1915
Here and þere himselue he gan to seche,
With lesinggis among, as his maistir him tawt;
ʒet wondir termes to him hatʒ he rawt.

Whann all þe breþerin in chapetre gadered were
Than seid he þingis hem þoutʒ ful meruelous.   1920
Oure fadere Norbert onto a eldeman þere,
Saddest & wisest aftir him of þat hous,
Asked him wheythir it were out perilous
To suffir þis man swech misty þingis to speke.
The othir man answered witʒ soft wordis & meke: 1925

fol. 28v "Suffir now, maystir, þis þing for a while.
It schal be wist ful weel and openly
Wheithir it comth fro þe fendis gile
Or elles it comth be reuelacioun fro hy."
Sone aftyr þis man felle seek sodeynly,   1930
He þat þese profecies þus gan expowne,
And whan he was in bed leyde adowne

Thann sette he his speche al onto þe heuene.
They cam aboute him sum to his counfort,
Of his breþerin be sex and be seuene,   1935
Summe of hem come for to report
What he wold sey of þat grete sort.
Of himselue he seyde first of alle
Grete þingis & many whech aftir schuld falle.

1880 *þe gret se*: the Mediterranean sea.
1895 *Alle þat come to me*: PL 1299D: 'Omnem qui venit ad me non ejiciam foras'
(John 6: 37); l. 1897 is a paraphrase of John 10: 29 and is not in *B*.
1914 PL 1299D-1300A: Danielis quoque unus ex eis prophetiam se scire asserebat, et
de ea quaedam duce mendacio loquebatur, ubi de quatuor, et septem et decem cornibus et
regibus propheta scribendo inducit et de Antichristo. See Daniel 7: 7-27.

Of othir felawis he spak meruelously alsoo: 1940
"This man," he seid, "þat stant here be my bed
I say on lede him the hye blis ontoo,
And ther was he with mech ioye ifed.
This oþir man þat stant here was eke led
To þat same ioye, ful his rithfulnesse.   1945
And þat þird man is he now, as I gesse,

That God hath ordeyned a bischop to be,
And þat man eke schal gouerne puple fele.
This man schal dwelle and deye in charite;
That man schal falle fro his goostly hele."   1950
Whann he had made al þis long apele,
He turned awey as þouȝ þat he wold ȝelde
His pore soule oute of þis worldly felde.

He lay stille as deed, þei sey, euene þe space
Of an houre alle hool, & þan þei gun rynge   1955
Euenesong belle. He left up his face
And alle his body. He roos withoute helpynge,
Went to þe qweer and sore gan to synge
Rith as þei dede whech his felawis were.
Ech of hem þat was astoyned with fere   1960

fol. 29r   Scorned hemselue of here illusioun,
           Beleuand þe wers al here lyf more
Ony swech troyloure with his ymaginacioun.
Ȝet was þere anothir felaw leyd in his hore
Into þe holy Apocalipse hard and sore   1965
Summe of hem sayd, "Behold who God aboue
Hatȝ visitid us neuly witȝ a touch of loue.

Lete us now lere these new reuelaciones;
Let us stody bysily þat we may knowe
The dragonis laboure and circulaciones,   1970
Who þat he wayteth bysily be rowe."
Othir wisere men þat were þere, I trowe,
Seyde þei wold not admitte no new prechoure
Til he was auctorized of Norbert here foundoure.

1989   g *added to* awaytyn *crowded before* of *and separated by an oblique*
                stroke
1996-2184 PL 1301B-03A

Than sey þe deuele he myth not þus avayle,   1975
And cast new witte new slaundir to make.
For euyr is he bysy in his assayle,
In his temptacyoun euyr wil he wake.
He hath a new sotilte now to him take:
To breke paciens and charite to confunde,   1980
Whech schuld most habundauntly in religious habunde.

For þese same too men hatȝ so set astaunce
That ich of hem is bisi othir to kille
Both in here wordes and in here contenaunce.
There is not elles but they wil fulfille   1985
Here desirous appetite, be it neuyr so ille.
So are þei sette in hertis crueltee,
But þat þei were lettid of grete charitee

Be bysi awaytyng of here breþerin aboute.
Wheythir þei were mad at on aftir þis tyme   1990
Mi book tellet not withouten doute,
Ne I myselue list not for to ryme
Neythir of here vertues ne of here cryme
But if I fond therfore sum auctoryte.
Me þinkith resoun þat it so schuld be.   1995

fol. 29v   This forseid enmye þat is so importune   xx
           In his awaytyng, and euyr schowith on hepe
Euele upon euele as is his elde custume,
On of þis houshold he gan to his powere repe;
So wood he was þat he gan stert and lepe.   2000
Thei were astoyned because Norbert was oute,
Therfore to put al þing oute of doute

1957 *roos*: MED gives several instances of *risen* used transitively. The line could possibly read, "And alle his body he roos withoute helpynge," for he uses *roos* intransitively in *Augustine* xv, l. 28.

1970 PL 1301A: Audiamus igitur eum, ut ab eo discamus quod de excelsis didicit in Apocalypsi per mentis excessum. See Apoc. 12: 1-13.

Thei bonde him fast & schet him in a hous,
Til þei had councell who þat þei wil werk.
This ilk spirit was holde so perylous,   2005
There myth no man, vnneth ony clerk,
Avayle aȝens him. So whann it was derk,
And late at eue, þe prioure, as þei seyn,
With certeyn felawis eythir thre or tweyn,

Is com to þe hous; but er he fully cam þere,   2010
The deule witȝinne cried al aloude,
With huge voys sore he gan to blere:
"Now schal he come, þe cursed prest & proude.
He schal now entre and sore on me croude,
This daffid fool with his barred cote.   2015
Cursed be he and hanged be þe throte!

Spere þe dore, men, & barre it sore and fast."
Thus cryed þe deuele, whan it was ful derk:
"That grete tre ouyrtwert I wil ȝe cast,
That he entre not to do here his werk;   2020
For he schal faile ful mekil of his merk,
Thouȝ he brynge þe crosse and eke þe belle."
This good man, soothly for to telle,

Was not astoyned, but entred in grete hast,
And to þe deuele he spak rith in þis wise: 2025
"What wordes are þese þat þou spekist in wast?"
The deuele answerd to him in þis gise:
"What þing askest þou, loke þou the avise
Wheythir askest þou now what þing it is
That I speke, or ellis what he is   2030

2019   tre *added above and to the right of* grete
2020   he *added to right and above* That *in a lighter ink*
2056   for *added above and to the right of* But

  2034 *bewe*: adj., contracted form of 'beau-sire'. MED does not give any instance
where it is used alone; it is, however, a rhyme-word.

fol. 30r   That speketh on to þe. Chese þis or þat,
For þis I telle þe now, in wordes fewe:
There is no man þat werith hood or hat
Schal wete eythir of me, I sey bewe.
Not þou þiselue, dotard, balled schrewe,   2035
Art þou a maystir? What hast þou to doo
Witʒ þis man or me? Go þi weye, goo!

Go betymes & loke þat þou be ware
That I venge me not sodeynly on the
With bittyr woundys & soris newe & bare."   2040
This man hath aspied now þe sotilte,
And knew be toknes þat a wikkid spirit was he.
Wherfore witʒ bold hert & myty deuocyoun
He mad onto him swech exorʒiʒacioun:

"I coniure the," he seith, "be þe strong vertu   2045
Of Iesu Criste, Goddis son aboue,
Whech on þe crosse witʒ woundis fresch & new
Ouyrcam þi powere, & fro þe þo gan schoue
His owne childyrn & broutʒ hem to his loue.
Be þis powere I bid þe þat þou not hide   2050
What þou art, but telle me in þis tide."

The deuel seyde: "Mayst þou congen me,
Be what vertu fayn wold I now knowe?"
The old man answered, witʒ myty charite:
"This Goddis vessel wold I ful fayn fowe,   2055
But for me schal þou not bowe so lowe.
For Cristis name I wil þou do þis dede.
Euery creature to serue him is bownde of nede.

He schal cunge þe þat sumtyme on þe crosse
Ouyrcam þi powere, whech þou ful falsly   2060
Vsurped to the, & he restored þat losse."
The deuele began to make a sory cry.
Thus he cried ful lowde: "Ey my, ey my!
What schal I do? I must now telle my name.
I am þat deuele, I am rith þat same   2065

Whech dwelt symtyme in þat fayre ӡong mayde
At Nyuygelle, whech mayde þo was browt
Before ӡoure Norbert where he his charmes sayde;
He lessed my powere and set me al at nowt.
If I had powere it schuld ful dere be bowt.   2070
Cursed be þat oure þat ӡoure Norbert was bore;
He and hise, þei contrary me euyrmore."

Thus is þis man certified in dede;
It was a deuele þat was witӡin þis man.
Therfore he þoutӡ that it was grete nede   2075
That he more help & counsell now schuld han
To avoyde þis wikked cursed Sathan.
He calleth þe couent and asketh what is best,
Thei seid alle: "Þis deuele hatӡ take his nest,

And is so bold he wil not for us owt,   2080
Lesse þann we fast, pray and do penaunce.
Wherfor to put al þing oute of dowt,
Lete us now vse þe same ordynaunce
Whech Crist oure lord with holy obseruaunce
Bad his apostoles that thei schuld vse,   2085
And neuyr þis councell for no þing refuse.

'This spirit,' he seide to hem, 'wil not oute
But with prayere and deuoute fastyng.'"
This holy couent cast hem for to loute
To Cristis ordynaunce. Þerfor both eld and ӡing   2090
Thei take here disciplines, deuoutly praying
That God schal spede hem in þis forseid dede,
And to þe hous anon streith þei ӡede.

2069   me *added above and to the right of* set
2104   in *added above and to the right of* ones *in a lighter ink and very*
                minute hand
2122   e *changed to* o *in* holdith

2067 See above ll. 1035 ff.
2088 Mark 9: 28.

They made haliwattir with grete deuocyoun,
A vessel ful ordeyned for that cause. 2095
Alle þe couent went on processioun
Syngyng and seying many a holy clause.
Whan þei cam þedir þe deuele no lenger wold pause,
But cryed with dene aloude into the sky:
"Arise felawes, aryse and that in hy! 2100

fol. 31r   We be more in noumbir þan þei, it is no dowte.
Lete us laboure and breke þis men as smal
As kyrnelis are with þe turnyng abowte
Of þe mylle, whann thei are ones in fal.
Go to, breke þese men, on ȝow I cal. 2105
Arise, felawes, arise owt of ȝoure den,
And help þat I were wroken of ȝon men."

The prioure answerd to þis grete thretyng;
"So schal þou doo, if þou haue powere,
And ellis schal þou not for al þi bostyng 2110
Ones be hardy for to touche us here."
Thoo began þe deuele as wood as fere
The clothis whech he had vpon to rende.
He ferde as þouȝ he wold make an ende

Of þat same man, whech he had obcessed. 2115
Thus he seid onto that olde chanoun:
"Wenest þou þi maystirchep ouyr us be dressed?
Wenest þou oure powere now to put adown?"
A childe stood there with a benetis crown,
And held þe crosse as was þan þe vsage. 2120
The deuele seyde openly with ful wood rage:

"For him I leue þat þis child holdith,
Him I drede, he is my tormentoure."
Lo, who þis deuele oure lord God now dredith,
Confessith him as for oure sauyoure. 2125
Fals Iewys despise him in here boure,
And eke so do þese fals cristen men.
This prioure comaunded his felawis nyne or ten

2119 The *childe* is an exorcist. He wears a corona or tonsure (*benet*) of an exorcist.

To lose þe bondes of þis ich caytyf,
And for to bryng him a litil more ny   2130
That þei may bathe him in þis bath of lif,
In holy water whech stood þere fast by.
A ful ȝong clerk of that cumpany
Sayde to þe prioure: "I dare take on hande
Alle alone with outen help or bande   2135

fol. 31v   To brynge him and lede where he schal be,
If ȝe wil bid me be holy obediens;
For þat schal make me strong inow, parde,
Aȝens þe deuele to make resistens."
The prioure considered þe mannis sapiens   2140
And eke his feith. He bad him do his dede;
For his good wil he was worthi mede.

No man halpe him with hand ne witȝ tonge,
But he broutȝ him alone lich a childe
Þat is led witȝ norce whil he is ful ȝunge.   2145
This man þat was before tyme so wilde,
Now is he made in maner meke and milde.
The deuele qwook is þis mannes presens,
Whech was so hardy to fulfille obediens.

Now is þe man put rith in the watyr.   2150
Thei seide here orisones and here coniuraciones.
The deuele began to iape and to clatyr;
But þe couent whech was of dyuers nacyoun
With on asent made now here prostracioun,
Wepyng, waylyng, praying witȝ good entent   2155
To Iesu oure lord God omnipotent.

So at þe last aftir many iapis þis fende
On þe tunge of þis man him sette;
Blak and smal was that sory prende,
Lich a letuse seed, þei sey, was his mette.   2160
He brente eke so sore þat he hette
Alle þe mouth, & made it lich flawmand fere.
The tunge was oute; al men myth se him þere.

2133   li *expunged before* clerk
2182   sum *written over an erasure*; space *added later; also in margin*
2185-2338   PL 1301B-04C

He spak boldly in open audiens:
"Now am I here, what wil ȝe witȝ me now?   2165
There is no man now in þis presens
Schal make me soo onto him bow
To forsake my dwelling, whech is scharp & row."
The prioure answerd: "Euyr hast þou be
A strong liere, for ȝet þou liest, parde.   2170

fol. 32r Lete no man leue þe, for þou schal, magre þi heed,
Voyde þis persone, elles we passe not hens.
Alle þe powere vndir my fote I trede.
I bid the now, here in this presens,
As þou owist to Criste obediens,   2175
That þou obeye to me for Iesu name here."
Alle þei felle down devoutly in here prayere.

Whan þis was seid, with stynk and mekil cry
He voyded þe body and fley to his place
Whereas he for trespas is ful worthi   2180
To dwelle for euyr. God lord of his grace,
To do sum penauns graunt us here sum space,
That þe deuele, whan we schal hens wende,
No powere ouyr us haue at oure ende!

This same spirit, whan he say non avayle   xxi 2185
   In his temptyng amongis þis holy flok
Othirwise, he cast him newly to assayle;
For fro þe braunches he goth now to þe stok.
Euene as þe wynde lifteth up a wullock
For very lithnesse, rith soo þese spiritis flye   2190
Fro place to place, and þat ful hastilye.

Rith soo fro þis place þis same spirith is goo
Streyt to Traiect þere owre Norbert was.
A certeyn bayli was in þat cuntre thoo,
That had þe charge both of corn and gras,   2195
And of alle a cuntre, both of hye and basse,
Whech longed onto a ful worthi prince þere.
Into þis man, as wood as ony bere

2193 *Traiectum*: ford, appears in a number of place-names for towns situated on a river: Traiectum ad Rhenum, or Vetus Traiectum (Utrecht), Traiectum ad Moenum (Frankfurt), Traiectum ad Mosam (Maastricht). It is most probably Maastricht here as it definitely is in l. 3991.

This deuele is entred rith for þis entent,
That he þat myth not amoungis þe childirn spede   2200
Of þis ich Norbert, now sewirly haþ he ment
On þe heed to venge him now in þis dede.
It is his tecch bataile euyr to bede.
Now was it haliday in that same cytee,
Whan þat þis man witȝ a huge menee.   2205

fol. 32v Is brout to cherch where as Norbert was
Synging his masse with grete deuocyoun.
Alle þe puple, the more and eke þe lasse,
With grete sobirnesse on kne felle adown,
Praying oure fadyr Norbert, alle witȝ o sown,   2210
That he schuld haue reuth on þis same caytyf,
And fro hym þis wikkid spiritȝ dryf.

The puple gadered sore on ilk a syde
To se þe conflict betwix þese parties too:
Wheythir þe deuele þat is prince of pride   2215
Schuld haue þe maystry, or ellis he schuld goo
Fro þis same man; þe preste schuld charge him soo.
Euene as he was in vestiment com fro his messe,
Onto his werk Norbert gan him dresse.

Summe þat stood aboute counceled him to spare   2220
His laboure as now tyl anothir day.
Thei seide for very labour he was wery and bare;
Therfor þei counceled him he schuld make delay.
"Go refresch ȝou þis nyth, & tomorow assay,
For þis day is ny ended and idoo."   2225
Oure fadere Norbert turned hem ontoo.

He spak in þis wise: "Be þe deueles envye
Deth entred into erde, & þere ȝet abideth.
Wherfor, if ȝe wil loke and dewly aspye,
ȝe schul weel wete his powere ȝet glideth   2230
In þe same malice, þouȝ he sumtyme him hideth;
For he may neuyr haue wil of repentaunce.
So malicious was his synful greuaunce.

2200   his *expunged*; þe *written above* it
2209   sobirnesse *written over an erasure*
2217   *MS period between* man *and* þe

Lete us lette him þat we may; it is grete nede.
For I sey ȝow sewirly þe cause þat he is here   2235
Is for to lette me of my meritory dede.
His entente is, if þat ȝe wil lere,
The hertis of þe puple wit slaundir to fere.
That þei schuld not þe word of God receyue,
But fro her hertis lithly it weyue.   2240

fol. 33r Haue ȝe not herd the wordes of treuth
That on this wise of this Sathan seith
He pulleth awey þe seed, & þat is grete reuth,
Fro þe hertis of hem þat are in oure feith?"
Alle þis auctorite before hem he leith,   2245
And forth to his exorcismes he hastith anoon.
He comaunded þe seke man schuld be leyd on a stoon

Euene be the autere. Tho made he there
New haliwatir with alle þe circumstaunce
That longeth þerto, salt and the othir gere,   2250
Rith aftir þe elde cherches ordynaunce.
Whann he had doo alle þis obseruaunce,
He took salt in his hand a good quantite
And to þis mannys mouth with fyngeris thre

He put alle þis salt. But anoon this goost   2255
Whech was withinne spat into his face
With angry wordes & witȝ ful grete boost:
"God ȝeue þe," he seith, "a ful euele grace.
Thi councell is now to lede me apace
Onto ȝon tubbe to my tormentrye,   2260
Onto ȝon aliwatir. ȝet schal thow lye,

ȝet schal þou faile, for no hurt I fele
Of al þi scorgyng, þi thretis I not drede;
Thi grete bondes greue me not a dele;
To wasch me now sikir it is no nede."   2265
Tho ded he þe wodman a litil ferþer lede
That he schuld not here what here councell was.
Alle þei consented, þe more and þe lasse,

2227 Wisdom 2: 24.
   2239 PL 1303C quotes Luke 8: 12: Quia venit diabolus ut tollat semen verbi Dei de
cordibus eorum.

That he schuld be brout to þis holy funt
And waschid therin a longe while.   2270
The deuele began sore for to grunt;
He cast him to lette hem with a fals gile
Alle þoo men þat dwelt witȝin þat myle.
He slaundred ful cursedly of here synnes olde,
Specialy of swech synnes þat were not tolde   2275

fol. 33v To þe preest be hem in confessioun.
Euery man fled awey for very schame.
The deuele slaundird hem so þorw þe town.
"This man," he seith, "lay be his dame
And þis ilk man for al his good name   2280
Hatȝ be a brothell alle þis twenty ȝere."
There abode no man his defautes to here,

But for it was eue and come was þe nyth,
Men counseled Norbert to go to his rest
And performe his dede at morow whan it is lith.   2285
He himself þoutȝ þe counsele was best.
Whan he was set at his smal feest,
There cam folk to him & seide: "Sere, þis man
Whech was late wood, now ful sobirly began

To wayle þe wordes whech þat he seyd ere.   2290
He repenteth him sore for his mysdede,
Praying alle men þat aboute him were
That with a pater noster and eke a crede
Thei schul pray to God he schuld bettir spede."
Thus ferd he al þat nyth & þe next day;   2295
Wherfore with þankyng men gun to God say:

"Gramercy, lord," þei seide, "þat þou can hele
And smyte alsoo rith as þou þiselue
Listist, þi fredom on to us now dele.
Euyr mote þou in oure hertes delue   2300
Thi swete deuocioun þat we may be ten or twelue
Serue þe lord." Thus seyde thei alle.
Now was þat nyth in þat cyte falle

2307   h expunged before lenger
2336   man added above and to the right of þis

A new distaunce and a cruell debate
Betwix þe cyteceynes, I knowe not þe cause. 2305
But Norbert schortly spared non astate,
Ne for no werinesse lenger wold he pause,
But told hem alle schortly in a clause,
The deuele had broken here vnyte.
In this wise onto pees reformed he þis citee. 2310

fol. 34r Than com þere men onto oure fadere ageyn.
They seyde: "Sere, þis man þat was amendid
Is now tormentid witȝ þat spiritȝ certeyn
That sekirly, but if þat he be tendid,
Alle ȝoure laboure in wast as now is spendid." 2315
Norbert seyde: "Suffir as for a while.
I telle ȝou treuly þis was þe fendis wile.

For whil he was bisy in þis dissencioun,
Whech was betwix þe men þat dwelle here,
This othir man had no vexacioun, 2320
But fro his torment rested þann ful clere.
Lete him vexe him a day or too in fere;
For to þis laboure the man is ful worthi.
If ȝe wil wete the cause I telle ȝou whi:

He was a bayly and many extorcionis dede 2325
In his office, as many of hem are wone.
Wherfor þe deuele onto oure lord God ȝede
As asked leue to doo as he had done,
That is to sey both at morow and none
To vexe his neybouris sumtyme witouten cause. 2330
And now I telle ȝou schortly in a clause:

Withinne schort while he schal be cured ful weel."
So was he sewirly, for as oure story seith,
He was thre dayis witȝouten rest or meel.
And þann oure Norbert, witȝ his deuoute feith, 2335
The holy gospell ouyr þis man now leith,
He is mad hool of maledye for euyr more.
Thus can oure lord recuren euery sore.

2338 Following this exorcism PL 1304C-1309B rehearses several incidents not found
in Capgrave: 1) The conversion of Godfrey, Count of Cappenberg, and the stormy

Now hath Norbert receuyed auctorite   xxii
    Of oure fadere þe pope and confirmacioun   2340
Of alle his ordre. Þerfor now is he
Come ageyn onto his mansioun.
Thei telle him now alle here tribulacioun
Whech þei haue suffered in his absens,
And he ful faderly counforted here consciens.   2345

fol. 34v   He had made a monastery ere þat he þens went
At Laudune, in þe subarbes it stant þei seye.
Pore men were þei aftir his entent,
Notwithstandyng he made it a abbeye.
It stant ful fayre upon þe grete weye   2350
Whech goth to town. Þere planted he swech braunches
That þorw þe world ȝet his plantyng launches.

The trees he sette þere swech frute þoo forth browt,
That ȝet it lestith, and euyr mote it lest.
O noble frute þou may not to dere be bowt;   2355
For of alle frutes me þinkith þou are best!
Owt of þe tree of lif þou took þi nest.
Euyr mote þou sprede in sweche schadowid space
That þou mote lede us to the welle of grace!

Oure fadire Norbert made þere eke fast by   2360
Anothir cherch; þei calle it Viuariense.
There made he an abbotte to kepe ful streytly
The holy religioun with grete prouydense.
He bad he schuld neuyr with hem dispense,
But thei were seek. Þanne suffered he   2365
That þei schuld menge here rigoure with charite.

2339-2457 PL 1309B-11A
2356   of *added above and to right of* For

---

situation it precipitated in his family when Norbert accepted him as a member of the
Premonstratensian Order; 2) Theobald, count of Blois, who petitioned acceptance but
was refused by Norbert on the grounds that he should marry (Capgrave mentions the
search for a bride for him ll. 2788 ff. below); 3) the cure of a blind demoniac; 4) the ex-
tirpation of Tanchelin's heresy in Antwerp and the grant of a church as an expression of
gratitude for this work.
  2339 Pope Honorius II on 17 Feb. 1126 in a letter "Apostolicae disciplinae sectantes
vestigia," gave the seal of approval to the order founded by Norbert. The document is
given in full in PL 166: 1249-51; excerpts in PL 1308 note 86.

But ȝet þis fende whech had to hem envye,
He folowid euyr in what weye he went.
He pursewid eke vpon his cumpanye
At here entering, whann þei to Vyuary were sent,   2370
As scripture seith: Assur with hem euyr went.
This is to seye, whidir þat goodmen goo
The wikkid spiritis folow hem euyrmoo.

For as I seide, þis same wikkid spirith
Entred in on of that same cumpanye,   2375
Whech man neythir be day ne nyth
Mith haue no rest but euyr began to crye.
And who he caute this wikkid maledye
I wil ȝou telle now in wordes fewe.
This same man was go owte to hewe   2380

fol. 35r   Into þe feld or elles to swech maner werk
As plowmen vse. And what with grete hete
Of his laboure — for he stood in his serk —
What for þe sunne sore he gan to swete
And for he thristid his lippis for to wete,   2385
He ran to a welle þat stood þere beside —
Tyme of þe day was euene þe nontyde.

The welle was clere, wide & eke ful cold.
Whan he cam thedir his heed witȝ grete hast
He put in þertoo. He loked and gan behold   2390
A wondir schadow, derk of schap, alle wast.
He sey therin þan durst he no þing tast
For very fere, but gan to renne and fle.
Euene in his weye a wondir persone met he,

Orible and derk, & þus he spak to him: 2395
"Whos man art þou? What dost þou here?"
Anon þis man þoutȝ þis person grym;
He durst not þerfore ȝeue him no answere,
But fel down wood sodeynly anon ritȝ þere.
Thus seith þe story: þe deuel had in him place;   2400
Anon he gan to rende himselue and race.

2361 Valsery, Beatae Virginis Mariae (or Vaussery, Vallis Serena), one of the arch-
abbeys. As in the case of St. Martin, it was taken away from the secular canons and given
to the Premonstratensians in the hope of reform (see l. 716 above and note). The year of

Othir men þat stered there aboute
Fownde þis man himselue þus rendyng.
They felle upon him þere a ful grete route.
And of oure tale to make a schort endyng,   2405
Thei led him to towne rith in þe euenyng.
Thei broutȝ him to Norbert, to loke what he wil seye.
Anoon as he sette upon hym eye:

"Beholdetȝ," he seith, "oure enmye, þe cursed feend,
Who he is bysy euyr to slaundir oure name.   2410
For in euery place where þat we schuld wende,
Before us he is euyr, haue he blame!
Alle þis doth he to appeyre owre fame,
That men schuld wene þis ilk vexacioun
Schuld folow euyr owre predicacyoun.   2415

fol. 35v   But oure lord God schal ȝeue us swech speed,
He schal not availe witȝ alle his þousand snaris."
Tho gan he conioure þe spirith as it was need,
That he schuld leue al his bysy fares
And fille þis man no lenger witȝ swech cares.   2420
He prayed oure lady deuoutly eke on his kne,
Of whom þe cherch was, þat for þe grete pite

Whech grew in hire whann hir son ded blede,
Sche schuld haue mercy & graunt þis man grace.
Whan he had prayed, þe puple gan take hede   2425
At þis wood man, specialy at his face.
He loked al sobir & gan no lengere race
With his handis as he had doo ere.
Thei felle on kne & þankid God rith there.

2409   enmye *written above* þe
2452   he *in left-hand margin*
2453   *long* r *added to* Afty *in a different ink*
2458-2513   PL 1313B-15A
2463   was *inserted above and to right of* depute
2464   of *added above and to the right of* not

---

its transfer is not certain: 1124 or as late as 1126. See *Monast. Praem.* 2: 537-539.
   2371 Ps. 82: 9. The incident referred to in the Psalm is recorded in 2 Kings 15: 19.

Thus þei seide onto þis noble man: 2430
"Now may ȝe rest of ȝoure grete laboure,
For blessed be God þat þis ilk Sathan
Hath now no lengere powere to deuoure."
But oure Norbert, whech had a goostly sauoure
In such knowyng more þan þe puple had,   2435
Spak onto hem aȝen witȝ wordes sad.

But specialy, whan he had felt þe grete stynk
Whech went oute at þe mannes nose,
He bad þei schuld not on þat maner þink:
"He is not goo ȝit, I wil ȝou not glose.   2440
The deuele doth þus for þis cause, I suppose,
He resteth awhile, þat we foles schuld wene
That he were go, but þe reuers schal be sene."

Euene as he seid, soo it felle in dede;
For in his absens þe man was vexed newe,   2445
And so tormentid þat of very nede
With bondis grete, myty, many & trewe
Thei haue him bownde: his ioyntis are al blewe.
Thus lay he stille alle þat long nyth.
The next day, whan comen was þe lith,   2450

fol. 36r   Norbert is goo to expulse þis fende,
He goth to cherch & seith his messe betyme.
Aftyr his messe streith ded he sende
For þis man, & ere þat it was pryme
He holid him both fro langour & fro cryme.   2455
God be euyr þankid in his seyntis alle,
And on here helpyng mote we calle!

Anothir þing þere is þat we schul not forȝete,   xxiii
   That fel at Premonstrate in here owne place.
It was his vsage morow & eue to trete   2460
Of holy lyf to hem and eke of grace.
So on a nyth it happed him to pace
The tyme whech depute was to exhortacioun,
For he weryed not of swech occupacioun.

Thei sette so longe þat it was ferre in þe nyth   2465
Summe of hem eke thristid wondir sore.
He comaunded hem to take with hem lith;
And, for þei had of othir drynk no store,
To a pitte witȝouten ony more,
Whech stood beside, he bad þei schuld goo   2470
And fette hem watir to slake here þrist soo.

Thei came aȝen whan here pot was ful,
But or þei entred here maistir lowde gan crye:
"What haue ȝe doon, iwis, ȝe be ful dul.
That watir þat ȝe brynge, I telle ȝou treulye,   2475
It is not clene. What nede me to lye?"
Thei seide alle þei waschid it or þei went;
There was no clennere vessell hens to Kent.

"We took þe watyr eke with good avyis.
What nedith ȝou to sey it is not clene?   2480
In ȝon watir are neythir rattis ne myis,
Ne no venym for soth, as we wene."
Thus seide þese messageris þan al bedene.
"Weel, pore owte," seith he, "in a cup and look."
On of hem a fayre white cup forth took,   2485

fol. 36v   He pored in watyr, he sey therin rith nowt.
The goodman cryed: "Cast þat watyr awey!"
Thei were ful loth for to offende him owt.
Wherfor, as men þat mut nedys obey,
Owte at þe dore forth rith in the cley   2490
They threw þe watir and filt anoþir ageyn.
Ȝet eftsones: "Þrowe it owt," he gan seyn,

"Lete no man drynk of þis watyr as now!
I forbede ȝou, for perel þat may falle.
For if ȝe drynk boldly, I tell it ȝow   2495
That þere is noon here of ȝou alle
But he schal repent or he passe þis halle."
And ȝet eftsones he bad hem fille þe cup
The potte was tome & in þe liftyng up

2465   it: *MS* is
2503   þei¹: *a small* i *added to* þe
2514-2653 PL 1315A-19C

Thei pored a tode, an orible in length & brede,   2500
Into þe cuppe. Sum come nyhere with lith;
Thei stert abak than for very drede,
So were þei agast whann þei sey þis sith.
The wondyr was grete, & gretter, I ʒou hith,
Than men be ware, for it was wynter tyde;   2505
Whech tyme þis vermyn are wont hem to hide.

They were astoyned, alle þat stood aboute,
Of þis merveyle, who þat it myth bee.
Norbert seyde: "Take and þrowe him oute;
It is oure enmye þat werkith þis sotilte.   2510
His fraude is more þan his strength, leue me.
A thousand craftis hath he us to deceuyue,
But fro his snaris oure good lord schal us weyue."

Anothir tyme bretherin of this hous   xxiiii
Went to the feld trees for to hewe,   2515
Summe of hem whech were solaciows
Walked aboute in the fayre swete dewe.
As þei walked þei founde there a schrewe,
A wolf þei founde whech had caute his pray,
A litil goot, and gan to bere it away   2520

fol. 37r   For to deuoure him, rith soo is his kynde.
Thei stert onto him & caute awey þe beest.
On of hem, þe mytiest, at his bak behynde,
Threw þis goot; he þouʒ to haue a feest
Whan he cam hom; oside he gan him wreest,   2525
In a pryvy cornere he hing him be þe feet.
There was he droppyng in his blood al weet.

The wolf folowid þe steppis of þe blood.
He þouʒ he had wrong þat he schuld so lese
Swech pray as he had caute to his food.   2530
He stood at þe ʒate; he myth not chese.
With his feet he gan clawe and brese
The erde vndir þe ʒate, as he wold com in.
Thei of þe hous herd a maner dyn,

2520 *litil goot* a misreading of the Latin *capreolum* (PL 1315A), a roe. The Latin for
goat would be *caper, capra,* or *capella.*

Thei loked oute þann and sey þe beest.   2535
Thei cryed owt upon him þat he schuld fle,
But he lay stille and kept his areest.
As a tame dogge doth, rith soo ded he.
They ronne to here maystir too or thre
And teld him þe caas what was befalle.   2540
Anoon he bad þei schuld be called alle.

They þat were gilty and had do þe dede,
Thei confessed hemselue who þei had doo,
And who þat þei onto þe feldis ȝede,   2545
Founde hem medelyng þese same bestis too,
And who þei took þe litil goot him froo.
"Ow," seith oure Norbert, "þe beest is ful trewe;
For ȝe ded him wrong, he wold not ellis ȝou sewe."

Thei asked mercy for that litil trespas,
As þouȝ þei had doo a grete synne;   2550
Swech was þe vsage of þat ilk plas.
Norbert bad hem: "Fet þe carkeys inne,
Bere it to þe wolf, þe more and þe mynne,
The body, þe skyn lete him haue alle.
We wil not þat anothir tyme he pleyne schalle   2555

fol. 37v   That Norbert his meny toke awey his mete;
Thus schuld we be noted of extorcyoun.
Take him þat is his euene in the strete,
Make not of þese to no dyuorcyoun."
Whan þis wolf had thus his porcyoun   2560
He went streyt to wood; þei sei him no more,
Thei herd him no lenger neydir berk ne rore.

Anothir of here breþerin eke kept scheep in þe feld,
And anoþir mannis schepperd asked him þis:
"If ony beest come now, þou hast no spere ne scheld.   2565
What wold þou doo þan, so haue þou blys,
If þat þou sey a wolf or ony of his
Take ony of þi scheep and bere it awey?"
This ilk innocent to him þoo gan sey:

2545   same *written above* þese
2584   *erasure after* þe

"For soth I wold bidde him in my maistiris name   2570
That he schuld ley down my scheep ageyn.
Me thinkith but he obeyed he were to blame."
Than aftir þis not longe, soth for to seyn,
This ich questioun was not spent in veyn,
But fulfillid in dede; for oute of þe wood   2575
Cam a grete wolf rennyng, as he were wood.

He cawt a scheep in his mouth & went
Forth to wood ageyn in ful grete haast.
He þat kept hem thoutʒ þat he brent,
So grete care had he for þat ilk waast.   2580
Lowde he gan crye with a grete gaast:
"Whedir gost þou, beest, whedir wilt þou goo?
Ley down that scheep, and do it now no woo!

In my maystiris name, I bid þe ley it down.
That þing þat þow beres, parde, it is not þin.   2585
Do it no harme neythir in throte ne crown,
For if þou do it, it wil turne the to pyin.
Ley dow(n) þat scheep, I sey, for it is myn.
Mi maystir took it me this same day to kepe."
The wolf witʒoute more leyd down þe schepe.   2590

fol. 38r   Anothir of hem was eke sent to kepe
The flook of scheep, & for he myth not weel,
Thei were so many, reule alle his schepe,
A ful long tyme, or it was vnderne seel,
There cam a wolf and at his feet gan kneel.   2595
He ran aboute and kept þe scheep alday.
A soleyn kepere for scheep and eke a gay!

Thus lay he stille, þe wolf rith be þe flok.
There durst no scheep al þat day so long
Go fro his felawis for perel of a knok.   2600
Thus kepte he hem, ʒet slept he among.
Whan euene was come, & silens bell rong,
These to keperis broutʒ hom here scheep,
Ful sadly and sobirly; non of hem leep.

2587   *MS period between* do it *and* it
2588   *MS* dow

Whan alle were in dryuyn at the gate,   2605
The ȝate was sperd and þe wolf witȝoute.
With his feet knokked he sore þereate,
As þouȝ he wold entre witȝouten doute,
He þoutȝ grete wrong þat had go aboute
Al þat long day, & had not for his trauayle   2610
Neithir mete ne hire to turne him to avayle.

Oure Norbert herd ful weel þat knokkyng.
"Lete in þat man," he seith, "þere is a gest."
Thei runne to þe ȝate both of elde and ȝyng,
Many of hem, and fond þe wolf þere rest.   2615
Thei cried upon him to fese him fro his nest,
But he nolde fle for no voys ne cry,
But be the ȝate ful stille gan he ly.

Norbert sey þis and asked his breþerin alle
What þis myth be. Thei were alle in dowte.   2620
Anon he ded þat othir brothir calle,
Whech here scheep at morow had led owte.
Whan he cam in, ful lowe gan he lowte;
"Wil ȝe wite," he seith, "whi this wolf is here?
He did þis day that he ded neuyr ere.   2625

fol. 38v Whann I was wery for very laboure & feynt,
He cam to help me and, treuly as I wene,
I schal no lesyng before ȝoure persone peynt.
I sey no dog ne man þese ȝeris fiftene
Kepe his scheep togidir alle bedene   2630
As ded þis wolf. He halp to dryue hem hom,
And neuyr sith from us wold he gon."

"Now," seith Norbert, "I knowe his menyng.
There was no man wold qwite him his labour.
Wherfor rithfully math he tarying   2635
To receyue of us now sum socoure.
Throwe him mete, lete him no lenger soioure."
Thei threw him mete, he caut it & went awey.
Anothir tyme þe same wolf, as þei sey,

2645   man *added above and to the right of* and
2654-2716 PL 1319C-20C

Cam to a childe kepte calueryn in the feld, 2640
Ded na harm but took breed of his hand.
O myty God þat al þing hast at weld,
Who þou makest merveyles in oure land;
These wilde beestis obeyin onto þe band
Of holy obediens, and man is þerto rebelle. 2645
Ful weel can scripture of swech vnbuxumnesse telle:

That þei þat wil not obeye to goddis lawe
Alle þing schal to hem euyr onbuxum be.
And specialy whann here soules are drawe
Owt of here body, and witȝ deueles too or thre 2650
Be broute before the grete mageste
Of oure lord God, alle creatures þan schul fith
Aȝen swech men as it is ful rith!

With many craftis, as we seide before, xxv
Were þei assayed þat dwelt þoo in þat place. 2655
The wikkid spirit wil euyrmore perse and bore,
With sundry assayes and with sundry cace,
To loke who he may renden men and race,
And brynge hem oute of þe trew rith weye,
That in his snaris he myth hem bynde & teye. 2660

fol. 39r He was so bysi in his temptacyoun.
With orible sitys hem to fere and fese,
There durst no man to no occupacyoun
Go oute o nyte to do himselue no ese,
So besy was he to brynge hem in dishese. 2665
O sleythi Sathan, thi whilis schal not availe
Ouyr þoo men þat here synnes cun wayle!

Of special fesyng ȝe may here, if ȝe list.
There was a man myth neuyr go alone
Into no place but anoon a mist 2670
Schuld be afore him & many of his fone.
At þe last he happed into þe ȝerd to gone
Late at eue to voyde swech neccessarye
As we witȝ diligens into oure bely carye.

2646 The following stanza, ll. 2647-53 is Capgrave's negative paraphrase of two
quotations from scripture in PL 1319C: 'cum placuerint viae ejus Deo, omnes inimici

Anon he sey on stand before his face,   2675
Blak and huge, with eyne clere as glasse,
Whech was ful bysi in his armes to brace
This ich man, and he astoyned wasse.
It semed onto him a body al of brasse,
Saue lich a man he was off stature,   2680
But mech largere than ony creature.

This man had often be vexid witʒ swech þingis,
And rolled his mynde if his feith were stronge.
He seide to himself: "Alle þese dissimulingis,
If I were hardy þei schuld not vexe me longe.   2685
Mi sith is deceyued, I trowe I loke al wronge,
Now, Iesu Criste, thi mercy lord I calle,
For I schal on him what euyr so befalle."

This man pursued; þe spirith fled awey.
He ran after boldly more and more,   2690
He caute a counfort newly in his fey,
For be þis deuele he gan to set no store.
The man ran lithly as doth a wilde bore,
He wend ha caut him, but he caut a tree.
He helde it fast, ʒet at þe last he   2695

fol. 39v   Loked wisely and sey it was an asch.
He turned aʒen hom to his celle.
Euyr aftir þat tyme he coude fro him wasch
Alle swech illusiones, were þei neuyr so felle.
Thus ouyrcam þis man þe powere of helle.   2700
There was anoþir eke in þat same occupacioun,
Whech was ivexed with swech a temptacioun.

2679   al *added above and to the right of* body
2693   ly *added in a minute hand above and to the right of* lith
2717-2779 PL 1320C-21B

---

ejus pacifici erunt' (Prov. 16: 7) et alibi: 'Pugnabit orbis terrarum contra insensatos'
(Wisd. 5: 21).

He sat in swech a hous & þe deuele eke
Euene aȝens owris moo than thre.
He durst neythir stere no ones speke,   2705
So aferd of this sith was he.
At þe last he þoutȝ : "Þis is but frelete;
If I durst rise, I trowe he wold goo."
With þat ich thoutȝ he crouched him þoo

Euene in the forhed, & up he roos þan.   2710
The deuele stood in þe dore, as he thoutȝ.
Whan he with grete feith to þe dore cam,
He groped fast, but he fonde noutȝ.
Neuyr aftir þat day he of swech þing routȝ.
Alle a mateyns tyme þei se he was þere,   2715
Wrestyng and wrastillyng in swech maner fere.

It is no wondyr þouȝ þe hed of hem alle   xxvi
    Sey swech illusioun whan his childirn smale
Were vexed witȝ þe same. Þerfor now I schalle
Telle ȝou of him a ful wondyr tale.   2720
He waked ny al þe nyth; þat mad him ful pale.
He had swech desire to wake and to pray,
So it happed on a festful day.

He had be occupied in seruyse and þe full,
With singing and preching, as was his vsage.   2725
Ȝet whan nyth cam, þouȝ his spiritis were dull,
Lef he alle mirthes, he held hem but dotage.
He went into cherch witȝ ful sad visage,
Set him on his kne, witȝouten ony lith;
For his purpos was to dwelle þere al nyth.   2730

fol. 40r As he turned him and loked behind his bak,
He say þe deuele, standyng lich a bere.
With his teth he made a wondyr crak.
He streyned his clawis as þouȝ he wold tere
And rende in peces alle þat stood there.   2735
The man was fesed of that grisely sith,
Specialy alone and also in þe derk nyth.

What schuld he do he nyst not weel for fere.
He loked forth and sey the dore was sperd.
With his fyngeris he crouched him rith there.   2740
He avised him weel þat he was sum deel lerd
Of swech fantasies þat he schuld not be ferd.
With myty voys al lowde he gan to crye:
"Thi wittis avayle not, Sathan, þouȝ þei be slye.

What abides þou, what wilt þou, cruel beest?   2745
Thi hokes, þi teeth haue now no powere
To sette on me no daungere ne areest.
It is but vanyte þat þou schewis me here.
Thi rolled skyn, whech is no þing clere,
Is but fantasie as þouȝ it were a rynde.   2750
Thi fyry throte I counte it but a wynde.

Alle these vanytees whech þou schewis to men,
Alle are þei fals; schadowis be thei alle.
Go þi wey! Ful weel þis mech I ken,
Ful weel knowe I þat þei schal sone falle,   2755
Whann Goddis mercy wil schyne upon us alle,
Or elles whan we calle onto his gras.
Allas, þou Sathan, weel may þou seye 'allas.'

Thou þat were þe merke of God aboue;
Thou þat were swech an aungell bryth!   2760
And for þou fleddist fro þat goodly loue
Whech þou had, þe loue of God almyth,
Now art þou dampned sekirly, as it is rith,
To dwelle in þerknesse, as þou apperist here.
Awey þou Sathan, awey þou raggid brere!   2765

2753   *red period between* fals *and* schadowis
2754   *MS badly stained*
2770   ne *added above and to the right of* feld
2776   *MS period between* tyme *and* treuth
2787   erle *written over an erasure*
2780-2933 PL 1321B-23C

 2767 2 Cor. 6: 14, not 2 Cor. 6: 1 (PL 1321B).
 2788 Theobald the Great (1090-1152), count of Blois and Champagne, was a grand-
son of William the Conqueror on his mother's side, and nephew of Henry I of England.

fol. 40v Thou dampned brond þat art euyr brent in helle,
Betwix lith & derknesse is no comparisoun;
Falshed with treuth may not iustly melle.
Go þi wey, and ley thi boost adown.
Thou may not noye neythir in feld ne town   2770
But þou be suffirid be oure lord aboue.
Thi crafty skole here it may not proue."

Thus voyded þis fend oute of his presens,
He myth not bere þe wordis to him sayde.
Falsheed to treuth may make no resistens   2775
No longe tyme; treuth may be affrayed,
But it schal neuyr be so fully alayed
With no falshed þat he schal fle his ground.
In Goddis seruyse euyr his loueris be found.

Now wil we telle of þe wondir auenture   xxvii 2780
    That fel to him whan that he was chose
To be a bisschop and for to bere þat cure.
Ʒe wil like it ful weel, as I suppose.
A wondir þing it is who God can dispose
To worchep a man, þat semeth ful onlikly   2785
As to oure doom, and eke ful onweldy.

There was a erle at þat tyme in Fraunce,
He hith Theobald, whech had a mariage
Procured be Norbert to his grete avaunce.
The day was set, as þann was the vsage,   2790
Where þei schuld mete with ful grete costage
At a cyte, I not what is the name,
Ne þouʒ I knowe not, I am not mech to blame,

In 1141 he is said to have refused the crown of England. Though engaged in several wars against his sovereign, Louis, he had a reputation for great personal piety and for magnificent largesse to the church. St. Bernard held him in high esteem; in a letter to Manuel the emperor of Constantinople he recommends Henry, Theobald's son because of the reputation of the father: 'qui propter veritatem, et mansuetudinem, et justitiam, diligitur et honoratur inter principes terrae.' Ep. 424, an. 1146 in *Recueil des historiens des Gaules et de la France* ed. Michel J. J. Brial; new ed. Léopold Delisle (Paris, 1878) 15: 607-608. When advised to marry by Norbert, Theobald replied: 'nullam in matrimonium ducam, nisi quam Dominus Deus per te mihi voluerit copulare' (PL 1308A). The bride Norbert found for him was Mathilda, daughter of Engelbert, marquis of Crayburg (Kärnten) in Austria, brother of Frederick, archbishop of Cologne and Hartwic, bishop of Ratisbon. See PL 1308, note 85.

Because myn auctour touchith no swech specialtee,
But renneth at large as him lest to doo.   2795
ʒet þis supposyng haue I as for me,
That þis mayde and hyr kyn alsoo
Were longing to Germayn where Norbert cam fro.
Whann þei to þe cyte were com alle in fere
The mayde ne hir frendis were not ʒet þere.   2800

fol. 41r   Ne no man coude sey wheythir þei come or nowt.
The erle was sory; he dempt þere was sum gile.
Mech cost was doo, and mech þing was bowt.
Many a place ded he for hire byle;
He had rydyn eke for hire many a myle   2805
With alle his men, þis was no litil cost.
And because Norbert was in þis matere a post

And principal werkere, þerfor is he now sent
To wite what cause is that this tarying
Is þus maad and frustrat his entent;   2810
Theobald wil of alle this haue knowyng.
The soth was þis: þe mayde was but ʒing
And what for trauayle, what for tendir age,
Sche took sekenesse in hire cariage.

Sche lay euene stille & myth no ferther goo.   2815
But of þis matere schul we sese as now.
Myn auctoure telleth of it not o word moo,
Because it longeth not to þe lyneal bow
Of Norbertes lyf, but rennyth þerfro al row.
He þoutʒ it was but a matere occasionate   2820
Whech broute þis Norbert to his grete astate.

2818   *small* to *added* to no *before* to
2833   drede: dr *written over an* n (?)
2836   *period between* mete *and* herfor

   2823 *Epire*: Speyer on the Rhine in the Lower-Palatine. A royal palace was built there
in the ninth century and in 1111 Henry V made it an imperial city.
   2830 The mark floated in the middle ages between one-half and three-quarters of a
pound of silver. After the Norman Conquest it was at 13 s. 4 d. i.e. 2/3 of a pound

Now rydith Norbert hastyly in his iornay,
Town be town, tyl he to Epire cam.
He þoutȝ to him it schuld be euyr and ay
Very vilony but if he this worthy man   2825
Mith knyt in mariage rith as he began.
Wherfore, þat he schuld spede þe bettir his cause,
He sent his bretheryn, schortly in a clause,

That were at Premonstrate to fede with pore men
Eyte mark of syluyr. He bad þei schuld fede   2830
Beside þoo fifty he left whan he went þen,
A hundred & twenty þei schuld þe bettir spede.
Vitaile was dere, & þei had ful grete drede
That þei schuld fayle, wherfor þei were loth
To fede so many, because þat for hem both   2835

fol. 41v   Thei boute here mete; herfor was Norbert wroth.
He wrote onto hem þei schuld þis noumbyr take,
For were þei weel apayde or ellis were þei loth,
His noble precept may þei not forsake.
Now lete hem cast here hedis togidir and wake;   2840
This hundred men be his eleccyoun
Must haue here mete of þe comoun refeccyoun.

Thirtene of hem schul be in þe hospital hous,
Twelue of hem eke in þe freytoure schul be.
He thoutȝ here offens, whech was so perilous,   2845
Mith not be amendid but with hospitalite.
For medycyne is swech forsoth, leue now me,
Contrarye with contrarie is often tyme releued,
As in phisik it is ful weel appreued.

---

though the buying power under all circumstances would be hundreds of times more than
today. When some 250 years later Chaucer has his Pardoner earning one hundred marks
a year, it undoubtedly was an enormous sum.
   2844 PL 1322A: septem vero cum canonicis essent in refectorio.

Thus lefte he hem and forth to a cyte he is goo.   2850
Epyre it is called; it stood rith in his weye.
There fonde he þe Saxones & with hem many moo
Before Lothary þe emperoure, soth for to seye.
The clerkis of Parthenopole, not on ne tweye,
But a grete noumbyr eke fonde he there,   2855
Rith for þis cause: before þe emperour þei were

To chese a bisschop, for here elde was ded.
There was a cardinale eke come fro Rome.
Many causes gunne þei bete and tred,
But þe first of alle & why þei þidir come   2860
Was for to chese, aftir þe elde custome,
A holy man whech myth gouerne þat plas.
President of þis eleccioun a holy bisschop was;

Thei called him Albon, bisschop of Metense.
Before his presens þese clerkes named thre   2865
Of whech Norbert of Goddis presciense
Onknowyng him, onknowyng his mene,
Was chose for on. Þis bisschop, þat was so fre,
Made a tokne to þe cheseris ful pryuyly
That þei schuld chese þis Norbert solemply,   2870

2852   he *added above and to the right of* fonde
2854   t *added to* weye
2875   for *above and to the right of* Ther

2853 Lothair III (1075-1137) succeeded Henry V in 1125, despite the Hohenstaufen claim, and was crowned Holy Roman emperor in 1133 by Pope Innocent II whom he had reinstated in Rome as the canonically elected pontiff. *Vita A* (MGH 701-703) portrays the decisive diplomacy of Norbert in this affair; *B* merely states that Norbert was prevailed upon to accompany the expedition (PL 1338B-1339A). See the notes on ll. 3530 and 3534 below for bibliography on the schism.

2854 *Parthenopole* (Gr. *parthenos* 'virgin, maid'): a learned form for Magdeburg; the usual form is *Magdeburgensis*.

2864 There is some confusion here. *Albon* should be 'Albero' (PL 1323A). He was not, as Capgrave says, bishop of Metz nor was he the president of this *ellecioun*. As *primicerius* of the Chapter of Metz he was instrumental in having his namesake Albero, bishop of Metz, deposed by Paschal II. Later he himself became bishop of Trier. Though passionately dedicated to the interests of the church, it is questionable whether he deserves the sobriquet *holy*, so generously bestowed on him by Capgrave. The president of the assembly was as *B* clearly states: 'quidam cardinalis, qui a Romana sede noviter ad-

fol. 42r   What for þe auctorite of þis worthi man,
          What for þe goodnesse and þe hye fame
          Of þis ilk Norbert — for no man reporte can
          Of him ne of his ony spot of blame —
          Therfor, as I seide, for his good name   2875
          These clerkis stert to him & leyd on him hand.
          For it happed Norbert that tyme to stand

          Amongis othir folk to se þe chaunce.
          Thus seide þe clerkis alle þat cheseris were:
          "This is oure wil, þis is oure ordinaunce,   2880
          That oure fadere Norbert, whech standith here,
          Schal take upon him rith at oure prayere
          To be oure bisschop and gouerne us alle.
          Or þis day seuenyth we wil him stalle

          At oure owne cost, for he is but pore.   2885
          He pleseth us þe bettir, we telle ȝou treuly.
          We wil not lich othir men oure bisschopis rore."
          This ich Norbert stood ful sobirly.
          He had no tyme to pleyne him ne to cry,
          Ne make non excuse, but to Lothary þe kyng   2890
          Was he led forth with outen tariing.

          Whan þe kyng herd þat Norbert was chose,
          He comendid heyly þe cheseris alle.
          He seide sewirly þei coude weel dispose
          For here owne cherch; þei had weel ifalle   2895
          Into þis vnite swech a man to calle
          That dred God and was of good lyf.
          His conuersacioun was iknowe ful ryf.

---

venerat' (PL 1322C); *A* is more precise in determining the legate as: 'Gerardus ... qui post Honorium papam, Lucius papa cognominatus, catholicae praesedit ecclesiae' (MGH 694). According to *A* it is the legate who advised the election of Norbert upon consultation with Albero and another bishop; *B*, which Capgrave follows, has Albero point to Norbert as the man to choose.

  2870 Capgrave following *B* has the electors determine the choice (PL 1323A); *A* has Lothair do it: 'Domnus imperator Norbertum ipse assignavit archiepiscopum' (MGH 694).

Wherfore to þe legate was he led anon;
There was he confermed with outen ony more.   2900
Thei went with him þe cheseris euerychon;
Thei sungyn and cryed ful lowde and sore.
Te deum laudamus, as is the lore
And eke þe custom of euery eleccioun,
Was sunge þere in his institucyoun.   2905

fol. 42v   Thus in þe myddis of a froward nacyoun
Was þis man sette to proue his paciens.
To no ese of himselue but to vexacyoun
Toke he þat lordchep and that residens;
To swech chaunce as God sent he ȝaue obediens.   2910
For þe puple he dwelt among of very propirtee
Are hard of beleue and sturdy, leue me.

Sclaues and Saxones are þei called be name;
The on of hem is named ful of scharpnesse,
The othir hath a vocable of heuy fame.   2915
For Saxone betokneth þe grete hardnesse
That is in a ston. Here hertis, as I gesse,
Were ful hard to goodnesse to brynge.
The othir meny, the Sclauys, in expownyng

Meneth as mech as scharpnesse of a nayl.   2920
Thus leuyth he þe eesy lyf of contemplacyoun,
And to actyf lyf he turnyth his sayl.
He hath now left the swete occupacyoun
Of Racheles scole & of all hire nacyoun.
He may not chese: Lya must be plesed,   2925
Because þat with childir sche is so icesed.

2934-3101 PL 1323C-25C
2940   *period after* fere

    2899 Capgrave's description of Lothair's reaction to Norbert's election is entirely his
own; *B* merely states that the legate confirmed it.
    2903 This liturgical hymn was normally sung at the end of Matins, but was also used
at the conclusion of chapters, synods and after the election of ecclesiastical superiors. *B*
makes no mention of the *Te Deum*.
    2913 Slavonia extended east from the Elbe to the Oder and up to the Baltic Sea;
Saxony from the Elbe on the east to the Eider on the north and the Rhine on the west.
The southern border was in a constant state of flux.

He had cast him first in his conuercyoun
For to go to þe heþen, þe feith hem to preche.
And for he lefte þis heuenly disposicioun.
Therfor oure lord God wold he schuld teche   2930
To þis sturdy nacioun to loke if he myth reche
To bryng hem to þe ʒok of holy buxumnesse;
This was his occupacyoun euyr, as I gesse.

Whech tyme he was confermed, thei hem led   xxviii
Hom to his cite where he schuld be stalled.   2935
Euery man was steryng, þere was no man in bed;
The day of his entre þei nede not to be called.
Whan he cam þedir it semt he was walled
Alle with men in euery side, so þik þei went þere,
Grete men and smalle alle ʒede in fere.   2940

fol. 43r The grete of þe cuntre were glad for þis cause,
For þei had a man whech was of grete name,
The smale men were mery, schortly in a clause,
And of this eleccion made ful grete game,
Because þe pore men þat were blynd & lame   2945
Schuld be refreschid be þis mannis comyng.
For it was reported he loued swech þing

Barfote went he in a ful pore wede,
A mantyl had he ouyrest white & þreedbare
Amongis alle þe puple ful lowly he ʒede;   2950
He took no more upon him þan þouʒ he ware
On of þe lowhest þat went among hem þare.
Thei entred into þe cyte & forth to þe paleys;
At þe grete ʒate stood porteris with baleys

2920 PL 1323B also mentions Mary and Martha as symbols of the contemplative and the active life. See V. Fumagalli "Note sulle 'Vitae' di Norberto di Xanten," *Aevum* 39 (1965) 349-350 and note 11.

2924 Gen. 29: 20.

2927 PL 1323C suggests a Jonah-type: 'Unde dispositionem divinam putavit effugere, inde cogitur obedientiam manifeste subire.'

2935 Norbert was the 13th archbishop of Magdeburg. Established in 967, it played an important role in the Christianization and colonization of the northeastern part of Germany. See J. Bauermann, "Umfang und Einteilung der Erzdiözese Magdeburg," *Zeitschrift des Vereins für Kirchengeschichte der Provinz Sachsen* 29 (1933) 3-43.

Whech knew not here lord, he was so pore.   2955
On of hem stert to him & þus he seyd þan:
"Beggeris inowe are in at this dore.
Therfor go bak, withdrawe þe, good man.
Thou schewist ful weel þat litil good þou can,
Make space for my lord, he comth ritȝ anoon.   2960
But þou go rummere. I swere be Seynt Ion

I schal make þe goo." The puple cryed lowde:
"What dost þou, losell, wotest not what he is?
That same man, þouȝ pore be his schrowde,
He is þe bisschop of this see iwis."   2965
The porter was aferd whann he herd þis,
He fled ful fast and wold a go awey,
But Norbert ded him calle & þus to him gan sey:

"Be not aferd, myn owne brothire dere,
Ne fle not for my sake, what euyr þou sayde,   2970
For I sey the treuly, þere is no man here
Hey ne lowe, woman ne no mayde,
Þouȝ þei avisement in here langage layde,
Coude a gessed þe treuth so weel as ded þou.
Thyn eyne be more clere, I telle the rit now,   2975

fol. 43v   That callest me a begger þan her eyne were
That chose me to worchep or to degree.
Hide not thiselue, ne fle not for fere.
Trost me sikirly, þou hast thank of me.
So art þou worthi, þou flaterist not, parde."   2980
O noble meknesse þat hast mad þi nest
In Norbertis herte and þere hast þi rest!

Euyr art þou stabil in þat same place,
And euyr wilt þou dwelle to his lyuys ende.
Thus was þis man stuffid al with grace;   2985
Thus began he in his exaltacioun to bende
His lyf al to mekenesse. Crist mot us sende
Euyr swech condiciones to rest in oure breest
Whech were ifounde in this noble preest.

2962   *period between* goo *and* The
2989   *erasure after* were

Whan he was entred to his possessioun, 2990
He had mende of þe apostle þat seith on þis wise:
To a bisschop, he seith, is gret perfeccyoun
Ouyr his owne hous to be a iustise;
That he sette þe gouernaunce in swech asise,
So þat it plese God aboue alle þing, 2995
And to his neybouris it be a fortheryng.

Thoo called he þe officeres þat longed to his hous
To wite what expens þertoo were dew.
To here her acounte was he desirous,
Because þat þis lordchep to him was new. 3000
His officeres com, alle þat were ful trew;
Thei ʒoue þer acounte of þe receytis alle,
But whan þei had doo to serue his halle,

Thei myth not suffise for half a ʒere,
Alle þe rentis & profitis þat longid to him. 3005
Thoo seide he anoon to a grete officere
That stood beside, a sere he was ful grym:
"This ich acounte is to me ful dym.
Was þis cherch neuyr bettir in his expense?"
This othir man, whech had long experiense 3010

fol. 45r Off alle þese rentis, answerd in þis wise:
"It was sumtyme endewid ful weel
And ful plenteuously in al maner asise;
That is to seye both in clothing and meel,
But now is it wasted ny euery deel. 3015
For summe þat were bisschopis here in þis place,
Thei ʒoue awey þe londes with sory grace

2991 1 Tim. 3: 4.
3011 In binding the MS one folio was unfortunately turned around. The folio marked
44 r, v, as marked in the MS book, has lines 3081-3150; the folio marked 45r, v, as
marked in the MS book, has lines 3011-3080.
3012 Norbert's policy of extending his Order at the expense of local communities
such as St. Mary's was one of the causes for the growing dissatisfaction of the clergy and
populace of Magdeburg. At one time he was forced to flee to save his life from the angry
mob. This dramatic episode and a second in which the Premonstratensians were
threatened with expulsion from St. Mary's (PL 1331B-1337B) are not recorded by
Capgrave.

To here bretherin & nevys, rith as hem lest.
Whech possessiones are kept now ful strong,
And þoo are not þe werst but rather þe best.   3020
It schuld be ful hard to redresse þis wrong,
Grete cause whifor þei haue had hem long.
The men be grete eke þat hem now holde,
Stuffid with lenage, of corage ful bolde."

"And is it thus," seide þis noble prelate,   3025
"It must be redressed in al goodly hast.
I wil not in this matere drede non astate,
For swech maner dreed comth not fro þe gast
Whech enspirith al þing with his swete tast.
I wil," he seith, "send oute in al hasty wyse   3030
To euery man þat they may hem avyse.

Thei falle not in þat sentens whech I wil proclame!
That whosoeuyr hath ony possessioun
Longyng to my cherch in Goddis name
I wil now charge hem, and on my benysoun,   3035
That þei resyne hem withouten condicioun,
And lete þe cherch haue his rith ageyn."
His messageris are sent, soth for to seyn,

Thorwoute þe diosise and proclamed þis þing.
Thei þat were gilty grucchid ful sore;   3040
Thei þat were clere seid it was a good beginnyng.
Thei sette be his maundment ful grete store;
The othir part seide he had leyd his ore
Ferther in the watyr þann he myth rowe.
But neuyrþelasse whan þei gunne knowe   3045

fol. 45v The lif of þis man þei were sumwhat aferd.
Thei were brideled be reson but ʒet wold not þei
Want here possession neythir feld ne ʒerd,
Pasture ne graunge, corn, chaf ne hey.
Than was he compelled upon hem to ley   3050
The bittir swerd of curs with auctorite.
Than were thei aferd, be too and be thre,

3040   cc *of* grucchid *written over an erasure; final* d *written over an* l
3042   *erasure of two letters after* sette
3080   *small* d *added to* excuse

Because þat if a man stande acursed a ȝere   3055
He is oute of the lawe, as þe cyuyle seith,
Ne in no corte schal he plete ne apere.
This grete perel before hem he leith.
Eke in as mech as þei were of oure feith,
Thei thouȝt grete synne here fadir to offende,
Wherfor þei sent to him þat þei wold amende   3060

Alle her defautes, & eke restore him his good.
Who is glad but he, for now are þei frendis
As on his side. But here bittir mood
Is not staunched, fro slaundir þei sey þat he schendis
Alle gentilmen aboute him, for fro hem he rendis
Here temperal lyuyng; in euele tyme cam he þere.   3065
Thus gunne þei his name aboute þe cuntre bere.

But þe man had take so sikir & pleyn a weye
Of treuth & rithwisnesse þat it avaylith nowt
Alle þe langage þat þei can clater and seye.
For he was clene þe lesse þerof he rowt.   3070
There was no cherch ne parsch but it was sowt
And visitid both be him and his officeris,
And alle to amending & norching of good maneris.

The prestis stered here puple for to teche
Who þei schuld leue onto Goddis plesaunce.   3075
To religious men he was a very leche;
He made here houses with ful grete puruyaunce.
And ouyr mysdoeris he set swech gouernaunce,
That þei were punchid hardily at þe fulle;
Thei were not excused be lettir ne be no bulle.   3080

fol. 44r Officiales and denes þat had gouernaunce
Ouyr þe puple he charged in Cristis name,
That þei schuld punch alle þe myschaunce
Whech regned in presthood, specialy þat defame
Of onclene lecchery whech defouled here name.   3085
He seide þer schuld no preste lyue about him
But he were chaast, loked he neuyr so grym.

The vicious men took this ful heuyly;
Othir were wroth eke; he took here good hem froo
Whech þei fro þe cherch had occupied wrongfully.   3090
This was þe cause þat þei and many moo
Spoke of him euele. Þei seide mech care & woo
Was com to þe cuntre sith that comelyng
Was þus entred for to be here kyng.

But he kept his constaunce at alle tyme,   3095
He wold not chaunge neythir for euele ne good,
For seide þei weel or seyde ony cryme,
Were þei sobre or ellis wer þei wood,
He chaunged neuyr his gouernaunce ne his mood.
Thus was he strengthid be Goddis grace aboue,   3100
That he dred neythir here hatred ne loue.

Before þe paleys, not fro it but litil space,   xxix
       There stood a cherch onto oure lady dedicate.
Thedir made he ful ofte tyme his pace,
Whech tyme þat he list to be desolate.   3105
He was þar sumtyme ful erly and ful late
In his contemplacioun, in prayere al alone,
Betwix God and him makyng his mone.

In this same cherch of chanones seculere
Was þan a college of twenty persones & no moo.   3110
Thei kept here obseruaunce in cloystir & in qwere
Mech þe bettir þat he cam too and froo
So often as he ded. But he desired þoo,
Because it was ny him, his breþerin schuld be þere.
He seide he himself wold al þe costes bere   3115

fol. 44v   Both to the pope and eke onto þe kyng.
He profered hem eke a bettir place þan þat.
This peticioun was not to here lykyng,
For þe chanonis of þe gret cherch seid him ful plat,
There schuld no man witȝ hood ne witȝ hat   3120
Take awey fro hem here possessioun;
For if he ded he schuld haue þe malysoun

3102-3143   PL 1325D-26B
3106   þar *added above* sumtyme *in a lighter ink*
3129   PL 1326B-28A
3144-3262   y *added to* þe *and written over an* n (?)

Of Iesu Criste and owre fader the pope
Whech had confermed it be many a bulle.
Thus was oure Norbert frustrate of his hope;   3125
But ʒet at the last his hert gan he up pulle,
And took vpon him auctorite at þe fulle,
That sith he was hed and souereyn of hem alle,
Nedys to his entent þey must bowe and falle,

Rather þan he to hem. Þis was the ende!   3130
At þe last thei consented to his entent;
To his obediens mekely gun þei bende.
So are þese twenty chanones to anoþir place sent
Forth with alle here cariage gladly þei went
Because þe place þei go to is more solacious,   3135
More plenteuous of mete, & more spacious.

His breþerin are entred eke to here possessioun.
He loued þei schul not fer fro him dwelle.
He was þere with hem in ful grete deuocyoun,
Both day and nyth, schortly to telle.   3140
He loued ful euel witʒ worldly þing to melle,
But þat he must nede of very offise.
Religioun, he seide, was very paradise.

The noumbre of his breþerin grew fast and sore   xxx
   Both in Sueue and Saxone cuntres ful wyde.   3145
In Sueue had neuyr be no religioun before;
In Saxone had þere be, but it gan sore slyde.
Here meknesse was distroyid witʒ sory pryde
Whech þei had caute of possessioun temporal;
For of euery religioun plente is the fal.   3150

fol. 46r   The cuntre al aboute gan grucch sore & seye:
"These ich newe comelyngis wil us ouyrgrowe."
Vpon Norbert eke euele langage þei leye.
Thei seid he was com thidir here cuntre for to sowe
With swech maner doggis as longed to his bowe;   3155
Thus woluys þe scheep gun hurt both & bith.
But þese good men were endewid with þe lith

3154   he *added above and to the right of* seid

Of very innocens whech hem defended.
But for alle here clennesse bityn thei were,
With ful bittir tungis whech were neuyr amendid,   3160
But labbyng and roryng as doth ony bere.
For þei þat dwelt witȝ him in houshold rith þere
Vndir his sidis, his sidis ful sore bytyn
Ful pryuyly with malice, & if ȝe wil wytyn

Euene as þe sautere seith of þe wikkid tungis: 3165
Nedderis venym is vndir swech tungis alle,
For thei laboure to destroye þe lungis
That are in a man & his entrayles alle.
Very serpentis me thinkith þat I may hem calle.
The seide of þis man þe kyngdames he schuld lese   3170
Both of Saxon and Sueue, Teutonie and Frese.

They seyd fals þerof, for he cam hem to lede
To þe kyngdam of heuene to þat blissid lif.
Thus are schrewis wont to qwite a man his mede
Whan a man is bysy and eke inquysityf   3175
Alle vicious lyuyng fro hem for to dryf!
But of special persecucioun wil we now telle,
Whech þat to Norbert at þat tyme felle.

The holy tyme is come in whech men are clene,
Lenten I calle it, when men of here synne   3180
Go onto cherch as þei are taute bedene
To þrowe awey þe filth whe⟨ch⟩ þei are inne.
Norbert for he loued soules to wynne
Sat al þat tyme ful besily in his place
To reconcile men fro synne onto grace.   3185

3161   doth *added above and to the right of* as
3163   *period between* his sidis *and* his sidis
3170   *MS* The; *Norbert usually has* Thei
3182   whe⟨ch⟩ *MS* whei
3197   *period after* schroof

fol. 46v The Lent went fast; Maunde Þursday is come,
    Whann of that sacrament a commemoracioun
    We maken ful deuly as is the custome,
    Nowt only we, but euery cristen nacyoun,
    For þann is tyme to make purificacyoun   3190
    Of alle here synnes þei þat Cristen be.
    Alle þis holy tyme ful dewly sat he,

    This same Norbert, bysy to reconcyle
    Synful soulis and brynge to charite.
    Thei cam onto him fer fro many a myle;   3195
    But among othir at þe dore where he
    Sat and schroof, with ful grete sotilte
    There cam a man in a mantell al ihid
    Whech with alle þat euyr he myth preye or bid

    Laboured to the porter þat he mytȝ come in.   3200
    Anon þe portere to his maystyr þis told:
    "There is a man withoute, sere, þat of his syn,
    If ȝe wold schryue him he seith he were behold
    Onto ȝow whil þat his lyf myth hold."
    "Lete him stande," seith Norbert, "stille withowte." 3205
    So stood he stille til alle þat were abowte

    Were serued and igo, but euyr he presed fast
    To entre to þis hous; but euene anoon,
    As Norbert sey him, he seid to him in hast:
    "Stand stille þere þou standist in name of Seint Ioon. 3210
    Come me no nyhere, meue not þi toon!"
    The seruauntis come in, & he bad þei schuld take
    This ich man & owt of his clothis him schake.

    Whann þat his mantell was itake awey
    Thann sey þei a knyf whech hing be his side,   3215
    Ful scharp igrownde: what neditȝ more to sey?
    It was ordeyned to make woundis wyde;
    Malice had made him a ful special gyde,
    To bringe in veniaunce, but oure blessed Iesu
    Wold not suffir his seruaunt þat was so trew   3220

3166 Ps. 139: 3, not Ps. 13: 5 (PL 1326D).

fol. 47r   To falle in perell ne in no myschaunce.
But whann þis man was caut þus openly
In his treson he list no thing to daunce,
But was sore aferd. Þoo þei asked him why
That he cam in with wepun þus priuyly.   3225
He teld hem pleynly in ful schort manere
That certeyn men, both prestis & seculere,

Had hered him þat tyme to þis entent,
That he schuld sle þe bisschop in þis manere.
They freyned & he told hem or he went   3230
What maner men & who many þat þere were
Whech him counceled þis treson for to rere.
Whann it was wist, grete merueyle alle þei hadde
That men þat were of wittis wondir sadde

And eke of councell witʒ þe bisschop þanne   3235
Schuld be so wikkid for to þink or doo
Swech a tresoun. Euery man gan banne;
But oure Norbert is not gouerned soo.
With mery chere and wordis according þertoo,
Thus seyde he þann to hem þat stood beside: 3240
"Wondir not mech þouʒ now at þis tyde

Owre cruell enmies haue entised þis man
To do this dede; for þis is þat same day
As þe gospell ful nobilly witnesse can,
In whech þe Iewis, witʒ ful grete aray,   3245
Sowt oure lord to bryng him to abay.
Weel were he alowid þat in ony houre
Of this day with myscheef or laboure

Mith suffre deth. Þerfor lete us now doo
As oure lord dede: forʒeue alle trespas.   3250
So myth we sekyrly scapen fro alle woo,
And sonnere falle onto þat goodly graas
Whech men schul haue before þe glorious faas
Of oure lord God, for þus counceled he:
Do weel to hem þat hate ʒou, whateuyr þei be.   3255

3243   þat *written over an erasure between* is *and* same
3263-3325   PL 1328A-28C
3264   Witʒ *added immediately before* clennesse

fol. 47v   ȝet for al þis, this retour is put in hold,
           For nowt elles but for he schuld hem fese
           That for to sende him of treson were so bold.
           He had not þere þouȝ no grete desese.
           Thus alle men þat wil oure lord plese   3260
           Schul scape daungeris, þouȝ þat þei be grete.
           For of þis matere we wil no lenger trete.

           Thus lyuyd þis bisschop in ful holy lyf.   xxxi
             Witȝ clennesse and stody was his moost laboure
           The mouled ydilnesse fro his soul to dryf;   3265
           To Goddis seruyse ȝede he euery houre.
           This was to þe world a ful swete sauoure;
           His good ensaumple was to sum men þere
           Very lyf as ȝe ful weel may lere

           In þe apostel; to summe eke it was   3270
           Deth and harm, to hem þat loued it nowt.
           Ȝete schul ȝe here, if ȝe wil list a cas,
           That with grete malys upon him was sowt.
           But of swech tresoun he ful litil rowt,
           So was his trust sette in God aboue,   3275
           Whom he serued both with fere and loue.

           His vsage was þoo, as we seyde wel late,
           To kepe þe seruyse both be nyth and day.
           Onto þe chauncell mad he many a gate
           With his chapeleynis, in ful prestly aray.   3280
           There was a clerk whech was þoo ful gay,
           Coragous and strong, malicious eke þertoo;
           Aȝens his ordre mech þing had he doo;

           Wherfore Norbert wold alday him snybbe.
           This same clerk was hired, as I wene,   3285
           Of certeyn men þat were onto him sibbe
           As of malice, of angir and of tene.
           "This sory bisschop," þei seid, "þat is so lene,
           Schal neuyr be in pees, but grucchin alle his lyfe.
           Go forth, þou man, take in þin hand a knyf,   3290

3244 Matt. 26: 47 ff. (Mark 14: 43 ff.; Luke 22: 47 ff.; John 18: 2 ff.).
3255 Matt. 5: 44.
3267 2 Cor. 2: 15-16.

fol. 48r   Wayte vpon him whan he to mateyns goth.
Take and serue him, þan schul we be in pees.
He is euyr chidyng, euyr angry and wrooth."
This ich clerk, withouten ony sees,
Hath leyd him pryuyly rith where þe prees   3295
Of clerkis schul com, whan þei to mateyns went;
Ful sikyrly wend he haue had his entent.

Thei came too and too as was þe vsage,
Clerkes ȝeden soo, and þe bisschop last.
This cruell man whech had take þis wage   3300
In his hert hatȝ determyned and cast:
"The hinderest man, go he neuyr so fast,
He schal haue þe wownde ere þat he pase."
But it happed þat nyth, of oure lordis grase,

Norbert in þe myddis of hem at þat tyde   3305
Went forth, ful mekely takyng no gret heed
At swech dominacyoun whech sound`tȝ` into pryde
Ful often tyme. Thus forth he ȝeed.
This clerk roos up with ful grete speed,
On him þat last went he leyd on ful sore,   3310
And þat ich man began to crye and rore:

"What are þou," he seid, "in vertu of God aboue,
That smytist me so and I greue þe nowt?
This maner brothirhod is not groundid in loue!"
"O," seyde þis theef, "almys haue I wrowt;   3315
That ilk man, whech þat I haue sowt,
He is skaped and goo or þat I wist."
And with þat word fro hem is he twist.

3292   him *added above* serue
3300   take *added above and to the right of* had
3305   þe: s *of* þes *imperfectly erased*
3308   *period after* tyme
3326-3465   PL 1328C-31A
3346   *MS* religio

Thei folowed after, but Norbe(r)t cryed: "Hoo!
Pursewe him nowt, lete him go his way.   3320
Do him no harm, lete him scape and goo.
Goddis will must be fulfillid ay.
If he haue powere to sle me, welkom þat day.
Thei slepe not alle, þei þat hedir him sent,
Thei wil not leue til þei haue here entent."   3325

fol. 48v   The innocent flok whech oure fadere left   xxxii
     At Premonstrate, þei gunne to falle in dwere,
Because here heed was þus fro hem reft.
For now are runne the dayis of too ʒere,
Sith þat Norbert to hem, both leef and dere,   3330
Cam not there. Wherfore sum men seyde
That ilk reule to whech thei were teyde

Mith not lest withoute a gouernoure.
Summe seyde þis: þat he schuld come ageyn.
"Who schul þe scheep doo in storm and stoure,   3335
Who schul þei doo in wyndis and in reyn
But if here schepperd he witʒ hem?" Þus þei seyn.
Summe seid it was best for to chese anothir.
Thus is þere differens betwix brothir & brothir.

Whan þat Norbert herd of þis affray,   3340
He was aferd lest þan þat trauayle
Whech he had planted schul now drye away.
Therfor with gouernaunce he will hem now rayle.
Withouten ledere þer may no man saile,
This wist he weel. Therfor he dede calle   3345
Off þis religio(un) þe saddest and wisest alle.

3326 The fact that Norbert continued his evangelistic apostolate after founding
Prémontré and the markedly active character of his foundations as bishop have given rise
to the view that Norbert did not envisage the development along contemplative lines and
the highly centralized system established by Hugh of Fosse, his successor. See Chas.
Dereine, "Les origines de Prémontré," *RHE* 42 (1947) 352-378; F. Petit, *La spiritualité
des prémontrés au xiie et xiiie siècles* (Paris, 1947).

Whan þei were come, he asked hem in fere
What was here councell, & who þat þei schuld doo?
Summe of hem þat stood be him there
Seyde þei wold dwelle witʒ him euyrmoo,   3350
For fro here maistir þei seide þei coude not goo.
Summe seyde þei wolde chese anothir place,
And leue þere as God wold send hem grace.

But alle consented vndir a prelate to dwelle
That myth hem sette in stedfast gouernaunce.   3355
Whan he herd þis, a schort processe to telle,
He took þis matere into contynuaunce.
He bad hem go hoom & kepe her obseruaunce,
Saue a fewe whech he held there stille.
He seide onto hem þat þis was his wille: 3360

fol. 49r Thei schuld avise hem sadly euerychon
Whom þei wold chese & he schuld on his side
Examine here meritis. Þere schuld no fauour gon
But witʒ mekenesse, witʒouten ony pryde,
And with charite þis matere wold he gide.   3365
Thus seide he to hem & aftir a grete while
His messageris sent he many a myle.

Men of credens, þei went to euery hous
Of þis ordre assignyng hem here day,
Whan þat þei schal, in tyme moost gracious,   3370
Haue here eleccyon onto Cristes pay.
As þei were assigned, so ded þei witʒouten nay.
Thei chose a man aftir his owne entent,
And of here choys letteris haue þei sent.

Thann happed it soo: þat man whech was chose   3375
Was dwelling þere, but Norbert kept it cloos.
For grete causes sewirly, as I suppose,
Of þis eleccioun wold he make no roos
Onto þe tyme þat he knewe his foos,
If ony were there. For euyr was his vsage   3380
To bere a matere with ful sad visage

A long tyme or he wold speke it owte.
He wold first proue euery mannys entent,
And ransake þe hertis of hem al abowte.
Thann wold he performe his appoyntment,   3385
And sey, "Seres, I suppose ȝe be bent
Alle with on hert to swech conclusioun.
Were it ordinaunce, were it eleccyoun."

This same man eke, whech was chose þus newe,
Thouȝ it were kept ful priuyly in counsaile,   3390
Alle þis councell ful pleynly þoo he knewe
Be reuelacioun, he knew it witȝouten faile.
Whil he lay praying & gan sore to wayle,
Oure lord appered to him, as he thoutȝ.
Norbert, his fader, to þat presens him broutȝ.   3395

fol. 49v   Oure lord put oute his rith hand ful hertly,
And receyued þis ilk same man þat tyde.
"Behold, lord," seid Norbert, "þis same is he þat I
Haue chose vndir me for to be þi gide
Ouyr alle þoo men whech þat wil abide   3400
In þat holy lyf of very religioun,
Whech haue made to þe here professioun."

Aftir þis reuelacioun mad upon þis wise
Onto þis man, Norbert ded him calle.
Whann Norbert was set amongis hem as iustise,   3405
And his breþerin were gadered aboute him alle,
He seid þus to hem: "My conceyt open I schalle
Al pleynly to ȝou my breþerin þat be here.
This ich man þat sittitȝ amongis us in fere

3386 PL 1329C: quatenus nullam faceret in causis ex abrupto definitionem, nisi prius, ut homo poterat, exquisisset voluntatem Dei, et hausisset de circumstantibus sensum meliorem.

3389 *This same man*: Hugo of Fosse.

3409 Capgrave's source does not mention the name of Norbert's successor. He is the *clerk* of Bishop Burchard (ll. 477 above), Hugh of Fosse. It is significant that Hugo is called the first abbot of Prémontré: 'Hic iacet Dominus Hugo, qui fuit primus Abbas huius Ecclesiae et rexit Ecclesiam istam cum universo Ordinis Praemonstratensi triginta quinque annis, feliciter et quiete. Obiit anno domini MCLXIV.' (C. L. Hugo, *Sacri et canonici ordinis praemonstratensis annales* (Nancy, 1734), vol. 1, col. 10).

Is chosen be God and eke be al þe hous   3410
Of Premonstrate to be abbot there.
Thouȝ þe occupacioun be ful perilous,
ȝet wil I bidde þe & pray þe both in fere
That þou take it, broþir, and haue no dwere.
God he schal help þe, whech hath þe chose."   3415
This othir man answered, as I suppose,

Rith on þis wise, þat sothly his entent
Hath euyr be, sith he to þat relygioun
Was first receyued, to be obedient
Onto his souereynes & what þei bad him don.   3420
"Vnto my powere," he seide, "I fulfillid it son;
Therfor I wil not refuse now þis charge.
I am not fre, I stand not at my large.

I wil go onto hem & with al my myth
I wil asay if ony profith may I doo.   3425
If þat I do it, þan wil I, as it is rith,
ȝeue grace and þank to God & no moo;
If I spede not, fro hem wil I goo,
And come aȝen, fadere, for vndir the,
And vndir thi comaundment euyr wil I be."   3430

fol. 50r   Aȝen onto him Norbert spak ful sone:
"Go forth, good sone, and be not aferd.
Goddis hand in alle þat is to done
Schal euyr be with þe. It is his vynyȝerd
Where þou schal werk, parde; þou art lerd   3435
Who þou schal doo. Go now on my blessing."
This ilk man þe nexte morownyng

Taketh his leue, & forth he went apase,
With too felawes, sad men for the nones.
He himself was abbot of that place   3440
Whech we call of Premonstrat þe wones,
A ful fayre place of tymbir & of stones;
On of þe othir was abbot of Antwerpense,
A grete place endewid with grete expense;

3459   *long r inserted between o and l of wold*

The þirde of hem was mad gouernoure   3445
Of Florifiense, where dwelt þe noble clerk,
Petir icalled, whech with grete laboure
Drowe on þe sautere a ful noble werk.
I wot ful weel I set not amys my merk
For I say þis book withinne fewe dayes.   3450
This same werk I proued at assayes.

Anothir abbot was made eke at Laudune,
Anothir at Vyuary, þe þirde at a place
Whech þat þei calle rith of elde custume
Good Hope. Thus with very grace   3455
Began þis ordre his braunches to brace,
And spryng in erde; for first were þei sex,
And aftir to grettir noumbir gun þei wex,

That al þe world is ful of hem now.
God ȝeue hem grace to kepe here ordre weel,   3460
And to drawe so depe in þat holy plow,
That þei turne not bak at no tyme ne ceel.
If þei do þus, mercy schal be here meel
In heuene blesse where þei schal dwelle.
Of othir þingis now I wil ȝou telle.   3465

3447 Peter of Herentals (1322-1391), canon and then prior of Floreffe. The work of
Capgrave examined was Peter's *Expositio super Librum Psalmorum*, completed, according
to the colophon, on 4 January 1374. Forty years after *Norbert* was completed the *Expositio* was printed. St. Norbert's Abbey, West De Pere, Wisconsin, has a copy dated
1480, though the place of origin is not given. See "Petrus van Herentals," *Nationaal
Biografisch Woordenboek* and A. L. Goovaerts, *Ecrivains, artistes et savants de l'ordre de
Prémontré* (Brussels, 1899-1920) 2: 40.

3457 Capgrave suggests that Norbert appointed all six abbots at this time. *B*,
however, makes it clear that the abbots of Laon and Valsery had been previously appointed (consecrati erant) and that the abbot of Bona Spes was appointed by the abbot of
Prémontré immediately after (statim post) his own appointment (PL 1330B). Of the five
abbeys (beside Prémontré) recorded here Capgrave has previously mentioned only two:
Laon (ll. 2346 ff.) and Valsery (ll. 2361 ff.); Floreffe and Antwerp and *Good Hope* were
not, since Capgrave did not use the chapters where reference was made to their foundation (see notes to ll. 1211 and 2338 above). The alphabetical sequence of the first four,
or arch-abbeys has no particular significance; the chronology according to *B* is: Floreffe,
Laon, Valsery and Antwerp.

3461 Luke 9: 62.

fol. 50v   His aduersaries, consideryng his paciens,   xxxiii
       What sorow and angir þat he had bore ful longe,
Consideryng eke his lif and innocens
Who he had suffered many a sory pronge
Of here venym, þei slaked sumwhat þe tonge,   3470
Araying hem to saluen aӡen swech wounde
Whech þei had mad and lay ӡet al onbounde.

Fourty mark þei sent him amongis hem alle
To amende with here formere greuaunce,
With whech þei had fro here lordchep falle.   3475
Thei asked forӡefte of alle here gouernaunce
And made to him a ful grete repentaunce
Of alle defautes whech þat þei had doo.
The castell ӡates opened þei alsoo,

Whech þei had sperd long tyme before: 3480
For sith he cam, he myth no entre haue.
Thei sette be him þan so litil store,
That non of his, swiere, ӡeman, ne knaue,
But if þei wold here lyues as þan laue,
Mith make no maystryes þere in no wise.   3485
Here hertis are now sette in othir sise.

Thei lete him in to alle his strengthis there,
With mech worchep & with ful grete prees.
Praising God with gladness & with fere,
Thay prayed oure lord þat he schuld encrees   3490
This mannes goodnes þat it schuld neuer sees.
Thus seid þei alle, and þat he worthi was
To be a bisschop of a bettir plas.

3466-3528   PL 1337-38A
3467   he *added above and to the right of* þat
3473   *abbreviation for* is *added to* among
3494   þei *written over an erasure*
3495   *MS* þe; *the usual form in Norbert is* þei
3498   *MS* he
3515   l *expunged after* Onto
3516   *MS* louel

For God, þei seide, had ful merveilously
Wrout for him, þe se it weel inow.   3495
Fro perel of deth whech ful sotilly
Was ordeyned for him, God fro him it drow.
Thus are ⟨þ⟩e tecches, whech were ful row,
Falle onto meknesse. Blessed be swech a lord
That þus can turne, þat þus can reule þe world.   3500

fol. 51r Thus hath mekenesse ouyrcome here cruelte
With gidyng of grace. God seid, so I wene,
That whosoeuyr haue humylite
He schal be heyued and þat schal be sene:
Hestir for meknesse was made a qwene;   3505
Norbert a bisschop was mad for þe same.
The world vseth not ofte swech maner game!

The þirde ȝere felle al þis good chaunce
Aftir he was chose, & sithin fully fyue ȝere
Ful nobilly helde he in gouernaunce   3510
Alle his puple whech was gadered þere.
Fro day to day he gan hem euyr to lere.
Alle religioun and alle maner honeste
Worchep to God aboue al thyng set he.

Onto oure feith he was euyr a tutoure.   3515
He loued therof so weel the vnytee,
That with his myth and al his laboure
Heresye and scisme ful greuously punchid he.
To desolate folk a fadere wold he be,
Faderless & widowys he susteyned witȝ his myth.   3520
Religious men eke both day and nyth

He visited ful weel, bylyng not only here wones,
But teching hem þe forme of religioun.
He took more heed at soules þan at stones.
His besynesse was al set to sauacyoun   3525
Of his subiectes, whech fro dampnacyoun
He drow euyr more, and euyr mot þe fame
Of his good dedis lest & eke þe name.

3503 Luke 18: 14.
3505 Esther 2: 17.

In þis same tyme, as elde cronicles seyn,   xxxiiii
Fel a scisme of whech is dool to here;   3530
But neuyrþelasse I must telle ȝou al pleyn
Swech maner þing as I fynde wrytin here.
Too popes regne⟨d⟩ at ones þat same ȝere
As now þei doo, God amende þe caas!
The o pope thus he named was   3535

fol. 51v Innocent þe secunde whech be dew eleccioun
Was made pope. Þe othir eke hith þus,
As þis story seith, Petir þe Leoun;
But othir bokes sey he hith Anacletus
Whatsoeuer he hitȝ, contrarye to Iesus,   3540
Whech is prince of pees, was he euyr founde.
The cause þat he was þus susteyned in þat grounde

Was his grete kynrod, for þei were strong
And meyntened him with al here hool myth,
Notwithstandyng þei ded ful grete wrong;   3545
For þis ich Innocent had only þe rith.
Be trew processe was he eke elith;
But þe othir with seculere hand kept þe cyte,
Made lawes and ordinaunces of whech is pite

To speke and here, but þat it must be doo.   3550
The statutes of holy faderes before,
This ich Petre took no heed thertoo.
Thorw ȝates & walles ded he þrille and bore,
Alle þoo strengthes rent were and tore
That stood aȝens him; and þoo þat were his   3555
Are bylid up with mech cost iwys.

This Innocent was fayn for to come awey
And saue his lyf with hise for a while.
Onto the emperoure Lothary, as þei sey,
Came he down fro Rome many a myle,   3560
Pleynyng to him of his wrong exile,
Praying him of help and þat in hast;
But if he help alle will turne to wast.

3529-3619   PL 1338A-39C
3535   *MS* regnes
3545   ful *added above and to the right of* ded
3546   t *added to* Innocen *over an erasure*

Thus seide þis pope onto this emperoure:
"Princes are gadered now on euery side 3565
To susteyne þe rith, þe fredom, þe hounour
Of holy church." To Rome wil þei now ryde.
Prelatis reden witȝ hem þe treuth to gide,
Amongis whech Norbert was chose for on.
Thus ryde þei forth in cumpany euerychon. 3570

fol. 52r Schort processe to make, þei are com to Rome
Witȝ grete prees & mech folk rydyng in fere.
The pope Innocent is set þere in his trone
Be þe strength of Lothary as ȝe may here.
And þe same emperoure, witȝouten ony dwere, 3575
Was crowned þere be þe popis hand,
A noble prince, þat durst wel tak on hand

A ful grete daungere for Cristes sake.
A worthi man in armes euere was he holde.
The elde cronicles witnes, I vndirtake, 3580
That he was in bataile ful hardy & bolde,
Wyse of councell eke, for neuer wold he folde
Ne falle fro þe treuth in no manere wise.
His manhod was proued at best deuyse

3583   no *added above and to right of* in

3530 Upon the death of Honorius II in 1130, four cardinals immediately proceeded with the election of Gregory who took the name of Innocent II. Cardinal Pierleone, with the backing of his family, gathered cardinals, priests and laymen to his own cause. His cardinals, perhaps five in number, elected him as Anaclete II. The schism lasted until 1138. See E. Mühlbacher, *Die Streitige Papstwahl des Jahres 1130* (Innsbruck, 1876; rptd. 1966); also Franz-Josef Schmale, *Studien zum Schisma des Jahres 1130* (Köln-Böhlau, 1961).

3534 The schism Capgrave refers to was precipitated by the Council of Basle on 25 June 1439 when it deposed Eugene IV, declared him a heretic and proceeded to elect Duke Amadeus of Savoy on 5 Nov. 1439. The Duke took orders and was solemnly crowned 'Felix' in Basle on 24 July 1440, three weeks before Capgrave completed *Norbert*. The schism formally ended with the dissolution of the Council in 1449 and the abdication of Felix. Cf. Hubert Jedin (ed.), *Handbuch der Kirchengeschichte*: III *Die mittelalterliche Kirche*: 2 *Vom kirchlichen Hochmittelalter bis zum Vorabend der Reformation* (Fribourg-im-Br.-Basle-Vienna, 1968) 572-588.

In many cuntrees, specialy in Cycile, 3585
In Saxone, in Almayne & ouyr al aboute.
The realte of Rome be many a myle
Was augmented be him witȝouten doute.
Of þis mannis praysing I wil no more oute,
But schortly conclude þat þis same emp(er)oure 3590
Loued Norbert soo þat vnneth no houre

Mith he be fro him: his lyuyng was so clene,
His doctrine so good, his ensaumple so swete.
But so mech trauayle had he, I wene,
This same bisschop, what witȝ cold & hete, 3595
In mystemperure, in drye and in wete,
That he took seknesse whech wold not awey,
But in schort tyme, sothly to sey,

It broute him to a ende; for aftir he was com hom
To Parthenople, his seknesse com ful fast, 3600
That foure monthis as stille as ony ston
Down in his bed ful lowe is he cast.
The lif þat we haue here may not euyr last,
Neithir in him ne in no othir with.
Thus tooke he leue of þis erdely lith. 3605

fol. 52v He went to þe othir þat is mech more clere.
He myth not euele deye, as Seynt Austyn seith,
For he lyued weel whil he was here
Both in gouernaunce and in his feith.
Thus is he rauyschid onto þat goodly heith 3610
Where Goddis presens is schewid euyrmore.
There hatȝ he his guerdon for his trewe lore.

Eyte ȝere, as we seyd, gouerned he
His bisschoprik with ful bysy holynesse.
The ȝere of oure lord, as wryten fynde we, 3615
A thousand a hundred foure & thirty, as I gesse,
Is þe date of his deth & his last sekenesse,
The Wednysday euene in Pentecost feest,
The eyte ydus of Iuny, as seith oure geest.

3590   MS empoure
3620-3710 PL 1339C-41A
3626   MS fudacioun

Whan he was ded þere felle a grete staunce   xxxv 3620
   Betwix þe hed cherch in þe same stede
And Seynt Mary cherch whech be his gouernaunce,
And be his prouydens, as ȝe ful wel may rede
Befor in þis book, it is no drede
He ordeyned there a hous of religioun   3625
Of his owne bretheryn & of his fu(n)dacioun,

And translate þens þe chanonys seculere.
This cherch made cleym in this wyse:
Thei seide because he was here bisschop þere,
And was in manere here lord and iustyse,   3630
It was grete reson, as þei gun deuyse,
That he schuld be byryid in þe heed plas,
Because þat heed of þat diocise he was.

The othir men made grete resonis why
That þei schuld haue him in possession.   3635
Here grete argumentis in swech kende þei ly:
Thei seide he wan hem with exhortacioun,
And broute hem owt of here owne nacioun
To serue God þere, wherfor sith þat he
Here fadere was, it semeth reson, parde,   3640

fol. 53r That he schuld logge among his childir dere.
Ferþermore, anothir resoun thei broutȝ
That or he deyid out of þis world here,
With weel avised speche & parfith thoutȝ.
He comaundid his body þat it schuld be broutȝ   3645
Onto his bretheryn, for þat was his will.
Who do þe reuers, þei þink he doth ill.

3607 PL 1339B: Neque enim, ut ait Augustinus, poterat male mori, qui bene vixerat.
The text in Augustine's *De Disciplina Christiana* reads: Non potest male mori, qui bene
vixerit (PL 40: 676). Norbert was canonized only in 1582. See E. Valvekens, "La
canonization de Saint Norbert en 1582," *Anal. Praem.* 10 (1934) 10-47.

Vpon þis stryf onto þe emp(er)oure þei sende.
For sekirly, þei sey only his iugement
Wil thei obeye, and non othir ende   3650
Schal þei pursewe. Þe messageris are sent
Rith fro both sidis, and þei þat went
Taryed eyte dayes or þei come ageyn.
In alle þis tyme, schortly for to seyn,

Is þe body bore fro place onto place,   3655
Fro cherch onto cherch where þei sing & rede
Diriges and masses onto Goddis grace.
Alle prestes aboute to þat seruyse ȝede;
The lewid puple þei seide here crede.
Thus was he kept alle þoo eyt dayes,   3660
For so long þe messageris mad here delayes.

And notwithstandyng þe wedir was so drye
That þe grasse in þe feldis was al tobrent,
And alle þing was, if I schuld not lye,
ȝet be myth of God omnipotent   3665
Whech wol not suffre his seruantis to be schent,
Norbertis body ȝaue neuyr no stynk
In al þis long tyme. Lord, whann I think

Of þe incoruptibilnesse þat sum folk haue
Aftir here deth, it is a demonstracioun   3670
Onto my reson, þat þei whech schul be saue
And led onto heuene aftir þe resurreccioun,
Schul bere here bodies with hem to þat mansioun.
For sith þe body may be clene þus alone
It schal be mech clenner whan he schal gone   3675

3648   *MS* empoure
3668   *MS period between* tyme *and* lord
3684   *MS* empoure
3696   *MS* solempmly

fol. 53v Forth in the felauchip onto þe blisse
With his soule þat schal schine ful brith.
Whereof al solace þei schal neuyr mysse
As þese elde clerkis in here bokes writh.
Alle þis is iseide for þis noble with, 3680
Norbert I mene, þat lay so longe on grounde,
And in his flesch was no sauoure founde

Of no onclennesse in no manere wise.
The messageris þat were sent to þe emp(er)oure
To be in þis matere a rithful iustise, 3685
Are now com hom with grete laboure.
Be mery, ȝe men, for the day is ȝoure.
ȝe Premonstratis euyr, mot God ȝou saue,
ȝoure hool entent in þis matere schul ȝe haue.

The body is bore to Seynt Mary cherch 3690
Where his breþerin dwelle. Þe emperour wil soo;
Aftir his comaundment men mut nedis werch.
Thus is he byryed and al þe offise doo.
Who sang þe masse or seid þe sermoun þoo,
ȝe gete not of me; myn auctour telletȝ nowt 3695
But þat his bodi solemply was browt

Onto þe erde & leyde before þe autere,
Halowid of þe crosse, sothly þus he seith.
Aftyr was he rered & leide in þe qwere
In a fayre tombe of a grettere heith. 3700
Thei þoutȝ it was encresing to here feith
And eke enhaunsyng to here religioun
Euery day of his graue to haue a visioun.

Thus lith he stille ful fayre in þe qwere
Abydyng in hope on Cristis mercy 3705
Whann he schal risyn, as we seid weel ere,
And apperen to þe dom with seyntis in þe sky.
Thei þat ful lowe now in þe ground ly
Schul rysyn þann into euyrlastyng rest;
There schal not hold hem cophre ne chest. 3710

fol. 54r Grete argumentis are þere, many and fele,   xxxvi
          That þis ilk man for his werkis vertuous,
And for þe penaunce he ded in his hele
Schuld be, be liklynesse, dwelling in þat hous
Whech as scripture seith is so solacious.   3715
For reuelacionis were had in this matere
Of certeyn persones, as ȝe may here.

The same day and oure þat he on deyid,
Whan þat his soule out of his body went,
There was a broþir of his þat long had he teyid   3720
To streyt lyuyng with al his entent.
This same brothir in a traunce was hent
Alle sodeynly where he sey his maystir goo
A ful fayre persone and white clothis alsoo.

This sey he þann, & in his hand he held   3725
A braunch of olyue ful fayre & ful grene.
Swech maner braunches had he seyn but seld,
But neuyrþelasse þis man as I wene
With dredful hert asked him bedene
Certeyn demaundes of whech þis was on: 3730
"Maistir," he seith, "whidir wilt þou goon?"

His maystir answerd & seid to him thoo:
"I come now fro paradise with þis olyue,
And streyth to Premonstrate now schal I goo
To plante þis braunche þere þat it may thryue.   3735
There is no man now dwelling on lyue
That hatȝ swech anoþir, þis dare I say."
Thus went he forth, he þoutȝ, in his way.

3711-3850   PL 1341B-44A
3748   s of as *blotted out*
3766   MS him
3771   h *in light ink added above and to the right of* w *of* with
3772   MS *erasure after* þat

The man told his breþerin þis auysioun.
Thei noted þe day in whech he it sey,   3740
For ferre fro Premonstrate stood her mansioun.
But within certeyn dayes men þat be þe wey
Rydyn, and went onto hem gun sey
That here maystir was ded; þan knew þei weel
Who þat he deyid at þat same seel.   3745

fol. 54v Anothir reuelacyon was had in þis wise;
There was a brothere, a preest he was, þei sey.
He þoutȝ his fadere, as he coude deuyse,
Appered onto him with stature fayre & hey,
Walkyng before him in a ful grene wey,   3750
But sodeynly, er þe mountenauns of an oure,
As he þoutȝ, he was turned to a floure.

And þis same floure aungellis hent anoon;
Thei bare it up forth into the sky.
This same man wook & þoutȝ his drem vpon,   3755
And dempt ful euene as it was hardyly
That þis same avisioun whech was so mysty
Ment not elles but þat his fadyr was goo
Fro þis world, his dreem ment rith soo.

Onto his prioure he ran in hasty wise,   3760
Praying him to graunt him now þis bone:
That he þat day myth to þat hye iustise
Comende þat soule as he was bounde to done
Of his fadere. The prioure answerd sone:
"What tokne hast þou þat þis man is past?"   3765
He told hi(s) drem onto him in grete hast.

The day was noted and founde ful stedfastly
That it was soo; blessed be God almyth
That for to schewe us is now so redy
Who þat his seyntis are ledde onto þe lith.   3770
There was amongis hem eke anothir whith
Þat was witȝ Norbert long tyme conuersaunt.
Aftir his deth he prayed God he schuld graunt

3715 1 Cor. 2: 9.

To sende sum tokne and eke sum answere
Wheythir his maistir were in blesse or nowt;   3775
Ful fayn wold he in þis matere lere;
With mech prayere bysily hath he sowt.
Oure blessed lord, þat hatȝ us so dere ibowt,
Wold not leue him alone þus desolaat
But ȝaue him answere, þouȝ it were rith laat,   3780

fol. 55r A grete reuelacioun and a ful fayre sith
He beheld his noble maystir whech was fro him goo.
As he lay in rest upon a holy nyth,
He þoutȝ he was rauyschid into a hous þoo
So fayre and so brith had he seyn no moo.   3785
It passed þe sunne, þe brithnesse þat was þere.
Amongis othir felauchip þat togidyr were

He beheld his maystir on whom his desire
Was ful sore sette, & whan he him sey
With brennyng loue, as man þat was on fyre,   3790
Before his feet al plat he gan him ley;
His wittis for ioye were ny awey.
"O maystir," he seyde, "for Goddis hye myth,
Telle me of þin astaat, and if al þis lith

Be to þin counfort and þi consolacioun."   3795
His maystir cam ny & lift him fro þe ground.
"Rise up," he seith, "fro þi prostracioun,
Myn obediensere, and weel be þou found,
In þis same ioye þat is eterne and round.
Thou wold fayn wite if I endewid were.   3800
Thouȝ þi demaund be hard, ȝet schal þou lere;

For who þat knokkitȝ bisili sumtyme schal in.
Come nyhere to me, & lete us sit adown.
I do þe to wite clensed of alle syn
Am I with mercy, whech is to me bown."   3805
This ma⟨n⟩ seye a sete as brith as ony crown,
Where Norbert was set in ful grete rest.
Swech wordes he seyd: "I am passed þe werst.

3806   *MS* may
3828   *MS* dek

For it is seyde to me 'come, my sistir dere,
Come sit in þi place aftir þi trauayle.'   3810
For to þe I telle my brothir þat art here
Þere may no desese aȝens me avayle.
I am in al qwyete saue in maner I wayle,
As aungellis doo, for fere of the doom."
Whan þis was seyd þe man awook soon   3815

fol. 55v   Hugely counforted be this avisioun.
Ȝet or he went fro him to his fadir he seyde:
"Fadir, I pray the of thy benysoun,
I pray þe eke, for loue of Mary þe mayde,
Telle me in treuth if þou were euel apayde   3820
That I cam not to the whan þou were seek?"
Norbert him answerd witȝ wordis ful meek:

"Thou schal come," and witȝ þis word anoon
The avision is goo, and counforted is þe man.
In swech maner wise þat his breþerin ilkon   3825
Sey him neuyr so myry as he was þan.
Of þese avisiones no more telle I can.
For þei be de(r)k, and so must thei be.
The apostill seith soo, leuyth now me:

That al þat euyr we se here of þe oþir lif,   3830
We se it as in a myrowre or in a glas.
Therfor in þis mater to be inquysitif
Grete perel it is, and euyrmore was.
We schal pray God to spare oure trespas,
And bryng us to blesse þer Norbert is inne.   3835
And specialy ȝe men, þat be of his kynne

And cleyme his fadirhood, loke þat ȝe hope
If þat ȝe folow þe steppis of his holy lif,
Ȝe schul come sumtyme to þat blessed cope
That witȝ largenesse of charite may fortȝ drif   3840
Alle debate and desese whech þat caytif,
The deuel of helle, acloyith men withal.
To þis entent down wil we fal

3802 Luke 11: 9.
3830 1 Cor. 13: 12.

On both oure knees, praying oure lord
To lede us and spede us in þis lif present, 3845
That we may kepe loue and concord.
And eke for to purchase very amendment,
So þat oure synnes may here be brent
Witȝ penaunce doying, þat we may haue grace,
In heuene blesse before Goddis face. 3850

fol. 56r These wordis folowand are drawyn ful schortly xxxvii
Owt of a book þat lith at Capenbregense.
Here foundouris lif is wrytin þere seriously;
But þei hemselue þus in schorter sentense
Brigged it thus onto the complacense 3855
Of here breþerin whech desired þis lif,
And of here desire were rith inquysitif.

In Westphale parties sprang a ful clere lith,
A post of þe cherch, a heuenely messagere,
Norbert called, so grete with God of myth, 3860
That ful of grace he was and of powere
Of ful grete continens, of eloquens a good skolere,
Formere and norchere of holy religioun,
Whech was eke causere of grete fundacioun

Off many houses þorw out dyuers londes. 3865
A prechoure of penauns was he witȝ þe best.
A trewe berere of Cristes owne sondes
Was he hold be est and eke be west.
Thus cryed he to hem þat lay þat tyme in rest
And knew not God arayetȝ; he seith þe weye 3870
Of oure lord and alle his styes ȝe feye.

Spirith of prophecye, and þat in wondir wise,
Had þis man; and, if ȝe list to here,
A speciall prophecye þis epistel doth deuyse:
Who þat in Westphale, aȝens a ful dere ȝere, 3875
He told hem alle þat were gadered in fere,
His breþerin, I mene, of hungir þat was comyng,
Whech schuld, he seid, come for here chastisyng.

3851-4089 PL 1343B-1350A (Additamenta)
3866   he *added above and to the right of* was
3878   come *added over* for; y *of* chastisyng *written over an* o *or an* e

And as he seide, so it cam in dede.
Grete hungir þere was of al maner vytayle,   3880
So sodeyn derth men to deth þoo ȝede,
That sodeyn pestilens gan hem soo assayle.
And in þis hungir, witȝouten ony fayle,
He bad his breþerin þat þei schuld not spare,
But ȝeue to pore þouȝ þat þei were bare.   3885

fol. 56v As he comaunded so ded þei til at þe last
Vpon a tyme þei ȝoue so mech away
That whan þei came onto here owne repast
Thei had rith nowt. Þann gun þei alle to say:
"Where is oure maistir? Lete him now assay   3890
His grete maystries." But he ful mekely:
"Breþerin," he seyde, "affray ȝou not forthi,

For it is writyn openly in Scripture —
If ȝe wil stody, ȝe may it pleynly rede —
'The rithful man whech God hatȝ in cure   3895
Schal not be suffered, withouten ony drede,
To dey for hu(n)gyr'." These men forth þei ȝede,
Thei fonde mete rith as here fadere seyde.
Whann othir men for hungir abouten deyde,

3897   *MS* hugyr

3851 The *Fratrum Cappenbergensium additamenta ad Vitam*, found as a supplement to all the earliest manuscripts of the *Vita B*, is little more than a series of *mirabilia* in the life of St. Norbert. It is very early, between 1155 and 1164 (see Wm. M. Grauwen, O. Praem., "Norbert et les debuts de l'abbaye de Floreffe," *Anal. Praem.* 51 (1975) 20), but contains little of historical value.

3852 Cappenberg, diocese of Münster, Westphalia, was the first foundation of the Premonstratensian Order in Germany. Godefried, son of Otto, count of Cappenberg, converted from his worldly and bellicose life, was accepted in 1122 by Norbert as a member of the Premonstratensian Order in the face of violent opposition from his family and particularly from his father-in-law, Frederick, Count of Westphalia. Norbert and Godefried emerged victorious and the ancestral castle of Cappenberg became a Premonstratensian monastery. Godefried died in 1127, and though never formally canonized, he was venerated locally as a saint. For his life see *ASS*, Januarii 2 (13 Januarii) 116-145, MGH, SS 12: 513-530 and the note on l. 2338 above.

3886 Isa. 49: 10.

3895 Prov. 10: 3, not Ps. 10: 3 (PL 1344B).

Alle that tyme thei had good plente.   3900
Blessed be swech a steward in a plaas!
Anothir þing felle eke in that cuntre:
Amongis his breþerin on seek þere waas.
He lay in þe fevyris, abidyng Goddis graas;
The man was spedful onto þe houses nede.   3905
Norbert streith onto his bed þoo ȝede.

"Rise up," he seyth, "I bidde in Goddis name,
Go do þis erand, for þou can do best."
This man þouȝ he had be mech to blame,
But he obeyid his fadere, as it was best.   3910
He roos up redyly fro his sekly nest;
He felt him hool, and hool was many a day
As fro þat seknesse. Blessed be God for ay!

Anothir þing is touched here alsoo
In þis epistil: who þat be inward counsaile   3915
Of þe holy goost, he and his breþerin þertoo
Chose hem a reule of whech þei myth not faile.
For there fynde þei al þing þat wil avayle
Onto good lyuyng and onto religioun.
This ich reule at þe first fundacyoun   3920

fol. 57r Of his clerkis þe noble Austyn mad.
But þis same reule more streytly for to kepe
Norbert hatȝ ment his breþerin eke be glad
Of þat streytnesse. Þei wil delue more depe
In here perfeccioun, morne, wayle and wepe,   3925
As men þat pleyne of þis worldly woo.
The streyt poyntis þat þei addid þertoo

Was harder habite and eke hardere mete,
Wollen cloþis next hem for to were;
Neythir fatte ne flesch wold þei not ete.   3930
This was þe wil of hem þat dwelt þere.
Ion þe Baptiste, þei seid, he schuld hem lere
Who þei schuld wynne heuene witȝ abstinense.
Thus was this ordre grounded in excellense.

The epistel seith eke þat Norbert on a tyme   3935
Sat in chapetir amongis his breþerin alle.
Whan euery man had accused his cryme,
Into othir daliauns goostly gan þei falle.
Norbert seyd þan: "Breþerin, to ȝou I schalle
Telle a tale whech þat I wil ȝe knowe.   3940
I knewe a man witȝin a litil throwe

That lay in stody and in his orisoun
A ful long tyme, þat God of his grace
Schuld sende to him sum reuelacioun
What reule he myth to his flok purchace.   3945
And as he lay rith before his face
Appered Seynt Austen, whech had þoo in hand
A reule of gold, as I vndyrstand.

Whech reule took he onto þat same with
Whom he appered to and þus sayd to him: "Sone,   3950
He þat þou seest, if þou be hold al rith,
He is Austen, bisschop sumtyme of Ypone.
Now hast þin askyng, now hast þou þi bone:
A reule vndir whech if thi childir hem cure,
Thei schul not drede aftir here sepulture   3955

fol. 57v The ferful doom, but sekyrly þereto stande
Before þat iustise and fauoure schul þei haue.
This dare I sauely on me take on hande,
If þei kepe þis, that þei schal be saue,
And go to blesse at that grete octaue."   3960
This same tale þat Norbert to hem told
Was of himselue sekyr, be ȝe bold.

It is þe manere of seyntes to do soo:
So ded Ion þe grete euangelist,
So ded Seynt Poule whan he wrote alsoo   3965
Who oute of þe world sodeynly he was twist
Vp onto heuene, & he himselue nyst
Wheithir his body was þere or nowt.
Of þis matere þe ende as now is sowt.

3964 John 19: 26; 20: 2; 21: 7.
3965 2 Cor. 12: 2.

Anothir miracule schal I now specyfye   3970
Of þis same man, and þat a wondyr þing.
He sang a masse ones at Florefye,
And sodeynly before his vsyng
He sey a drope of blood where it hyng
Rith on þe patene. His dekne stood by.   3975
He hith Rudolf, and he called him more ny.

"Seest þou, brothir," he seith, "þat I now se?"
The othir seyde: "Maystir, weel inow."
Both were þei gode, it schuld not elles be
That swech a visioun gracious to hem drow.   3980
Norbert was ny fallen into a swow,
But of deuocyoun sore he gan to wepe,
And aftir þat with his lippes to swepe

The blood away fro þe fayre patene.
He wasched it weel whann masse was idoo.   3985
This same religioun of custome, as I wene,
Wascheth here patenes of vse euyrmoo,
Whech custom grew ful long tyme agoo.
Of þis same dede, sothly as I suppose,
This same epistel writith þus in prose.   3990

fol. 58r   At Traiect eke is a wondir sith.
A pees of silk with aungellis þidir was broutȝ;
The puple sey it, who with bemys bryth
Out of heuene down to þe cherch þei soutȝ,
And leyd þat silk, ful merueylously iwroutȝ,   3995
Vpon þe toumbe where Seynt Seruase lay,
Whech was deed newly þat same day.

This same silk Norbert, whan he was þere,
Desired to see. Þe prestis answered sone
That here elderes up þei ded it spere   4000
In a hucch whech þei durst not ondone.
There was no man þat dwelt vndir þe mone
That in þat hucch was hardy onys to look,
So grete dreed of it þoo þei took.

3994   n *above and to the right of* dow

But his peticioun was graunted at þe last.   4005
The hucch is opened, and ful sodeynly
The silk fley out and to þe roof in hast
He mowntith up; alle þe puple it sy.
There hing it still ful merueylously;
Summe were astoyned, summe were aferd   4010
Lest þe grace of God were now isperd.

Fro here cherch þei dempt it wold awey,
But it hing stille lich a bird flikyryng.
Norbert ful sadly onto hem þus gan sey:
"We schal sone se what is þe signifying.   4015
Go we to masse in hast & make no tarying."
He made him redy, & whan he was at messe,
Oute of þe roof þe silk þo gan it dresse,

And cam ful esely down on to þe qwere.
He leyd him euene upon þe armes too   4020
Of oure Norbert that stood at þe autere.
He took it to him with grete deuocioun þoo,
Falt it togidir witȝouten ony moo,
And leyde it there where it was before.
Here may ȝe proue be very open lore   4025

3979 vocatoque fratre Rodulpho sacrista nostro, ejus tunc diacono (PL 1347A).

3987 This detail is Capgrave's own and can be documented. H. J. Lentze, "Der Messritus die Prämonstratenserordens," *Anal. Praem.* 26 (1950) 143 refers to M. Van Waefelghem, *Liturgie de Prémontré: Le liber ordinarius d'après un manuscrit du xiiie et xive siècles* (Louvain, 1913) p. 95, where there is a directive to wash the paten. Lentz says: "Jüngere Hss kennen noch Abwaschung der Patene mit Wein über dem Messkelche, die vor der Ablutionen der Finger vorgenommen wird. Sie schieben zwischen 'ad altar' und 'postea' den Satz ein: Postea aspergat vino patenam et infundat in calicem."

3991 *Traiect:* Maastricht. See note to l. 2193 above.

3996 Servatius (or probably Serbatios), whose relics were venerated at Maastricht from the 6th century.

4007 *ASS*, Maii 3 (13 Maii) 219, in connection with the life of St. Servase, tells of a piece of silk which was stolen from the treasury of the saint's shrine and worn at the celebration of the saint. The perpetrator was the Duchess of Lotharingia who was conscience stricken and confessed her fault. There is no mention among 11th-century miracles of the incident mentioned by Capgrave.

fol. 58v   That in þis bisschop Seruase þus inamed
Was ful grete vertu schewid be God of myth;
And in oure fadere Norbert euyr onblamed
Was ful grete feith both be day and nyth;
For his prayere was so clere and bryth,   4030
He myth not want þing þat he wold haue.
Thorw his prayere þe sunnere God us saue!

There was a man eke I vndyrstand
Whech was ful cruell and ful couetous.
He dwelt be a place whech þei clepe Boneland.   4035
He kept fro hem here londys and here hous,
ʒet dede he þing þat was more perilous:
For certeyn rentis held he to his bane,
That longed to þe cherch of Partenopolitane.

And notwitʒstandyng þere durst no man for dreed   4040
Speke onto him a word of þis matere:
ʒet oure Norbert boldly onto hem ʒeed.
He teld him þe perel and eke þe grete daungere
Whech he offendid God with his powere.
The man answerd ful sone to him agayn: 4045
"I haue no land fro ʒou, soth to sayn;

This þat I haue, it is myn herytage,
Whech ʒe schal not, no, non of ʒou alle,
Haue fro me. I haue be at grete costage;
I haue made þeron both houses & eke walle.   4050
Lete be ʒoure laboure, clepe no more ne calle.
ʒe gete here ryth nowt, þere is no more to seyn;
ʒe haue ʒoure part, turne now hom ageyn!

Norbert answerd: "Man, þou schal rew ful sore
Alle þis extorsioun, and alle þis couetise."   4055
He turned his bak, he seid to him no more.
But his thretyng be þe hey iustise
Was executed, and þat in wondyr wyse.
For þat same ʒere of enmyes was he slayn;
And þann þe cherch entred þe londys agayn.   4060

4073   he *above and to the right of* aspied

fol. 59r   Anothir tyme in þe emperoures hoost
Whilis þat he was, þis noble Norbert I mene,
He happed to come onto a noble coost
Onto a cyte Augusta, as I wene
So it hith. There was his prophecye sene,   4065
Whech him was graunted of oure lord Iesu
To haue in brest, prophecye good and trew.

It was his vse whan he to cherch schuld goo
To knele down threis & þus þan wold he say:
"Pees to þis hous, pees be here euyrmoo,   4070
Pees rest upon ʒou withouten ony nay."
Thus sayde he there þat ilk same day
And aftir aspied he þat pees dwelt not þere
Amongis þe puple þat aboute him were.

Onto his dekne seyde he þan specialy: 4075
"I haue desired, my broþir, a ful long tyde,
That pees schuld dwelle here in þis cumpany.
It wil not be; he is oppressid witʒ pryde.
Lete us go hens, lete us walk more wyde;
Here is no rest and þat schal sone be sene."   4080
As he seyde þann, so it felle bedene.

4035 *Boneland*: 'Apud locum qui Bonlandt dicitur; ubi nostrorum quoque fratrum floret coenobium' (PL 1348B). This is probably Bolanden near Hagen in the diocese of Mainz. The Premonstratensians came to Bolanden in 1160. The connection with Magdeburg is not at all clear; it was at a considerable distance from Magdeburg and in a different diocese. The question here, however is not of ecclesiastical property or canonical rights but rather *vini redditus, qui proprie erant Parthenopolitane Ecclesiae* (PL 1348B).

4064 *Vindelica Augusta* or *Augusta Vindelicorum*: Augsburg, an ancient city in Bavaria.

4070 The formula of peace (PL 1349A) 'Pax huic domui et omnibus habitantibus in ea' is an ancient liturgical one used by priests on visits to homes where they administered the sacraments. It is based ultimately on the injunction of Christ, Matt. 10: 12.

4081 The predicted event took place in August, 1132. An attack on the papal legate by the Augsburg citizenry, further exacerbated by a fracas between shopkeepers and the royal retinue, developed into an armed battle. In retribution Lothair destroyed the fortifications of the city and left the city in ruins. Norbert, with Lothair at the time, was instrumental in saving the life of the bishop of Augsburg. Cf. Friedrich Zoepfl, *Das Bistum Augsburg und seine Bischöfe im Mittelalter* (Munich-Augsburg, 1955), pp. 125-126.

For þe emperoure, þat was ful iuste & ful trewe.
For certeyn trespaas þat þe puple had doo,
Of þat cyte here hedis of he hewe.
This knew þis man long or it felle soo.   4085
Swech merveyles ded he and ȝet many moo,
But in þis epistil is no more now told.
For matere fayleth, I am no lenger bold

Onto ȝoure reuerens of þis man to wryte.
Mi noble fadere, norischere of us alle   4090
And specialy of me, wolde God I coude endyte
Sum goodly þing witȝ whech I mytȝ now calle
Onto ȝoure grace, and in ȝoure seruyse falle.
But now conclude I, as ȝe ȝoue comaundment
Be ȝoure messagere þat ȝe to me sent.   4095

fol. 59v Go litil book to hem þat wil þe rede.
Sey þou were made to þe abbot of Derham;
Fast be Stoke it stant wvtȝouten drede.
It is to lordes and gentilys alle in sam
And eke to pore men a very Iulianes ham.   4100
The abbotes name was called at þat tyde
The good Ion Wygnale, þat neuer wold him hide

4090   isc *of* norischer *written over an erasure*

4088 Capgrave passes over in silence the cure of a demoniac, the final episode reported in the *additamenta* (PL 1343B-50C). Nor does he append the 24 verse hymn, "Felix
Norbertus, primus ordinis hujus" (PL 1350).

4097 West Dereham Abbey of the Assumption of the Blessed Virgin Mary was
located in the diocese of Norwich, Norfolk, approximately 15 miles from King's Lynn. It
was founded in 1188 by Hubert Walter, Deacon of York, and later Archbishop of Canterbury. It was suppressed in 1539. Only the granary survives. See J. C. Cox, "The
Religious Houses of Norfolk," *A History of Norfolk*, The Victoria History of the Counties
of England (Westminster, 1908), 2: 414-418.

4099 *Iulianes ham*: home of hospitality. Having unwittingly killed his father and
mother, Julian established a hostel by a broad and dangerous river and helped travellers
across the river, and together with his wife ministered to their needs. He was venerated as
the epitome of the hospitable man, and thus Chaucer in the Prologue to his *Canterbury
Tales* describes the Franklin as "Saint Julian he was in his contree" (l. 340). For a complete history of Julian and the various confusions of identity, the documents and history
of the cult see B. de Gaiffier, "La Légende de S. Julien l'Hospitalier," *Analecta Bollandiana* 63 (1945) 145-219.

4102 John Wygenhale alias Saresson (or Sareson) was abbot of West Dereham from

For no gestis but rather he wold hem seke.
The freris name þat translate þis story
Thei called Ion Capgraue, whech in Assumpcion weke   4105
Made a ende of alle his rymyng cry,
The ȝere of Crist oure lord, witȝouten ly,
A thousand foure hundred & fourty euene.
Aftyr þis lyf, I pray God send us heuene!

ffeliciter

1429 to 1455. Of noble birth, he was educated at Cambridge University where he received a degree in Canon Law (A. B. Emden, *A Biographical Register of the University of Cambridge to 1500* (Cambridge, 1963), p. 655). His name appears frequently in ecclesiastical documents in Norfolk in the 15th century, recording offices he held and benefices granted to him. For a number of years he was Vicar General of the bishop of Norwich and also served as archdeacon of Sudbury. His will in the Norwich Archive Centre dated 14 January 1461 precludes the possibility that he died "in or shortly before 1459" as suggested by H. M. Colvin, *The White Canons in England* (Oxford, 1951), p. 323 n. 2. Capgrave, however, in the *Tretis* which he had promised to append to his *Gilbert*, refers to Wygenhale "þat deyed last." But *Gilbert* is dated 1451! (See *The Life of St. Gilbert*, ed. J. J. Munro, EETS, O.S. 140 (London, 1910), p. 142.) Capgrave's portrayal of Wygenhale is corroborated by the description in the mortuary roll which announced his death to various religious houses in England: 'Honoratus non minus a dominis quam ab universa familia; inter peritos disertus, cunctis se amabilem et gratum exhibebat; erat enim aspectus hilaris, vultu serenus, sermone jucundus, in conversacione affabilis, suis pariter et extraneis gratus et benignus, mitis, misericors, omnibus virtutibus congruebat.' For a description of the precious mortuary roll and its subsequent use see: J. G. Nichols, "On Precatory or Mortuary Rolls, and Particularly of One of the Abbey of West Dereham, Norfolk," *Memoirs illustrative of the history of Norfolk and the city of Norwich communicated to the annal meeting of the Archaeological Institute held at Norwich, July 1847* (London, 1851), pp. 99-114.

GLOSSARY

This glossary is selective in that it does not include words presumably familiar to the reader of modern English, nor forms readily recognizable from their context. For example, *bold* (l. 88), an adjective, is not glossed; *bold* (l. 1865), a verb, is. Again, *leue*, meaning 'stop' (l. 138), 'live' (l. 539), 'believe' (l. 1448) is recorded, but *leue*, meaning 'leave' (l. 188) is not. The first occurrence of a given word is usually glossed, and in the form it has at that point in the text; subsequent appearances are not cited except to note variants. In the alphabetical sequence, vocalic *y* is treated as *i*; *ʒ* appears under *g*, except where it represents *z* as in *neʒing*. I have, however, kept the scribe's *i* and *v* where modern conventions use *j* and *u*.

ABBREVIATIONS

adj.	adjective	*interj.*	interjection	*pret.*	preterite
adv.	adverb	*intr.*	intransitive	*reflex.*	reflexive
aux.	auxiliary	*n.*	noun	*sg.*	singular
comp.	comparative	*pl.*	plural	*superl.*	superlative
conj.	conjunction	*pp.*	past participle	*trans.*	transitive
fig.	figurative	*pr.*	present	*v.*	verb
imper.	imperative	*prep.*	preposition	*var.*	variant
impers.	impersonal	*pres.*	present	*vbl.*	verbal

abay   *n.* state of being checked in pursuit, 3246.
abite   *n.* habit (garment of a religious order), 1336.
able   *adj.* suitable, fit for, 233.
acloyith   *v. pr. 3 sg.* beset, harrass, 3842.
acord   *v.* agree, 728.
adrad   *pp.* afraid, 176.
affray   *n.* disturbance, 3340.
affrayed[1]   *pp.* disturbed, alarmed, 2776.
affrayed[2]   *pp.* worn away, 1005.
agate   *adv. var. of* **ongate**, straightway, immediately, 497.
alderis   *gen. of* **al**, all of them 1268.
algate   *adv.* by all means, 811.
Almayn   *n.* Germany, 456.
alyauns   *n.* association, help, 56.
among   *adv.* meanwhile, 1056.
ankeris   *n. pl.* hermits, recluses, 1261.
anoyed   *pp.* upset, troubled, 532.
apalled   *pp.* anxious, weary, 81.
apase   *adv.* quickly, rapidly, 830.
apele   *n. acc. sg.* supplication, appeal, 1951.
aray   *n.* array, display, 1048.

araye *v. pr. 3 sg.* provide with, prepare, 1901.

aspied *pp.* detected, found out, 988.

assayde *pp.* tested, tried, 1006.

assayes *n. acc. pl.* attempts, attacks 311.

assyse *n.* judgment, 593; fashion, 1313; **al maner asise**, various forms, 3013.

astate *n.* rank, 3027.

astert *v.* start up, begin, 892.

astoyned *pp.* stunned, bewildered, 176.

aube *n.* alb (an ecclesiastical vestment), 1050.

autere *n.* altar, 272.

avaleth *v. pr. 3 sg.* doff, remove, 966.

avaunce *v.* advance, progress, 1376.

avaunt *v.* boast, praise 854.

avyis *n.* deliberation, judgment, 2479.

bayli *n. var. of* **baillif**, agent, steward, 2194; *pl.* **baleys**, 2954.

balled *adj.* bald, 2035.

bande *n.* promise, agreement, 2135.

bane *n.* edict, proclamation, 4038.

ban(ne) *v.* curse, 614; condemn, 3237.

bare *adj.* manifest, real, 109; ? unprotected, 2222.

barred *pp.* striped, ornamented with horizontal bars, 2015.

basse *adj.* low-lying, low, 2196.

bede *v.* offer, present, 2203.

bedene *adv.* all together, at the same time, 2483.

bend *v.* bring down, 264; submit, 796; *pp.* turned, 1222.

benet *n.* exorcist; **benetis crown** form of tonsure worn by exorcists, 2119.

benysoun *n. used as adv.* **on my benysoun**, by all means, certainly, 3035.

bere *v.* clamour, shout, 1145.

besy *adj.* industrious, intent, 403.

bete¹ *v.* beat, 1453; overcome, correct, 1603.

bete² *v.* treat, discuss, 2859.

bewe *n. var. of* **beau sire** (*see note to line 2034*).

biggid *pp.* establish, found 835.

bile *v. var. of* **bilden**, to construct, build, 1621; *pres. p.* **bylyng**, 3522; *pp.* **bylid**, 1803.

blynne *v.* desist, refrain, 1390.

boystous *adj.* rough, coarse, 380.

bold(e) *v.* be encouraged, to cast off restraint, 1865.

bolnyd *pp.* corpulent, distended, 963.

bone *n.* boon, favour, 3761.

borde *n.* jest, joke, 1434.

boure *n. pl.* abodes, enclosures 2126.

bown *pp.* sent, given, 3805.

brace *v.* embrace, 2677; join, fasten together, 831.

brase *v.* 831, *var. of* **brace**.

brast *v. pret. of* **bresten**, force out send out, 276.

brennyng *pres. p. of* **bren**, 411; *pp.* **brest**, 1015.

brere *n.* briar, 1616; *pl.* **breris**, 770.

brese *v.* break into small pieces, 2532.

brothell   *n.* wretched person, scoundrel, 2281.

buxumnesse   *n.* obedience, 2932.

cace   *n. var. of* **cas**, device, scheme, 2657.

caytyf   *n.* wretch, 2129.

calueryn   *n. pl.* calves, 2640.

carkeys   *n.* carcass, 2552.

cast   *v. pret. 3 sg.* (*reflexive*) proposed, schemed, 905.

ceel   *n. var. of* **seel**, period of time, 3462.

chase   *v. pret. 3 sg.* chose, 755.

chaunce   *n.* happening, fortune, 267.

chaunge   *n.* exchange, replacement, 754.

chere   *n.* geniality, good cheer, 59; appearance, 491.

chesen   *v. pret. 3 sg.* **chase**, chose.

child   *n.* servant, 137.

circulationes   *n. pl.* changing from one element to another, 1970.

cyuyle   *adj.* civil law 3054.

clatering   *n.* chattering, idle talk, 946.

clatir   *v.* babble, prate, 949.

clere   *adj.* pure, praiseworthy, 2749.

cloos   *adj.* secret, private, 3376.

clut(t)e   *n.* patch, rag, 1410.

cobbe   *n.* herring's head (or tail), 1582.

college   *n.* fraternity, assembly, 776.

comande   *pres. p. of* **comen**; **in tyme comande**, in time to come, 1641.

comelyng   *n.* newcomer, intruder, 3093.

comonyng   *n.* participation, conversation, 686.

comoun   *v.* communicate, share, 709.

comounte   *n.* community, 1263.

complacense   *n.* **onto the complacense**, for the pleasure (or satisfaction) of, 3855.

conceyt   *n.* notion, thought, opinion, 709.

condiciones   *n. pl.* personal traits, habits, attitudes, 122.

condicioun   *n.* nature, quality, 126.

congen   *v.* ask one to leave, dismiss, 2052.

coniure   *v.* adjure, exorcise, 1041.

connaunt   *n.* agreement, pact, 520.

consciens   *n.* moral sense, sense of fairness, 661.

contynuaunce   *n.* **took into contynuance**, deferred, 3357.

conueniently   *adv.* suitably, properly, 826.

cope   *n.* top, summit (*fig.*), 3839.

corage   *n.* inclination, desire, intention, 187.

coragous   *adj.* lustful, lascivious, 3283.

corious   *adj.* artistic, exquisite, costly, 383.

costage   *n.* expenditure, cost, 2791.

couert   *adj.* guarded, secret, 703.

counfort   *n.* assurance, relief, 890.

crake   *v.* speak loudly, crow, 1110.

credens   *n.* authority, reputation, 3368.

crouched   *v. pret. 3 pl.* **Thei crouched hem**, they blessed themselves, 1863.

croude *v.* exert pressure on, force, 2014.

cun *aux. v.* can, know how to, 2667.

cunnyng *n.* experience, wisdom, 1085.

cuntenaunce *n.* bearing, 1559.

cure *n.* effort, work, 403.

cure *v.* care for, guide, 3954.

daffid *adj.* foolish, idiotic, 2015.

daliaunce *n.* conversation, 3938.

dam *n.* pond, stream, 397.

daunger *n.* **Put me in daunger**, run the risk, 7.

debate *n.* conflict, wrangling, 467.

decaluacion *n.* removal of hair, 1144.

defaute *n.* lack, defect, 650.

dele *n.* **no deles**, not at all, 943; **sum dele**, somewhat, 1446.

delite *n.* **fill his delite**, take his pleasure, satisfy himself, 920.

delue *v.* bury, plant, 2300.

dempt *v. pret. 3 sg. of* **deme**, judged, 888; **demyng, pres. p.** imposing penalties, 1386.

dene *n. var. of* **dine**, shouting, uproar, 2099.

dere *n.* harm, injury, 1008.

dere *adj.* grievous, oppressive, 3875.

dere *v.* wound, grieve, 1133.

desees *n.* death, demise, 1254.

desese *n.* distress, inconvenience, 467.

desesy *adj.* disturbing, troubling, 249.

desised *pp. var. of* **decised**, decided, arranged, 1715.

deuyse *n.* **at best deuyse**, perfectly, clearly, 3584.

discried *v. pret. 1 pl.* described, told, 512.

dishese *n.* disquiet, vexation, 2665.

ditʒ *v. var. of* **dighten**, prepare, make ready for use, 1900.

diuinacyoun *n.* prophecy, 1491.

dyuorcyoun *n.* separation, exorcism, 1194.

dominacioun *n.* influence, prevalence, 319.

dool *adj.* painful, distressing, 3530.

downgate *n.* a tumbling down, a falling apart, 1626.

dred *v.* honour, revere, 1731.

dresse *v.* **oute of his clothis dresse**, undress, 1158; **gan him dresse**, began to move, proceed, 1167; *pp.* arranged, ordered, 356.

dwere *n.* doubt, perplexity, 3327.

edifies *n.* building, 1614.

ey *n.* **at ey**, clearly, manifestly, 1452.

ey *interj.* alas, 2063.

eyres *n. pl.* heirs, 1295.

elith *pp. of* **eliten** elected, chosen, 3547.

endewid *pp.* endowed, provided with, 55.

endyte *v.* dictate, compose, 1404.

entended *v. pret. 3 sg.* intended, 601; be intent on, 1230.

entent *n.* purpose, 240; **take entent**, notice, 927.

erde *n.* earth 553.

erdely   *adj.* earthly, worldly, 3605.

ereyn   *n.* spider, 254.

erraunt   *adj.* arrant, wandering, 853.

euene   *adv.* **(fourty dayes) euene**, exactly, 191; **oute euene**, right out of, 254; **ful euene**,
      very directly, 1540.

euerydeel   *adv.* completely, entirely, 967.

exorȝiȝyoun   *n.* exorcism 1860.

expleite   *v.* relate, explain, 439.

fayn   *adj.* joyful, delighted, 109.

fayre   *adj.* average, fair, 111.

fallest, *v. pres. 2 sg.* reach, attain, 875; **was fallen**, happened, 959.

fares   *n. pl.* practices, 2419.

fede   *v.* stimulate, lead on, 1217.

fey   *n. var. of* **feith**, loyalty, faithfulness, 2691.

feye   *v.* cleanse, purify, 1055.

feyne   *v.* pretend, feign, 887.

feyned   *adj.* false, deceitful, 1576.

feynted   *adj.* stinted, limited, 1762.

feysing   *ger.* frightening, terrifying 2668.

fele   *adj.* many, 1948; **many and fele**, good, proper, 3711.

fende   *n.* fiend, devil, 981.

fendly   *adj.* diabolically, fiendishly, 889.

fere[1]   *n.* fire, 169.

fere[2]   *n.* fear, 257.

fere[3]   *n.* **in fere**, altogether, 2322.

fere   *v.* frighten, terrify, 2238.

fere   *adv.* far, 74.

fesed   *pp.* pursued, terrified, 132.

festful   *adj.* festal, solemn, 2723.

fyrid   *pp.* inspired with courage, 643.

fyth   *v. var. of* **fighten**, fight, struggle, 424.

flikyryng   *pres. p.* fluttering, wavering, 4013.

folde   *v.* falter, grow weak, 2582.

fone   *n. pl.* foes, enemies, 2671.

fore   *adv.* before, ahead, 1048.

forȝefte   *n.* forgiveness, remission, 3476.

fortheryng   *n.* advancement, 2996.

fowe   *v.* cleanse, purify, 2055.

fre   *adj.* noble, good, 2868.

freyned   *v. pret. 3 pl.* asked, inquired, 3230.

freytoure   *n.* refectory, dining room, 2844.

freke   *n.* brave man, warrior, 584.

frelete   *n.* weakness, 2707.

frentyk   *adj.* delirious, crazed, 612.

gaast   *n.* anguish, perturbation, 2581.

gay   *adj.* gallant, 2597.

gate   *n.* **in his gate**, on his way, 430.

ȝede   *v. pret. 3 sg. of* **gan**, went, 962; **ȝeed**, *pret. 3 sg.* 3308.

ȝekyng   *n.* itching, 273.

ȝelde   *v.* yield, give up, 1952.

gelous   *adj.* **gelous suspicioun**, distrustful, 1555.

ȝeman   *n.* yeoman, manservant, 3483.

ȝerne   *adv.* eagerly, quickly, 1135.

gesse   *v.* guess, presume, 122.

gyde   *n.* guide, 75.

gile   *n.* treachery, dishonesty, 1928.

gise   *n.* manner, 2027.

glideth   *v. pres. 3 sg.* passes stealthily, 2230.

glose   *v.* explain away, falsify, 2440.

goostely   *adv.* spiritually, 745.

ȝore   *n.* long while, 215.

gore   *v.* pierce, stab, 1850.

gouernaunce   *n.* deportment, conduct, 1556.

grase   *n.* favour, God's grace, 201.

grope   *v.* ponder, scrutinize, 322.

grucch   *v.* grumble, disagree, 158.

gun   *v. pret. 3 pl. of* **gan**, began, 922.

ha   *pron. var of* **he**, 2694.

hale   *v.* draw, pull, 12.

hardy   *adj.* bold, 897.

hardyly   *adv.* certainly, assuredly, 3756.

haunted   *pp.* practiced, exercised, 909.

heil   *adj.* healthy, sound, 519.

hele   *n.* health, 1183.

hende   *n. var. of* **ende**, 1587.

hent   *v.* regain, capture, 259.

hepe   *n.* **on hepe**, in great quantity, 1997.

here   *n.* hairshirt, 377; **hayir**, 380; **hayre**, 1472.

herre   *n.* hinge, *fig.* **oute of herre**, out of order, 549.

hye   *v.* hasten, 1732.

hise   *pron.* his own, his people, 3558.

hith   *v. pret. 3 sg. of* **hate**, was called, 98.

holdith   *v. pres. 3 sg.* guards, protects, 2122.

hole   *adj.* whole, sound, 1400; **all hool**, entirely, 1955.

holid   *v. pret. 3 sg. of* **holen**, cured, saved, 2455.

honeste   *n.* decorum, 1511.

hore   *n.* oar, 1964.

houe   *v.* float, rise to surface, 256.

houeve   *n.* oven, 1423.

hucch   *n.* box for relics, 4001.

iangeleris   *n. pl.* wranglers, quarrelers, 1745.

iape   *v.* act foolishly, be unruly, 2152.

icesed   *pp. var. of* **seisen**, possessed of, in possession of, 2926.

ich   *adj.* same, 473.

ydiotes   *n. pl.* uneducated, ignorant persons, 1899.

iette   *n.* fashion, mode, 1410.

yȝe *n.* eye, 762.

ilk *adj.* very, same, 72.

innouuacyoun *n.* renewal, 1792.

inquysityf *adj.* keen to carry out a decision, 777.

instaunce *n.* **mad instaunce**, entreated, asked, 1107.

intricacioun *n.* entanglement, complexity, 225.

inuectif *adj.* abusive, denunciatory, 337.

ioly *adj.* festive, convivial, 154.

yrous *adj.* angry, 628.

isene *v.* realized, discovered, 824.

iutice *n.* ecclesiastical judge, 332; arbiter, 3405.

ken *v.* know, 948.

kende *n.* species, 263.

kynde *n.* nationality, 99; character, 882.

kynrod *n.* stock, family, 49.

knaue *n.* boy, servant, 2483.

knyth *n.* knight, 425.

kose *n. var. of* **cors**, body of a living person, 145.

koye *adj.* quiet, discreet, 96.

labbyng *pres. p.* to talk foolishly, blabber, 3161.

lak *n.* **put ... lak,** reproach, blame, i.e. they considered the work a gross error, 1746.

lalle *v.* speak out, cry out, 1159.

large *adj.* generous, free, 125; lax, liberal, 932.

late *v.* let, rent, 1588.

launches *v. pres. 3 sg.* springs up, shoots up, 2352.

leche *n.* physician, 392.

leef *adj.* pleasing, dear, 50; **lef**, 73.

lees *n.* lie, falsehood, 174.

lef *n.* leaf (of a book), 1283.

leke *v. impers.* **him not leke**, did not please him, 740.

lenage *n.* lineage, pedigree, 3024.

lende *n.* give, grant, 749.

lenys *n. pl.* lines (written), 20.

leonis *n. gen. sg.* **leonis (rage)**, lion's (rage), 913.

lere *v.* teach, instruct, 315; *pp.* **lerd**, trained, knowledgeable, 3435.

lese *v.* release, part with, 961.

lesyng *n.* falsehood, 2628; **with lesinggis**, 1917.

lest *adj.* less, 1291.

lest[1] *v. impers.* **as hem lest**, as they wished, 1314.

lest[2] *v.* endure, 2354.

lette *v.* hinder, delay, 911.

lettirrure *n.* learning, erudition, 32.

leue[1] *v.* leave, abandon, 138; *pret. 3 sg.* **lef**, 2727.

leue[2] *v.* live, 539.

leue[3] *v.* believe, trust in, 1448.

leue *n.* permission, 1449.

leuene *n.* flash of lightning, 132.

lewid *adj.* uneducated, ignorant, 326; **lewid couent**, lay monastery, 1806.

lich *adv.* alike, 1511.

lyn *v.* rest, lie, 459.

list *v.* **if þat ȝe list**, if you wish, 19.

lith *adj.* agile, 112.

lome *n. pl.* tools, weapons, 1851.

long *adj.* tall, 111.

longing *pres. p.* **was ... longing onto**, attached to, connected with, 89.

loo *interj.* alas, 1547.

lore *n.* precept, 2903.

losell *n.* worthless fellow, 2963.

loueday *n.* day for settling disputes, 642.

loute *v.* bow, obey, 2089; **lowte**, 2623.

low *v. var of* **laughen**, laugh, 1187.

lyuelood *n.* sustenance, 1633.

magre *prep.* in spite of, 2171

mayn *n.* strength, virtue, 110.

maystries *n. pl.* mighty deeds, 3891.

male *adj.* evil, 1756.

maner *n.* kind, sort, 2534.

mansioun *n.* home, 2342.

marys *n.* swamp, marsh, 397.

math *v. pres. 3 sg.* makes, 2635.

maundment *n.* command, 3042.

mede *n.* reward, compensation, 1600.

medelyng *n.* interference, fighting, 1810.

mekil *adj.* much, 2021.

melle *v.* mix, associate, 2768.

mende *n. var. of* **mynde**, mind, 774.

mene *n.* common men, 114; **menee**, crowd, 2205; community, household, 1621.

mene *v.* mean, intend, 656.

menge *v.* blend, combine, 2366.

mere *n.* morass, 1617.

mette *n.* measure, 2160.

myngis *v. pres. 3 sg.* admonishes, persuades, 1228.

mynne *adj. comp.* less, 2553.

mischeuys *n. pl.* misfortunes, 844.

mystily *adv.* mystically, spiritually, 796.

myty *adj.* sound, stalwart, 1462.

mood *n.* mind, 262.

mouled *adj.* moldy, 3265.

mountenans *n.* **mountenans of an oure**, period of an hour, 3751.

mote *v.* must, bound to, 450; **mut**, 923.

neyh *v.* approach, near, 1825.

neȝzyng *n.* a sneezing, 277.

nys *adj.* wanton, weak, 1559.

nyst *v. pret. 3 sg.* did not know, 3967.

noye *n.* trouble, annoyance, 236.

nonys *n.* **for þe nonys**, for the nonce (a tag line), 671.

norched *pp.* brought up, 198.

norture *n.* breeding, 210.

not *v. from* **ne witen**, not to know, *pres. 1 sg.*, 2792.

noted *v. pret. 3 sg.* observed, 720.

noute *n.* nothing, 250.

observaunce *n.* rite, ceremony, 1151.

occasionate *adj.* incidental, 2820.

octaue *n.* solemnity, **that grete octaue**, the Last Judgment, 3960.

on *pron.* one, 1667.

ones *adv.* once, 1435.

onkende *adj.* unkind, ungracious, 723.

onþank *n.* ingratitude, 1153.

opened *v. pret. 3 sg.* expounded, explained, 1081.

or *conj.* before, ere, 288.

orisones *n. pl.* prayers, 252.

ouerest *adj. superl.* topmost, 2949.

ouerlede *v.* lead, be superior to, 1763.

out *pron.* aught, somewhat, 1923, **owt**, 2488.

pace *n.* passage, 1062.

pace *v.* pass, go, 1198.

pay *n.* **onto Cristes pay**, to please Christ, for Christ's pleasure, 3371.

pament *n.* pavement, floor, 1202.

parde *interj.* certainly (*lit.* 'by God'), 2138.

parsch *n.* parish, 3071.

pase¹ *n.* distance, path, 198.

pase² *n.* Pasch, Easter, 828.

patene *n.* golden plate for Eucharist, 289.

perse *v.* pierce, 2656.

pyin *n. var. of* **pyne**, grief, sorrow, 2587.

pileres *n. pl.* supports, columns, 1061.

pipelyng *adj.* whistling, piping, 881.

platly *adv.* bluntly, plainly, 558.

pleyene *v.* complain, 2555.

plesaunce *n.* **doth þat plesaunce**, do honour, 801.

plith *n.* condition, predicament, 878.

pouste *n.* strength, authority, 1874.

prees *n.* crowd, throng, 1778.

preiudicioun *n.* prejudice, bias, 1346.

prende *n.* impress, impression, 793.

pressed *adj.* oppressed, 1037.

preue *v. var. of* **proue**, to make good, establish, 535.

prik *n.* goad, spur, 159.

prys *n.* value, price, 231.

pryuyly *adv.* secretly, 147.

processe *n.* story, narrative, 3571.

profir *n.* proposal, offer, 208.

pronge *n.* pang, affliction, 3469.

puluir *n.* **puluir Wednisday**, Ash Wednesday, 916.

pursue *v.* persecute, 149.

puruyaunce *n.* providence, foreknowledge, 143.

quarter *n.* quarter (of a year), 735.

qwek *v.* tremble, 1127; **qwake**, 1180; **qwook**, 2148.

qwere *n.* choir (place where monastic offices were performed), 1594.

qwite *v.* repay, requite, 2634; **qwyte** *pp.* freed, redeemed, 1172.

race¹ *v.* tear away, slash, 19.

race² *v.* carve out, engrave, 838.

rayle *v.* regulate, set in order, 3343.

rathere *adv.* more truly, more correctly, 888.

rawt *pp. var. of* **wrouʒt**, devised, 1918.

real *adj.* true, actual, 30.

recuren *v.* cure, 2338.

reed *n.* opinion, advice, 1281.

reft *pp. of* **reaven**, rob, deprive of, 1152.

rehersed *pp.* recited, 1078.

rem *n.* realm, 1267.

rennyng *vbl. n.* running, 1176.

rere *v.* raise, rear, 1024.

reue *n.* reeve, manager, 852.

reuest *v. pres. 2 sg.* rob, deprive of, 1147.

rewe *v.* pity, 485.

ryf *adj.* numerous, plentiful.

ryf *adv.* **went ful ryf**, went very frequently, 1876; **iknowe ful ryf**, very well known, 2899.

rynde *n.* shell, rind, 2750.

ryng *n.* ring (knocker), 1713.

ring *n.* bond, 1808.

rith *adv.* right, exactly, 39.

roos *n.* **make no roos**, make no move, 3378.

rore *v.* bellow, proclaim loudly, 1072.

rout *n.* company, group, 371.

routʒ *v. pret. 3 pl. of* **rechen**, cared about, 1684.

row *adj.* unkempt, crude, 1616.

rowe *n.* **be rowe**, in turn, 1971.

rowt *pp. of* **rechen**, cared about, 3070.

rummere *adv.* **go rummere**, make room, 2961.

runge *pp.* sounded, made known, 1083.

sacry *n.* consecration (of the Mass), 253.

sadnesse *n.* seriousness, discreteness, 180.

sam *adv.* **in sam**, all together, 4099.

sautir *n.* Psalter, psalms, 1084.

sauacyoun *n.* salvation, 864.

sawte *n.* attack, assault, 997.

scapen *v.* escape, evade, 160.

schent *pp.* disgraced, confounded, 151.

schete *v.* shoot, 989.

schoue *n.* display, show, 897; **clowde schoue**, cloudburst, 884.

schoue   *v.* thrust, cast away, 165; force away, free, 2048.

schrewe   *n.* evil person, rascal, 2035.

schryue   *v.* prescribe penance, absolve, 391.

scorned   *v.* taunted, derided, 1056.

seche   *v.* seek, contrive, 222.

sedy   *adj.* full of seeds, fruitful, 845.

seel   *n.* period of time, season, 2594.

seyn   *adj.* holy, 1043.

seyn[1]   *v.* say, report, 301.

seyn[2]   *v.* see, perceive, 3727.

sekirnesse   *n.* security, 236.

sentens   *n.* opinion, sense, 226; statement, 1606.

serk   *n.* shirt, 2383.

seruyse   *n.* church services or offices, 203.

sese   *v.* cease, desist, 2816; **seste**, finished, concluded, 602.

sew   *v.* follow, pursue, 23.

sewirly   *adv.* surely, securely, 1279.

sibbe   *adj.* related, akin, 3286.

sidis   *n. pl.* **undir his sidis**, on either side, 3163.

signacule   *n.* mark, seal, 894.

sikirly   *adv.* certainly, 914; **sikir**, 920.

simulate   *adj.* false, pretending, 896.

sise   *n.* order, manner, 159.

sith   *n.* sight, vision, 1670.

sith   *adv.* then, afterward, 1286.

sitys   *n. pl.* pains, sorrows, 2662.

slawhere   *adj. comp.* duller, more spiritless, 1304.

sleythi   *adj.* cunning, crafty, 2666.

smet   *v. pret. 3 sg. of* **smite**, struck, blew, 167.

snybbe   *v.* reprove, rebuke, 3284.

sodekyn   *n.* subdeacon, 434.

soioure   *v.* wait, delay, 1797.

solacious   *adj.* agreeable 2516.

soleyn   *adj.* singular, exceptional, 2597.

sondes   *n. pl.* messages, gifts, 195.

sore   *adv.* earnestly, eagerly, 189.

sory   *adj.* miserable, painful, 169.

sotilte   *n.* cunning, 3197.

souereynte   *n.* sovereign power, 731.

soupith   *v.* swallow, sip, 260.

sown   *n.* sound, voice, 2210.

sownyng   *n.* a swooning, faint, 162.

space   *n.* space (of time) 2182.

specialtee   *n.* detail, 2794.

sped   *v. pret. 3 sg.* succeed; *trans. impers.* give success to, 3845.

spedful   *adj.* helpful, resourceful, 3905.

spere   *v. imper.* lock, fasten, 2017; *pp.* **sperd**, 2606.

stede   *n.* place, location, 295; **steed**, 293.

stered *v. pret. 3 sg.* inspired, guided, 221.

sterynge *n.* guidance, direction, 1223.

sterten *v.* be startled, flinch, 1074.

steuene *n. dat. sg.* voice, 781.

sty *n.* path, way, 1706.

stood *v. pret. 3 sg.* **stood in**, consisted of, 882.

stoon *n.* stone floor, ground, 2247.

stoure *n.* battle, 3335.

streit *adj.* strict, 1446.

strengthis *n. pl.* strongholds, 3487.

subarbes *n.* suburbs, outskirts, 463.

sunner *adv.* sooner, 4032.

swage *v.* assuage, pacify, 571.

sware *adj.* square, 836.

swech *adj.* such, 13.

swiere *n.* squire, 3483.

swow *n.* swoon, 3981.

tak *n.* clasp, hold, 1744.

tan *v. inf. of* **take**, 696.

targe *n.* charter, seal, privilege, 1250.

tase *v. pres. 3 sg. var. form of* **takes**, 1200.

tecch *n.* custom, habit, 2203.

teche *v.* teach, 668; *pp.* **iteyt**, 711.

teye *v.* bind, tie, 1386; *pp.* **teyid**, 192.

teld *pp. of* **telle**, told, 659; *pret. 3 sg.* **teld**, 959.

tende *v.* attend, pay attention to, 148.

tene *n.* vexation, sorrow, 248.

thy *n.* thigh, 408.

tyth *adj.* dense, heavy, 1743.

tosed *v.* pulled apart, 9.

trantes *n. pl.* tricks, strategems, 1100.

trete *v.* treat, consider, 886; *pret.* **ted**, 2859.

tryacle *n.* antidote, remedy, 264.

troyloure *n.* deceiver, guiler, 1963.

tuycioun *n.* keeping, custody, 1040.

turbuled *pp.* troubled, 586.

twist *pp.* detached, separated, 3318.

þere *rel. adv.* where, 823.

þrille *v.* pierce, bore, 3553.

þrote *v.* cut the throat, slaughter, 1824.

veniaunce *n.* vengeance, 3219.

very *adj.* true, 1520.

verytees *n. pl.* truths, 764.

viage *n.* voyage, 130.

vyleny *n.* discredit, evil, 26.

visite *v.* investigate, examine, 322.

vnbuxum *adj.* unbending, disobedient, 1560.

vnderne *adj.* morning, 2594.

vnnethe   *adv.* scarcely, with difficulty, 1903.

vnto   *prep.* **vnto my powere**, to the extent of my ability, 3421.

voyded   *pp.* freed, 980; expelled, 981.

voute   *n.* vault, 247.

waymenting   *n.* lamenting, mourning, 1197.

waioure   *n.* wager, pledge, 955.

wast   *adj.* solitary, wild, 2390.

wede   *n.* clothing, 31; **in his wede**, in his hire, pay, 1771.

weyue   *v.* remove, divert, 1897.

weld   *n.* **at weld**, under command, dominion, 2642.

weldest   *v. pres. 2 sg.* possess, own, 567.

wene[1]   *v.* think, suppose, 246; *pret.* **wende**, 488.

wene[2]   *v.* turn, direct one's steps, 520.

werch   *v.* act, strive, 3692.

werne   *v.* refuse, prevent, 704.

whik   *adj.* living, 836.

white   *n.* dairy products, 941.

wynse   *v.* kick against, be recalcitrant, 158.

wite[1]   *n.* punishment, penance, 1474.

wite[2]   *n.* witness, **Idoþe to wite**.

wite[1]   *v.* know, 157; *pres. 1 sg.* **wote**; *pret. 3 sg.* **wist**; *inf.* **wete**, 2034.

wite[2]   *v.* blame, 21.

with   *n. var. of* **wiht**, creature, 15.

witte   *n.* mind, 812.

wone   *adj. var. of* **wune**, accustomed, 2326.

wondir   *adv.* amazingly, 2466.

wonys   *n. var. of* **wune**, dwelling, 672.

woon   *n. pl.* woes, troubles, 1356.

wosy   *adj.* slimy, 1624.

wreest   *v.* put aside, ? hide, 2525.

wreke   *v.* harm, 914.

wringist   *v. pres. 2 sg.* break away, 156.

wullock   *n.* tuft of wool, thistle-down, 2189.

BIBLIOGRAPHY

MANUSCRIPT

San Marino, California. The Henry E. Huntington Library. MS HM 55, fols. 1-59. [The Life of St. Norbert, John Capgrave.]

WORKS OF JOHN CAPGRAVE

Capgrave, John. *Chronicle of England*. Ed. Francis C. Hingeston. (Rolls Series 1.) London, 1858.
———. *Liber de illustribus Henricis*. Ed. Francis C. Hingeston. (Rolls Series 1.) London, 1858.
———. *The Life of St. Katharine of Alexandria*. Ed. Carl Horstmann; intro. F. J. Furnivall. (Early English Text Society, O.S. 100.) London, 1893.
———. *Lives of St. Augustine and St. Gilbert of Sempringham, and a Sermon*. Ed. J. J. Munro. (Early English Text Society, O.S. 140.) London 1910.
———. *Ye Solace of Pilgrimes*. Ed. C. A. Mills; intro. H. M. Bannister. London, 1911.

SECONDARY SOURCES

Backmund, Norbert. *Die mittelalterlichen Geschichtsschreiber des Praemonstratenserordens*. (Bibliotheca Analectorum Pramonstratensium 10.) Averbode, 1972.
———. *Monasticon Praemonstratense, id est historia circariarum atque canonicarum candidi et canonici Ordinis Praemonstratensis*. 3 vols. Straubing, 1949-1956.
Bader, Walter. *Die Stiftskirche des Hl. Viktor zu Xanten. 1.1 Sanctos: Grabfeld, Märtyrergrab und Bauten unter dem Kanonikerchor vom 4 Jahrhundert bis um oder nach 752-768*. Kevelaer, 1960.
Bale, John. *Illustrium Maioris Britanniae scriptorum*. [Wesel, 1549.]
Bauermann, J. "Umfang und Einteilung des Erzdiözese Magdeburg." *Zeitschrift des Vereins für Kirchengeschichte der Provinz Sachsen* 29 (1933) 3-43.
Browe, Peter. *Die eucharistischen Wunder des Mittelalters*. (Breslauer Studien zur historischen Theologie, N.S. 4.) Breslau, 1933.
Colledge, Edmund. "The Capgrave 'Autographs'." *Transactions of the Cambridge Bibliographical Society* 6 (1974) 137-148.
———, and C. Smetana. "Capgrave's *Life of St. Norbert*: Diction, Dialect and Spelling." *Mediaeval Studies* 34 (1972) 422-434.
Colvin, Howard M. *The White Canons in England*. Oxford, 1951.
Cox, J. C. "The Religious Houses of Norfolk." *A History of Norfolk*, vol. 2. Ed. William Page. The Victoria History of the Counties of England. London, 1906.
de Gaiffier, Baudouin. "La Legende de S. Julien l'Hospitalier." *Analecta Bollandiana* 63 (1945) 145-219.
de Meijer, Alberic. "John Capgrave, O.E.S.A." *Augustiniana* 5 (1955) 400-440; 7 (1957) 118-148, 531-575.

Dereine, Charles. *Les Chanoines réguliers au diocèse du Liège avant Saint Norbert.* Louvain, 1952.

——. "Enquête sur la règle de Saint Augustin." *Scriptorium* 2 (1948) 28-36.

——. "Les origines de Prémontré." *Revue d'histoire ecclésiastique* 42 (1947) 352-378.

——. "Le premier Ordo de Prémontré." *Revue Bénédictine* 58 (1948) 84-92.

——. "Vie commune, règle de Saint Augustin et chanoines réguliers au xie siècle." *Revue d'histoire ecclésiastique* 41 (1946) 365-406.

de Ricci, Seymour and W. J. Wilson. *Census of Medieval and Renaissance Manuscripts in the United States and Canada.* 2 vols. New York, 1935-37.

Destombes, Cyrille-Jean. *Histoire de l'église de Cambrai.* 3 vols. Lille, 1890-1891.

Emden, Alfred B. *A Biographical Register of the University of Cambridge to 1500.* Cambridge, 1963.

Engelskirchen, H. "Nova Norbertina. Neue Forschungsergebnisse über Norbert von Xanten." *Analecta Praemonstratensia* 22-23 (1946-47) 132-140; 24 (1948) 158-161.

——. "Zur Bekehrung des hl. Norberts." *Analecta Praemonstratensia* 31 (1955) 344-345.

Fredeman Elta J. "The Life and English Writings of John Capgrave." Ph. D. Dissertation, University of British Columbia, 1970. [*Dissertation Abstracts International* 30 (1970-71) 6009-A.]

Fumagalli, Vito. "Note sulle 'Vitae' di Norberto di Xanten." *Aevum* 39 (1965) 348-356.

Gallia Christiana, in provincias ecclesiasticas distributa. Ed. Denis de Sainte-Marthe, *et al.* 16 vols. Paris, 1739-1877; repr. Paris, 1899.

Goovaerts, André Léon. *Ecrivains, artistes et savants de l'ordre de Prémontré.* 4 vols. Brussels, 1899-1920.

Grassl, B. F. "Der Prämonstratenserorden, seine Geschichte und seine Ausbreitung bis zur Gegenwart." *Analecta Praemonstratensia* 10 (1934) 1*-129* [supplement with separate pagination].

Grauwen, Wm. M. "S. Norbertus." *Analecta Praemonstratensia* 41 (1965) 310-311.

——. "Norbert en Gennep." *Analecta Praemonstratensia* 42 (1966) 132-133.

——. "Norbert et les debuts de l'abbaye de Floreffe." *Analecta Praemonstratensia* 51 (1975) 5-23.

——. "Norbert van Maagdenburg (Gennep, Xanten)." *Nationaal Biografisch Woordenboek.* Brussels, 1968, 3: 610-625.

——. "Norbertus, aartsbisschop van Maagdenburg 1126-1134." Ph. D. dissertation. Brussels, 1971.

——. "De 'Vitae' van Norbertus." *Analecta Praemonstratensia* 42 (1966) 322-326.

Grundmann, Herbert. *Religiöse Bewegungen im Mittelalter* (Historische Studien 267.) Berlin, 1935.

Heijman, H. Th. "Untersuchungen über die Prämonstratenser-gewohnheiten." *Analecta Praemonstratensia* 2 (1926) 5-32; 3 (1927) 5-27; 4 (1928) 5-29, 113-131, 225-241, 351-373.

Herman the Monk, *De miraculis S. Mariae Laudunenis.* Ed. Roger Wilmans. MGH, SS 12: 653-660.

——. *Liber de restauratione Monasterii Sancti Martini Tornacensis.* Ed. G. Waitz. MGH, SS 14: 274-327.

Hugo, Charles Louis, *Sacri et canonici ordinis praemonstratensis annales.* 2 vols. Nancy, 1734-1735.

[Innocent III.] *Die Register Innocenz III.* Ed. Othmar Hageneder and A. Haidacher. (Publikationen der Abteilung für historische Studien des Oesterreichischen Kulturinstituts in Rom, 2, 1.) Graz-Cologne, 1964, vol. 1.

[Jacques de Vitry] *The Historia Occidentalis of Jacques de Vitry.* Ed. John F. Hinnebusche, O. P. (Spicilegium Friburgense 17.) Fribourg, 1972.

Jedin, Hubert. *Handbuch der Kirchengeschichte*: III *Die mittelalterliche Kirche*: 2 *Vom kirchlichen Hochmittelalter bis zum Vorabend der Reformation.* Fribourg-en-Br.-Basle-Vienna, 1968.

Koch, K. and E. Hegel, *Die Vita des Prämonstratensers Hermann Joseph von Steinfeld.* Köln, 1958.

King, Archdale A. *Liturgies of the Religious Orders.* London, 1955.

Lancelin, H. *Histoire du diocèse de Cambrai.* Valenciennes, 1946.

Lefèvre, Pl. "L'Épisode de la conversion de S. Norbert et la tradition hagiographique du 'Vita Norberti'." *Revue d'histoire ecclésiastique* 56 (1961) 813-826.

Lefèvre-Pontalis, Eugène. *Le Château de Coucy.* Paris, 1909 (?)

Leland, John. *Commentarii de scriptoribus Britannicis.* Ed. A. Hall. 2 vols. Oxford, 1709.

Lentze, H. J. "Der Messritus die Prämonstratenserordens." *Analecta Praemonstratensia* 25 (1949) 129-170; 26 (1950) 7-40; 127-151; 27 (1951) 5-27.

Lucas, Peter J. "Consistency and Correctness in the Orthographic Usage of John Capgrave's *Chronicle*." *Studia Neophilologica* 45 (1973) 323-355.

——. "John Capgrave, O.S.A., (1393-1464) Scribe and 'Publisher'." *Transactions of the Cambridge Bibliographical Society* 5 (1969-1971) 1-35.

——. "John Capgrave and the *Nova legenda Anglie*: A Survey." *The Library*, Ser. 5, 25 (1970) 1-10.

——. "Sense Units and the Use of Punctuation-Markers in John Capgrave's *Chronicle*." *Archivum Linguisticum* N.S. 2 (1971) 1-24.

Madelaine, Godefroid. *Histoire de Saint Nobert*, 3rd. ed. 2 vols. Tongerloo, 1928.

Mannl, O. "Zur Literatur über der heiligen Norbert." *Analecta Praemonstratensia* 35 (1959) 5-14.

Moore, Samuel, S. Meech, H. Whitehall. *Middle English Dialect Characteristics and Dialect Boundaries.* (University of Michigan, Language and Literature, Vol. 13, Essays and Studies in English and Comparative Literature.) Ann Arbor, 1935.

Mühlbacher, Engelbert. *Die Streitige Papstwahl des Jahres 1130.* Innsbruck, 1876; reprinted 1966.

Munby, Alan N. L. *The Formation of the Phillipps Library from 1841 to 1872.* (Phillipps Studies No. 4.) Cambridge, 1956.

Nichols, J. Gough. "On Precatory Rolls, and Particularly One of the West Dereham, Norfolk." *Memoirs illustrative of the history of Norfolk and the city of Norwich communicated to the annual meeting of the Archaeological Institute held at Norwich, July 1847* (London, 1851), pp. 99-114.

Nova Legenda Anglie. Collected by John of Tynemouth *et al.* Ed. Carl Horstmann. 2 vols. Oxford, 1901.

Petit, F. "Pourquoi saint Norbert a choisi Prémontré." *Analecta Praemonstratensia* 40 (1964) 5-16.

——. *La spiritualité des prémontrés au xiie et xiiie siècles.* (Études de théologie et d'histoire de la spiritualité, 10.) Paris, 1947.

——. "Les vêtements des Prémontrés au xiie siècle." *Analecta Praemonstratensia* 15 (1939) 17-24.

Petrus de Herentals. *Expositio super librum psalmorum*. Cologne, 1480.

Recueil des historiens des Gaules et de la France. Ed. M-J-J. Brial; new ed. Léopold Delisle. Vol. 15. Paris, 1878.

Rosenmund, Richard. *Die ältestes Biographieen des heiligen Norbert*. Berlin, 1874.

Sacrorum conciliorum nova et amplissima collectio. 31 vols. Ed. Giovanni D. Mansi. Florence [and Venice], 1759-1798.

Sanctus Norbertus, Praemonstratensis Ordinis Fundator, Archiepiscopus Magdeburgensis. (Ed. Johannes Chrysostomus van der Sterre, 1665). PL 170: 1235-1364. [*Vita B*]

Schmale, Franz-Josef. *Studien zum Schisma des Jahres 1130*. Köln-Böhlaus, 1961.

Schneyer, Johannes Baptist. *Repertorium der lateinischen Sermones des Mittelalters, für die Zeit von 1150-1350*. Münster, 1972.

Semmler, Josef. *Die Klosterreform von Siegburg. Ihre Ausbreitung u. ihr Reformprogramm im 11. u. 12. Jhr.* Bonn, 1959.

Valvekens, E. "La canonization de Saint Norbert en 1582." *Analecta Praemonstratensia* 10 (1934) 10-47.

———. *Norbert van Gennep*. Brugge, 1944.

Valvekens, J. B. (ed.) "Acta et decreta capitulorum generalium Ordinis Praemonstratensis." *Analecta Praemonstratensia* 42 (1966) i-ix, 1-22; 43 (1967) 23-102; 44 (1968) 103-224; 45 (1969) 1-96. [Supplement with separate pagination.]

Van Waefelghem, Michel. *Liturgie de Prémontré: Le Liber ordinarius d'après un manuscrit du xiii⁰ et xiv⁰ siècles*. Louvain, 1913.

Van Waefelghem, Raphaël. *Les premiers statuts de l'ordre des Prémontré*. (Analectes de l'ordre de Prémontré, 9.) Brussels, 1913.

———. *Répertoire des sources imprimées et manuscrites relatives à l'histoire et à liturgie des monastères de l'ordre de Prémontré*. Brussels, 1930.

Verheijen, Luc. *La Règle de saint Augustin*. 2 vols. (Études augustinennes.) Paris, 1967.

Vita Norberti Archiepiscopi Magdeburgensis. Ed. Rogerus Wilmans. MGH, SS 12: 683-705. [*Vita A*]

"Vitae BB. Vitalis et Gaufridi, primi et secundi abbatium Saviniacensium." Ed. E. P. Sauvage. *Analecta Bollandiana* 1 (1882) 355-410.

Weyns, N. J. "Petrus van Herentals." *Nationaal Biografisch Woordenboek*. Brussels, 1970. 4: 663-672.

Wright, Cyril E. *English Vernacular Hands from the Twelfth to the Fifteenth Centuries*. Oxford, 1960.

Zak, A. "Episcopatus ordinis Praemonstratensis." *Analecta Praemonstratensia* 4 (1928) 64-68, 173-186, 294-311, 406-413; 5 (1929) 49-56, 132-147, 239-249.

Zoepfl, Friedrich. *Das Bistum Augsburg und seine Bischöfe im Mittelalter*. Munich-Augsburg, 1955.

SCRIPTURAL CITATIONS

Numbers in brackets refer to line numbers and/or notes.

Genesis	3: 21 (382); 29: 20 (2924)
Exodus	13: 14 (827); 27: 2 (831)
Numbers	21: 11 (831); 22: 28 (139); 33: 44 (831)
1 Kings	19: 12 (881)
2 Kings	15: 19 (2371)
Esther	2: 17 (3505)
Psalms	7: 13 (989); 34: 15 (175); 82: 9 (2371); 139: 3 (3166)
Proverbs	10: 3 (3897); 16: 7 (2646); 18: 19 (538-9)
Wisdom	2: 24 (2227); 5: 21 (2646)
Isaiah	11: 2 (1239); 49: 10 (3897); 60: 14 (791)
Daniel	7: 7-27 (1914)
Matthew	3: 4 (378); 5: 44 (3255); 7: 6 (606); 10: 12 (4070); 15: 13 (1749); 25: 29 (1583); 25: 35-37 (354); 26: 47 ff. (3244); 28: 3 (1353)
Mark	9: 28 (2088); 14: 43 ff. (3244)
Luke	8: 12 (2239); 9: 51 (1643); 9: 62 (3461); 11: 9 (3802); 18: 14 (3503); 22: 47 ff. (3244)
John	6: 37 (1895); 10: 29 (1897); 18: 2 ff. (3244); 19: 26; 20: 2; 21: 7 (3964 ff.)
1 Corinthians	2: 9 (3715); 13: 12 (3830)
2 Corinthians	2: 15-16 (3267); 3, 1-6 (840); 6: 14 (2767); 12: 2 (3965)
1 Timothy	3: 4 (2991)
Hebrews	4: 13 (1567)
James	1: 27 (351); 5: 20 (360)
1 Peter	4: 8 (360-4)
Apocalypse	12: 1-13 (1970)

INDEX

Numbers in roman type refer
to lines and/or notes, in italic to pages.

Abbot of Derham. *See* Ion Wygnale

Adam, 382

Additamenta fratrum cappenbergensium, 3, 12-13, 3851, 4088

Albon (Albero), 2864

Almayn(e). *See* Germayn(e)

Amadeus, Duke of Savoy, 3534

Anacletus. *See* Petir þe leoun

Andrew, Saint, 2

Antony, 807-812

Antwerpense (St. Michael's), 3443, 3457

Apocalipse, 1965

Apostle of the Wends. *See* Euermode

Assumpcion weke, *1,* 4105

Assur, 2371

Augusta (Augsburg), 4064, 4081

Augustine, Life of Saint. 5, 10

Austin Friar, *2*

Austin (Austen) Seynt, 51, 1294, 1329, 3607, 3921, 3947, 3952

Balaam's asse, 139

Barnad, Francis, *3 n. 4*

Bartholome(w), 695, 698, 716, 750, 756, 1767, 1723-29

Basle, Council of, 3534

Beauvais, Council of, 1730

Bernard, Saint, 2778

Boneland (Bolanden), 4035

Brocard (Burchard), *15 n. 59,* 471, 509, 814, 3409

Bury, John, *8 n. 27*

Cameracense (Cambrai), 472, 503, 783, 814

Cambridge, *7 & n. 22*

Cantica Canticorum 1073

Capenbergense. *See Additamenta*

Capgraue, Ion, 4105; life, *7-8;* works, *9,* extant works: *Commentarius in Genesim, 8 n. 24; Commentarius in Exodum, 8 n. 24; Life of St. Norbert,* MS HM 55, *1,* description, *1-2* contents, *2-3,* history, *3-4,* scribe, *4-7,* language, *7,* source, *11-13,* treatment of source, *13-15,* characterization, *15-16; Life*

of St. Katharine, 7 n. 22, 8 n. 27, 9 & n. 31, 10; Life of St. Augustine, 5, 10; Life of St. Gilbert, 5, 10 & n. 38; Tretis of the orderes, 6 & n. 16, 10 n. 38, 11 & n. 39; Ye Solace of Pilgrimes, 5, 6 n. 16, 8, 9, 11 & n. 40; Super Actus Apostolorum, 8 & n. 28, 9 & n. 32; Chronicle of England, 8 & n. 29, 9, 11 & n. 41; De fidei symbolis 8 & n. 29, 11 & n. 42.

Capgrave, John (the elder), *7 & n. 22, 9*

Cappenberg Chronicle. See *Additamenta*

Charta Caritatis, 1265

Clarke, Richard, *3 & n. 4, 4 n. 6*

Clarke, Samuel, *4 n. 6*

Cloyne (Cluny), 673

Colayne, Coleyn (Cologne), 87, 300

Colroys (Coriletum), 625

Concordia, 65

Conone (Cuno), 321, 387

Conrad of Constance, 246

Coty, 1730

Coucy, 754

Cuno, Abbot, 184

Cycile (Sicily), 3585

Cycile (Saint Cecilia), 379

Danyeles profecies, 1913

Derham, *1,* 4097

Deuele, Sathan, 846-903, 904-980, 988-1029, 1817-1890, 1996-2184, 2185-2338, 2367-2457, 2458-2513, 2654-2700, 2701-2716, 2717-2779.

Egipt, 827, 830

Engelbert, 2788

Enguerrand I, 1730

Epire (Speyer), 2823, 2851

Epping, Essex, *4*

Ereyn (spider), 254, 260, 279, 246-294

Ermensendis, 1211

Estern, 460, 824

Eue, 382

Euermode, 785, 787, 796, 806

Eugene IV, 3534

Felix, Pope. *See* Amadeus
Florefye, Florefiense, 1211, 3443, 3446, 3457, 3972
Freden, 128
Frederik, (Archbishop of Cologne), 88, 190, 2788
Frensch (builders), 1753
Frese, 3171
Frixlare (Fritzlar), 316, Council of, *14*

Gelas (Gelasius), *14*, 190, 386, 666
Gemlacum (Gembloux), 541
Gerard, 2864
Gereon, Saint, *14*, 1211
Germayn(e), Almayne, 85, 99, 456, 752, 2798, 3171, 3586
Glotony (Glotenye), 970, 1321, 908-980
Godfrey of Cappenberg, *14*, 758, 2338, 3851
Gratian, 1784
Gregory, the Great, *3*

Hadwidis (Hedwig), 98
Hartwic, Bishop, 2788
Henry Hungtington Library, *1, 10*; Manuscript HM 55, *1-7*
Herdbert, 98
Heribert, 300
Herman, Joseph, 246
Herman the Monk, 503
Hermits of St. Augustine, *7*
Herry ȝe ȝonger (Henry V), 75, 90, 2853
Hestir (Queen Esther), 3505
Holy Year (1450), *8 n. 26*
Honorius II, 2339, 3530
Hubbard, Rev. Arthur, *4*
Hubert, Walter, 4097
Hugo of Fosse, 498, 514-539, 3326-3441
Hyginus, Pope, 1784

Ingeramne (Euguerrand II), 1736
Innocent (II, Pope), 3536, 3546, 3557, 3573
Innocent (III, Pope), *12 n. 49*, 1479, 1481
Instituta Generalia, 1265
Ion, Seynt (Baptist), 377, 3932
Ion, Seynt (Evangelist), 2961, 3210, 3964
Iordan, 1882
Iulianes ham, 4099

Jonah, 2927

Kalixt (Callistus II, Pope), 670, 678, 750
Kent, 2478
King's Lynn, *7-8*, 21

Ladbrooke, Newington, *3 n. 4*
Laudune (Laon), 695, 1723, 2347, 3452, 3457
Leland, John, *9 & n. 30*
Lothary (Emperor), 88, 2853, 2870, 2890, 2899, 3559, 3574, 4082
Lucius, Pope, 2864
Lya, 2925
Lydulf, 307

Magdeburg, 2854. *See* Parthenopole
Marien-Freden, *See* Freden
Martha and Mary, 2920
Martin V, Pope, 1331
Mathilda, Queen, 321
Mathilda, wife of Theobald, 2798
Maunde Þursday, 3186
Mechlin, General Chapter of, 1331
Metense (Metz), 2864
Moore, Bishop, *3 n. 6*
Mortuary Roll, 4102
Moyses, 832

Newington, Ferdinand, *3 n. 4*
Newton, K.C., *4 n. 5*
Niemeyer, Gerlinde, *14 n. 53*
Niuigelle (Nivelle), 807, 1030, 2067
Norbert, Life of: birth, 78, character, 111-127, conversion, 128-129, ordination, 190-196, attempt to reform Xanten canons, 197-245, spider miracle 246-294, preparation for ministry, 295-315, rebuke by council, 316-392, wandering preacher, 393-427, beginnings of an Order, 428-539, peacemaker, 540-658, preliminaries to religious life, 659-833, early trials, 834-1029, exorcism, 1030-1211, spiritual leadership, 1212-1407, community virtues, 1408-1538, false disciples, 1539-1604, building Prémontré, 1605-1799, diabolical persecution, 1800-2338, monastic expansion, 2339-2515, wolf stories, 2516-2653, satanic apparition, 2654-2769, Theobald's bride, 2780-2821, monastic charity, 2822-2849, election to episcopate, 2850-2933, installation, 2934-2989, administration, 2990-3066, pastoral work, 3067-3101, the canons of St. Mary's, 3102-3143, persecution, 3144-3176, attempts on his life, 3177-3325, provisions for the Order, 3326-2465, victory over hate, 3466-3528, Roman schism, 3529-3570, journey to Rome, 3571-3593, death, 3594-3619, burial, 3620-3710, appearances after death, 3711-3850.

Norwich, *4 n. 6*, 4097
Nova Legenda Anglie, 10 n. 35

Orgliaunce (Orleans), *14*, 430

Palme Suneue, 435
Papebroch, Daniel, *12 n. 44*
Parthenopole (Magdeburg), *15*, 2854, 2935, 3600, 4039
Pascase (Paschal II), 73, 2864
Paston Letters, 916
Pentecost, 3618
Petir (Peter of Herentals), 3447
Petir þe leoun (Pierleone, Anaclete II), 3538, 3552
Petir, Seynt, 373, 464
Phillipps Library, *3*
Phillipps, Sir Thomas, *3 & nn. 2-4*
Poule, Seynt, 146, 840, 3965
Powis, *3 n. 3*
Premonstrat(e) (Prémontré), 754, 757, 758, 823, 1213, 1604-1764, 2459, 2829, 3327, 3411, 3441, 3734, 3741

Racheles scole, 2924
Registers of the General Archives (Augustinians), *7 n. 22*, 8-9
Reymys (Rheims), 678, 1534
Rode (Klosterrath), 302
Rome, 74, 2858, 3560, 3567, 3571, 3587
Rudolf, 3976
Rule of St. Augustine, *3*, 48, 1280-1330, 3914-3960

St. Giles, *14*, 386
St. James, Westminister, *3 n. 6*
St. Martin's. *See* Laudune
St. Michael's. *See* Antwerpense
St. Norbert's Abbey, 3447
St. Trudo, chronicler of, 316
St. Victor's church, 93

Salamon, 539
Saresson. *See* Ion Wygnale
Sathan. *See* Deuele
Saturninus, Saint, *3*
Savile collection, *3 n. 1*
Saxones, 2852, 2913, 2916, 3145, 3147, 3171, 3586
Scisme, 3518, 3530-3574
Sclaues (Slavs), 2913, 2919
Seruase, Seynt, 3996, 4026
Sigebergense (abbey, 184, (priory), 300
Speyer. *See* Epire
Stoke, 4098
Sueve, 3145, 3146, 3171

Tanchelin, *14*, 2338
Te Deum, 2903
Theobald, *14*, 2338, 2788, 2811, 2836
Thomas (de Marle), 1730
Traiect (Maastricht), 2193, 3991
Trier, 2864
Troye, 92, 235
Tynemouth, John of, *10 n. 35*

Valens (Valenciennes), 433, 435, 463, 540
Viuariense, (Valsery), 2361, 2370, 3453, 3457
Vita S. Norberti, Vita A, 12-13 & nn. 51-53;
Vita B, 11, 12 & n. 46, 13-16 & nn. 52-63;
Harleian MS 3935, *14*
Vitalis of Savigny, 246

Walter, Hubert, 4097
Watford, Hertfordshire, *4*
Westphale, 3858, 3875
William the Conqueror, 321
Wolf, 2514-2562, 2563-2590, 2591-2638, 2639-2653
Wygnale, Ion (Wygenhale alias Saresson), *1, 2, 10 n. 38*, 4096, 4102

Xanten, 93